THE DARK STORY OF EMINEM

NICK HASTED

OMNIBUS PRESS

London · New York · Sydney

(A Division of Music Sales Limited)

Cover designed by Fresh Lemon
Picture research by Julie Barber & Nick Hasted

ISBN: 978.1.84938.458.2
Order No: OP53559

Exclusive Distributors:
Music Sales Limited,
14–15 Berners Street,
London W1T 3LJ.

Music Sales Corporation,
257 Park Avenue South,
New York, NY 10010, USA.

Macmillan Distribution Services,
56 Park West Drive,
Derrimut, Vic 3030,
Australia.

Typeset by Galleon Typesetting, Ipswich.
Printed in the EU.

A catalogue record for this book is available from the British Library.

www.omnibuspress.com

For Stacey Shelley,
the bravest person I know,
who helped me write it.
With love.

CONTENTS

INTRODUCTION

FEVER

FEBRUARY 8, 2001. The storm clouds of anger and outrage have been building for weeks, from politicians and students, gay rights campaigners and women's groups, reporters for homophobic tabloids and liberal broadsheets. As Eminem sleeps in the private jet ferrying him from Paris to the opening Manchester engagement of his UK tour, the British are reviling, dissecting and supporting him with an intensity reserved only for the most terrible folk devils, and startling pop stars.

He is being pursued from America by accusations of real violence and hurt: his own mother, Debbie Mathers-Briggs, wants $10 million for the distress he has caused her; his wife Kim is considering divorce, and has recently slashed her wrists over his raps' insensitive insults; they say he pistol-whipped a man for kissing her, and waved a gun at another, all in one night. But it's the raps on his last record, *The Marshall Mathers LP*, the thoughts in his mind, that disturb and distress Britain most. He claims to have slaughtered O.J. Simpson's wife, to have armed the Columbine killers. He taunts women, and homosexuals. He wants to kill his father, and his mother, and his wife.

That's why 100 gay rights protesters gather outside the Manchester Evening News Arena in the hours before he takes the stage, why his hockey-masked, chainsaw-wielding image is on the cover of every newspaper the next morning, why the police will barge into his dressing room after the show, only to find him vanished, slipped away in the night.

It's hysteria whipped to a frenzy rarely seen since The Sex Pistols, sucking in commentators and members of the public with no normal interest in pop, and, like a fever, with those people it passes quickly. But, as I take the train to attend that Manchester show, I know Eminem has provoked deeper discussion. *The Marshall Mathers LP*, and in particular its recent number one single 'Stan' – the schizoid, self-reflective story of an

Eminem fan's mad love for his idol – has stopped all my friends cold. One female friend semi-seriously offers sex for any spare ticket I might find. Another friend who only likes classical music plays 'Stan' over and over at a party, fascinated. And whenever Eminem's name is mentioned, it's impossible to talk about him for less than an hour, and then someone new will start the conversation again. Is it all right to laugh at him? Is it okay to adore him?

He is simply too arresting, too ambiguously, coherently furious to ignore. On *The Marshall Mathers LP*, he has danced with glee on every embarrassing social fault-line in America, embraced every disgraceful and awkwardly hateful side of his country, from bullying misogynist machismo to homophobia. And his excuse, advanced during this tour? "Pardon the cliché, but I'm just a product of my environment. America made me."

He grew up, it's been revealed, on the wrong side of the tracks, a white boy in the black half of Detroit's poorest district, the son of an impoverished single mother. He was beaten almost to death and shot at by his black neighbours for his skin colour. And yet, the heroes of this racially abused white were black rappers; and now he walks among them, wildest of them all, like some twisted photo-negative of a Civil Rights dream.

American politicians and pressure groups shake nervous fingers at his unnatural pre-eminence. But Eminem's music skips around its earnest accusers, because he is more sophisticated than them, in a way as important as his racial transgressions. As a child fan of gangsta-rap's fantasies who grew up in the real (if, for him, wrong) ghetto, he understands perfectly the difference between exaggerated art and grim reality. This has freed him to explore extreme emotional places that his country – so much happier censoring rappers than addressing real racially divided ghettos, poverty and gunplay – would rather think didn't exist.

All these things run through my mind as I enter the Evening News Arena minutes before this lightning rod figure takes the stage. The protesters have melted away long ago. Only the 28-year-old Marshall Mathers himself is left, to face the expectations of 16,000 young fans, and the fascination of the rest of Britain, waiting to hear what the monster really looked like, and the awful things he did.

But the man I watch for the next 90 minutes is the very opposite of a monster. Instead, when the horror movie hockey mask in which he enters is removed, his charisma fades like the Wizard of Oz. He looks short and slight, gym-work not obscuring the vulnerable, pasty, playground victim he once was. An expensive set and a cartoon intermission, and the sharing of rapping duties with his band of adolescent Detroit friends, D12, all seem designed to distract attention from the most infamous, supposedly fearless pop star in the world.

He doesn't look likely to pistol-whip anyone, or to rape his mother. Instead, he concentrates on gently talking to the mostly teen or under crowd, making sure these children are in on the joke; trusting them not to do as his lyrics suggest. He ludicrously makes them all claim they're drug addicts, to bring these people who like him closer, and push his credulous, adult critics away. The great misogynist even brings a teenage girl fan on stage, and treats her with such deference she could be his own daughter. He seems desperate to destroy the hysteria he's provoked, to return to being an entertainer. In the flesh, his extremist art and timid reality seem separated by chasms. His rage only resurfaces at the end, when, rounding on his critics, he barks the chorus of another of his infamous hits: *"I am whatever you say I am."*

In truth, he's so much more, and less. The real story of who he is begins 28 years before, and 4,000 miles away. It takes us back to the eerie industrial ruins of Detroit, USA.

1

GROUND ZERO

FLASHBACK. In Detroit, you can never go back far enough. People who talk glibly of the Death of the American Dream do so only because they've never been to this place, and seen the corroded, crudely hacked up corpse of a century of false hopes for themselves. Read the history books before you arrive, and you realise the city in which Eminem had to make his way is the end of every kind of American line.

Its rise was swift and promising enough. At the 19th century's start, it was little more than a break in the Midwestern wilderness, a settlement known only to trappers from the French Canada it nearly touched. "De troit" was French for the straits, the narrow riverway down which they rowed, as they slipped between nations. But by 1805, the state of Michigan's first governor, Judge Augustus Woodward, was already planning to transform it into "the Paris of the West", a perfect new city of rationally designed parks and boulevards. This was the first dream Detroit dashed.

Still, in 1825, when the Erie Canal linked Canada's Great Lakes to New York, it was chosen as the staging post for the settlement of America's Northwest. In 1884, a railroad linking Detroit and Chicago added to its importance in the growing nation; although typically, this was one of the last such routes to be built. By the 20th century's dawn, its downtown district was bustling and thriving in the style of grand American cities like New York, factories, bars, civic buildings and homes clustering together. But Detroit's would be the last such urban area to be attempted in America, as a new, suburban life beckoned; and it would suffer the most sickening decline.

Such a fall would have seemed unimaginable when Henry Ford, born in nearby Dearborn, watched the millionth Model T roll from his factory in 1915, in a Detroit he had turned into the boomtown centre for the automobile industry he had started and ruled. His high factory wages

5

sucked in families from as far as Palestine, Eastern Europe and the American Deep South. They rioted outside his gates in the clamour for those jobs, and by 1921 Detroit's population had quadrupled, to a million. War work in the Forties brought a fresh surge, many of them Southern blacks, seeking opportunities away from their oppressive homes. Detroit was named "the arsenal of democracy" then, or simply Motor Town. It had the highest-paid blue-collar workers in America, its factories spread for miles, their machines turned incessantly, growth seemed the city's permanent condition. But the segregated, devastated wasteland called "Amityville" by Eminem, or simply Shitville, was already being built, behind that veneer.

The segregation of its black and white citizens now defines Detroit as much as the Model T did. It was in the boom decade of the Forties that this time-bomb was set, as the city's black population doubled, but the streets they were allowed to live in barely moved. Real estate covenants forbidding black occupation, white hostility and government collusion kept them hemmed into decaying districts like downtown's Lower East Side, otherwise known as "rat alley", for the rodent bites its cramped residents suffered, in homes absentee white landlords let fall apart as rents rocketed, in a ghetto stuffed to bursting point. Family life was strained, residents became transient, crime and squalor rose. Whites had their preconceptions confirmed. So when, in the Forties, the auto industry Detroit had birthed began to abandon its factories, following capitalism's logic into cheaper suburban sites, white citizens fled with it. As civil rights legislation also challenged racial covenants in the city, whites entered new suburbs, which spread almost endlessly into barren hinterland. Past Detroit's northern city limit, the long highway 8 Mile Road, these townships were not physically separate from Detroit. But legally, their vast grids of new bungalows, carved into "city" limits and school catchment borders, could not be penetrated. Protected by subtler real estate racism, and neighbourhood associations who harassed and attacked black "invaders", as they had previously in the city, these new suburbs became a white world.

South of 8 Mile, an ordinary road as uncrossable as the Berlin Wall, blacks were abandoned, living among the cadavers of the factories that had tempted them from Dixie. Tax dollars had left for the suburbs too. In the black world of downtown Detroit, jobs, money and hope disappeared daily. And in 1967, this place of invisible apartheid became a site of race war, a vision of where such iniquity could lead.

There had been one race battle already, back in the boom year of 1943, a little after *Life* had realised: "Detroit is dynamite: it can either blow up Hitler or blow up the US." 34 had died then, 25 of them black, in a 3-day battle finished by federal troops. That lit the fuse. And the 1967 eruption, in a decade of race riots, was the most vicious in America since the Civil War. In other cities in the Sixties, there had been order in the destruction, a concentration on white-owned businesses, a statement being made in the flames. Detroit was already too far gone. Sparked by a police raid on an after-hours drinking joint one hot July night, black rioters torched indiscriminately. A Vietnam general and nearly 5,000 paratroops were needed to pacify the city. In five days, 43 people were killed, 30 by law officers. There were 7,231 arrests. 2,509 buildings were looted or razed. Vacant lots from those days still pock Detroit. "It looks like Berlin in 1945," Mayor Jerome Cavanagh said, looking at his smashed city. "America's first Third World city," it was also dubbed.

That was five years before Eminem was born. The riot's ash hasn't yet been buried. In 1967, a third of Detroit's citizens were black. Now 80 per cent are. The quality of life in the metropolitan area that includes its suburbs is quite high. But in Detroit itself, it's as if some organic, irreversible decay has set in. Since 1950, its population has shrunk by a million. Over 10,000 houses and 60,000 lots stand empty. A third of its citizens are beneath the poverty line. Many live in zones of hardcore unemployment, prospectless. In the Seventies and Eighties, when the race lines of other American cities blurred, Detroit's hardened. It was de-industrialised, deadbeat. 8 Mile Road was the scar that showed its character.

There was a better history Eminem was heir to, a musical heritage of exceptional richness. In the early Sixties, black Detroiters Berry Gordy and Smokey Robinson had founded Motown (a contraction of Motor Town), and quickly gathered other local talent including Marvin Gaye, Stevie Wonder, The Temptations, The Supremes, Martha Reeves, and The Four Tops to the label. From Gordy's modest home, with the wooden sign "HITSVILLE U.S.A." on its roof, a hit factory was built to specifications as tight as Henry Ford's. An Artist Development Department groomed raw teenage talent, while house musicians The Funk Brothers and house writer-producers including Robinson and Holland, Dozier & Holland maintained immaculate standards on smashes from 'Stop ! In the Name of Love' to 'I Heard It Through The Grapevine'. Sent on a dangerous tour of the apartheid South in 1962, Gordy warned his stars they were representing "all of Detroit". And, according to Gordy's own accommodating beliefs, these records made in his seething, schismed city spent much of the Sixties integrating the pop charts with visions of yearning uplift, till they had fulfilled his boast to be "the Sound of Young America".

Detroiters' more complex, harsh reactions to the music, though, were proven when Martha & The Vandellas' 'Dancing In The Street' became a rallying cry for thousands in the 1967 inferno. The label's departure for LA in 1972 signalled the closure of another reason for hope in the city.

The more brutal realities of Detroit in the Sixties were translated into not only later Motown records like Gaye's *What's Going On*, but the grinding proto-punk garage rock of the MC5 and Iggy Pop's Stooges. Pop said his sound was partly a product of the pounding noise of the city's remaining auto factories, and garage rock continues to thrive in Detroit, oblivious to fashion, in bands like The White Stripes and Von Bondies.

Equally pivotal was the early Eighties creation of Techno, by three young middle-class blacks, Derrick May, Juan Atkins and Kevin Saunderson, living in rural Belleville, 30 miles from the city. Representative of the obscure fact that, as Atkins told Simon Reynolds, depressed Detroit is "[also] the city that has the most affluent blacks in the country", they made a kind of post-industrial, art-dance music, from influences including Kraftwerk and George Clinton. On tracks like May's 'Strings Of Life' they made sounds of eerie, funky electronic beauty, the first to directly respond to the cavernous, closed factories that now littered Detroit, where they were only marginally liked.

As a major inspiration for the European rave scene which eventually popularised Es among Eminem's set, May's influence on the rapper can faintly be traced. The decline from popular music of aspiration to cultish music of devastation, though, shows more clearly where Eminem entered Detroit's lineage.

In music, industry and politics, he lived in a place whose glory days had nearly gone. In a nation which by the Nineties was ruled by hip-hop, from East or West coasts, he rapped in the middle of nowhere. He was like the working-class men still scrabbling for auto jobs in the city. He lived in the home of Hitsville. But the Hit Factory had closed its gates.

Take a journey around Detroit today, though, and you'll find new landmarks, staging posts in Eminem's own story. Like his music, they're inseparable from the fallen, fractured state of the city itself.

Midtown is as good a place as any to start. Walk through Wayne State University's campus, towards the grand industrial skyline which was once the city's heart, and you drop into an alien landscape, composed of all the things Detroit has lost. You can walk for 15 minutes, and not see another soul. It's like touring Pompeii, soon after the volcano. The sense of some natural disaster is imprinted on every empty building. Rows of roughly cemented windows look like wet mould. The paint on every wall of what were once factories is peeling. It's as if these streets have been dredged from underwater. Asbestos is left open to the air, hundreds of windows are simply smashed. One vast building's roof is ripped off, and inside it seems a crashed plane of junk has landed nose-first, ploughing through its floors, filling it to the brim. The wind moves the debris, as if it's alive. Nearby are great empty parking lots, long deserted alleys, wild grass patches. This nearly silent wreckage is peaceful and calming to a visitor. Only when bored youths appear in the distance do you remember people were meant to live and work here, and that Detroit is dangerous at night now, because they can't.

Turn right along the old city limit, Grand Boulevard, and you've entered the Lower East Side, still the ghetto's rotted core. There are charred frames of houses turned to ash here, cracked roofs, large muddy lots. Destroyed things aren't replaced down here, just left as gaps and ghosts. Eminem lived here for a while, with Kim and Hailie. But not long enough to make you stop. To get where you're headed next, you could speed up Gratiot, the freeway that splits this old neighbourhood. You'd move fast and see nothing, the way most whites from the suburbs like it; it would help explain how this place has gotten so isolated. But Eminem had no car, growing up. And going slower, a different way, will keep you to his path.

So keep going, straight across Grand Boulevard. Before long, you'll be on 8 Mile Road. Eminem has talked about it so often in interviews, naming it "the racial borderline", even calling his film *8 Mile*, so large does it loom in his mind, that you expect a simmering ghetto cauldron. It is certainly Detroit's central fact, the end result of its racial history, the track Eminem boldly crossed onto the wrong side of, to make "black" rap music. But walk as far as you like along it, as it runs the length of Detroit's northern edge, and its potency is invisible. It looks like just another American highway. It is lined with auto repair shops, warehouses, cheap motels. It is only when you choose a side of it that 8 Mile's mystery is unlocked, and you truly start to step in Eminem's shoes.

Turn right, back down into Detroit, towards 7 Mile (you can count a lot with numbers in this place; they go up to 19 Mile, and down into hell). Depending which junction you choose, you might not be sure on which side of Eminem's border you've fallen at first. Walk one way, and you could be in a leafy English suburb, with mock-Tudor stone houses, substantial with wealth. Except every person you see is black. This is Bagley, one of Detroit's oldest black middle-class districts. Keep going along 7 Mile and the ghetto soon appears. There are more broken-windowed factories, burned houses, scrubland. There are outposts of life, too: schools, churches, recording studios. Every face you see is black again. In Detroit, skin separates you.

Eminem lived here on 7 Mile, for a while. The Hip-Hop Shop where he honed his rapping skills was there (it's now moved), so were his black friends in D12. And, as a teenager, he lived with his mother just south enough of 8 Mile, in a small, two-storey home, one of three white families on his block, behind the sprawling, ugly Bel-Air mall. And it was outside this mall that black teenagers stripped him to his underwear and jammed a pistol to his head, because he was white, before a passing, armed white trucker saved his life.

"If they grew up in Detroit, in the city," Eminem complained to *City Detroit* magazine of his critics, when he first tasted fame, "they would know what the fuck is going on. They would know why I feel the way I do, and why I say the things I do. When you're white and in hip-hop, everybody wants to know your background. You have to come from the 'hood. And I don't see the point in it. But it's like, okay; if everybody in the world wants to know where I came from, then this is where I came from. And I'm gonna show you."

The day before, he had done just that, taking MTV to his old home behind the mall. But he was being too defensive, back then. And he was only telling half the story. He was never just some white foundling, abandoned in a black world. The boy who as a national star would give himself new names and identities at will understood Detroit's dangerously split personality from both sides. Step off 8 Mile the other way, into the white suburbs, and you're still walking in his world.

You've left Detroit altogether now, according to the statutes barring its borders. You're now in the city of Warren. Like 8 Mile, it is a place hardly anyone would have heard of, if Eminem hadn't left it.

It is a sprawling grid of small, one-storey frame houses, replicas of the crumbling East Side it was built to replace, in the decade of the suburban dream, the Fifties. In the years afterwards, smashed windows, arson and violent threats greeted black Detroiters who tried to join whites' flight to it. Eminem's grandmother, Betty Kresin, lived in a trailer park here, and Eminem spent much of his youth there too. He has called this place "the white trash capital of the world". Not for the last time, he exaggerated for effect. Walk through Warren to the school where he spent the most years, Lincoln Junior High, and the white ghetto you expect from his interviews is hard to find.

It has the feel of a quiet English coastal town, off-season. It certainly isn't the home of people made wealthy by whiteness. It is just where Detroit's white working class retreated to, as their own futures shrank. The strolling teenagers of 7 Mile, or the cramped bustle of the Lower East Side, are absent. Adults drive to and from here in their cars, some to factory jobs, still. More kids stick in school. American flags flutter in yards. Neighbourhood Watch signs are prominent. The few, white faces you can see are working on their small gardens. Their subtly, determinedly different wood houses are often chipped, as on 8 Mile's other side. Some toys are left in the street, slovenly, but safe. There are wide mud alleys between the backs of some streets. The impression is of a place just keeping itself above the flood-line. "White trash" is too harsh.

Lincoln Junior High is on the corner of one of the wider avenues. A Drive-Thru Pizza place, a Rustproofing shop and a fire station are the nearby landmarks. "Thoughts and Prayers are with the Rescuers and Victims", says a post-9/11 sign in this peaceful-looking, loyal American backwater. A white boy is crossing the school's large parking lot suspiciously early in the day, with a rapper's low jeans and lope.

Eminem was here from 1986 to 1989, when, at 14, he quit education, to rap. It is the only school where he stayed long enough to make friends. When his nomadic mother moved again to Detroit, he walked two miles back every day, so he could keep them. So this is as close as you will ever get to picturing his school days.

Those were over a decade ago, of course. But the long corridors, metal lockers, and din of fractious, spirited adolescents can't have changed much. Only a small, significant number of black faces, and a few more white boys with a hopeful hint of hip-hop style suggest time's passing. Principal Paul Young has been here three decades. In Eminem's time, he was an English teacher. His take on Warren differs from his ex-pupil's.

"It's very much a blue-collar neighbourhood, of hard-working, honest people," he says in his office. "It has areas that are very poor, and areas that are relatively well-off. Quite a few families moved here from the South, to work in the auto industry. To some extent, it's been hit by that industry's decline. And it's an older neighbourhood. Some of the folks who have retired from the industry have moved further north. The area's become somewhat more transient. When homes go up for sale, in many cases, they're turned into rentals. As a result, the population's become more fluid, and lost some of the sense of community it used to have. But it's always supported the schools."

His view of 8 Mile, a short walk from his school gates, is sanguine too. "At one time, there were some racial issues here," he admits. "But I think that 8 Mile symbolism is less true today than it might have been when Eminem was a youngster. I think one of the reasons is that many of the whites who moved in to Warren from the South have retired and moved on. It's now their kids that are here, and they're more culturally aware, and more tolerant of diversity. Our school's much more diverse than it was even 10 years ago, when he was here."

Eminem's own life suggests how much Detroit's racial divide has frayed along the edge of 8 Mile, in recent years. But think of the unbroken black faces less than a mile to the south of Lincoln, and the small number of black children in its classrooms, and the gap remains stark. Walk down these corridors with Paul Young, and white and black children look up at you suspiciously, wary of a stranger.

Peer into the lunchroom where Eminem used to eat, and you start to see the child he once was. The food is cheap, ladled out in a small serving room by what in Britain would be dinner ladies. Boys and girls sit at small round tables eating quietly. One boy is dressed as a military cadet. Another has pink punk hair. But no one still here has such distinct pictures in their mind of Eminem.

"When he was here, he was Marshall Mathers," Young says. "I wasn't even aware of him then. Because I didn't have him in any classes. And his attendance wasn't very good. Certainly he's a very popular person now. I've had film crews and newspaper reporters turn up here, wanting to walk in and talk to the children. He was only here three semesters. When he left, I don't know where he went. I checked once with our counselling office, and there was no record of any other school asking for his transcripts. I heard at one time that he might have gone to an adult education programme someplace. But he was not a graduate. He only got to ninth grade.

"There are one or two teachers still here who had him in classes. But he was nothing out of the ordinary. It's not like he was suspended a lot, or had a lot of fights. He was a pretty okay kid when he was in school.

I looked through his records, and I don't see anything like he was expelled, or suspended. Not good attendance. Not good grades. But he stayed pretty much to himself. He was here. He wasn't any trouble. He was kind of nondescript. He didn't make a big mark."

When Eminem remembers Lincoln in interviews, it's usually to rage at an unnamed teacher who told him he'd never amount to anything. With an irony he must see as sweet vengeance, he's now recalled in its corridors only for being the success he is today.

"I'm interested in the fact that he's made a name for himself," Young says. "The coolest thing is that when I tell kids, 'Marshall Mathers went to Lincoln High School,' they go, 'Oh, that's neat.'"

There is one more thing to see here, on the way out. Open a thick, heavy door, and you're in a darkened auditorium. There is a plain wood, half-moon-shaped stage area, flush with the rows of seats looking at it from the shadows. Eminem performed in a talent show here once, the first time this shy, nondescript boy pushed himself forward in public. He didn't win, of course. His talent hadn't yet been found.

There is another school out here in the suburbs that figures importantly in his story. To reach it, you now have to bear north-east, till you've left Warren, and risen above 10 Mile, into the township of Roseville. The neat rows of identical, two-storey clapboard houses announce you're in a slightly better neighbourhood now. And Dort Elementary School, a small, low building, looks an inviting place to start your education. But it was in Dort's playground that Eminem, aged 10, was shoved into a snowbank so hard by an older boy who had been bullying him for weeks, De Angelo Bailey, that his brain haemorrhaged, and he fell into a coma for five days. The song 'Brain Damage' on *The Slim Shady LP* recounts the attack. Its central impact on his life, and mind, can only be guessed at. It happened during playtime, on a schoolday, according to interview accounts. But here, even more than at Lincoln, Eminem's passing seems to have left no trace.

Principal Betty Yee came here 11 years ago, long after the incident.

But she has had to look into it before. "You know why Dort has become so famous?" she asks a passing teacher. "They think Eminem was a former student here, from years ago! He had an accident out on the playground. So we're in the newspaper, I guess. But we have no record of him attending, apart from the situation that happened on the playground, many years ago. And you know what? From what I remember, it was on a weekend."

If Eminem, in his wandering childhood, did ever alight at Dort for more than one vicious, weekend hour, seeing it now, he could not have been luckier. All the facilities that might have helped him are on hand, from a music room to experts to help pupils "who need extra reinforcement". The children look happy and involved in their work. This is as far from the ghetto, or any suburban hell, as you can get. It is also far from the run-down trailer park where Eminem spent much of his time this side of 8 Mile. But as Yee talks, you begin to wonder if all the bad things that scarred him can be the fault of the places he was raised.

"Roseville is a blue-collar community, of hard-working parents, who really do want the best for their children," she says, echoing Lincoln's principal. "For me, it's a good community."

When you reach the playground itself, the place where Eminem's brain was jarred and his body shut down when he was just a boy, the violence is easier to picture. A plain stretch of concrete ground in the open air, empty of children now, only playthings at one end break up its hard surface.

"Yes, I can't imagine," Yee says, looking out. "The playground is pretty much the way it was, except we've added equipment – swings, and monkey bars. They weren't there, way back when he was pushed."

Walking away from this brutal landmark, Yee runs into an ex-pupil she recalls better than any place of education seems to remember Eminem. The teenager happily recites a motto she learned in her Dort days: "If my mind can conceive it, and in my heart I believe it, with hard work I *will* achieve it." "We do it every day, after our Pledge of Allegiance," Yee explains. You wonder if, in an uprooted life which could have moved him through Dort too swiftly for any record, Eminem was taught such an all-American promise, to battle in his head with the sneering dismissal of that high school teacher, as he forged his utterly American path to self-creation and success. But all anyone knows for sure about what happened to him here is the sudden, spilled blood he left on its concrete, and how close he came to being a corpse.

Bear south-east now, for one last stop. You are leaving Roseville, for St. Clair Shores, close to the wealthy white enclave of Grosse Point, and to Lake St. Clair, where the Detroit River rolls. You're leaving Eminem's schooldays, too, and looking for an adult milestone: Gilbert's Lodge, the restaurant where he worked between 1996 and 1998, right up until worldwide fame seemed to snatch him from everything he had known before.

You head down Harper, a bit beneath 9 Mile. Shady Lane stands opportunely to the right. The future Real Slim would have seen it every day. Walk across Gilbert's Lodge's gravel car park, and cement bear-prints lead you into a mock-hunting cabin. Stuffed pheasant, bear, sturgeon and snow-shoes are mounted on the walls. There's a long bar, and TVs showing sport. Groups of working-class families and friends sit eating and laughing in shadowed corner booths. "BUY AMERICAN. EAT HERE", says a sign. The food is straight domestic, burgers and meatloaf. This is the place the unknown Eminem worked the most, out of sight behind that bar, as a short-order cook. A waitress comes to take your order. Her name is Jennifer Yezvack. And at last the trail you've followed, which has seemed so faint, glows white-hot. As she speaks, it is as if Eminem has only just left the room.

"He's here in Detroit right now. I just talked to him," she says. "When he's doing something downtown he comes in here, Friday and Saturday nights. Then it gets too crazy, and he has to leave. He's loyal to Detroit. He still goes to all the bars downtown – Lush, Pure, all the different clubs, he hangs out at Marilyn's, on Monroe. He has to call ahead so that everybody can be taken care of. But he still hangs out."

Newspaper reports say, though, that Eminem now has to live far from downtown, and from Warren, in some plush outpost of the wealthy. But as Yezvack recalls the reasons, zigzagging casually through intimate details of his life, you know that his roots here, at least, are still strong.

"Yeah, there were a lot of problems in his last house," she says. "It was on a main road, people could just come into the backyard. People were looking in the windows, stealing stuff from the house, from the mailbox, from the lawn. So he lives in a gated community now. His main goal is living a normal life, with his daughter, and that is the honest to God's truth. His daughter is everything to him, and he wants her life to be as normal as it can. She knows who her father is, though. Hailie knows Daddy can't go to the movies like any Joe Dad would. Even though he *does* – he's put a baseball cap on and gone to the movies with her. I'm like, 'You're crazy !' But he just sneaks right in, and sneaks right out. But she's in school now, and the other kids at school know who she is. It's hard, just too hard. People are too starstruck. Everybody's just flabbergasted that someone made it in this area, that they can approach. So they do."

What was he like when he worked here, when he was just Marshall Mathers, you wonder. Yezvack talks on freely, with no apparent fear that Detroit's most powerful son will swoop down on her and exact a paranoid vengeance. In this place, even now, it seems Eminem can feel trust for old friends.

"I know him, and he hasn't changed to me at all," she says. "He's a very nice guy. He's not how he comes across in public. He was very quiet when he was here. I mean, he was always a smartass, sarcastic, but only every now and again. He was never mean or harmful to anyone, although him and I used to argue all the time, and he was quick, very quick with his responses. When he was here, he had no enemies. He just did his own thing. He was very into his music, always. Not even girls, really. Kim he was with, but he was never into drinking, never did drugs, nothing like that. He would bring a change of clothes into work, and from the minute he was finished, he would change in the break room in the evening and go round one of his friends' houses to rap. We knew he was going to do it. We were all happy for him. He kept saying it forever, when he was here – 'All I wanna do is rap.' He was always involved downtown. He'd go to open mics, all that stuff. I've been through a lot with him, over the years. We dated, on and off. He's a good guy. It's all a show, in a sense. We're talking about Marshall," she says casually, to a manager.

You digest the inadvertent gossip, that Yezvack was probably seeing Eminem at the same time as his fractious, notorious relationship with Kim, his now ex-wife, mother of his child, and brutalised subject of his songs. And a moment later, you're brought one last step towards your quarry.

"Who was here," Yezvack politely asks, "so I can tell him?"

You tell her your name, knowing this is the closest your life will brush his. You ask if you could speak to him like she does, anyway.

"No," she smiles, "he doesn't even like it when I talk this much."

So you say goodbye, and you leave Detroit, and you go back home, and start to think about the things you've seen and heard. You can see what Eminem loves about his fallen, forgotten city. It's a place that educates you in how race and money work in America, every day you walk its streets. It's a place so hard, it leaves no room for the illusions peddled on his country's coasts. It's one reason he makes the music he does. Of course, Eminem is not just the city he's from. He's the things he's done, too, and the people he was with. So you go back again, to the day he was born.

2

MOTHER'S BOY

Everything about Eminem's early life is unstable. Details of homes, relations, schools, jobs, all shimmer and fluctuate from one reminiscence to the next, as if nothing stayed still long enough to be sure of, and no one cared enough to take notes. Even his date of birth was a matter of conjecture till recently, the rapper seemingly pushing it forward two years in interviews, apparently wanting to be even more of a prodigy than he was. After the date was challenged by his mother last year, new publicity quietly started to admit he was born on October 17, 1972. Immediately, all the other "facts" and dates assumed about him pre-fame lock into a different, more believable shape. But still, many things have stayed in flux, maybe for good. You can even take your pick of names. But in the years before the world got to know him, he was always Marshall Mathers.

His mother, Debbie Mathers-Briggs, was the one constant factor in all that time, the itch he would scratch with escalating, obsessive violence on his subsequent records. She was just Debbie Briggs, a 15-year-old girl, when she met the 21-year-old Marshall Bruce Mathers, Jnr. in 1970. Her family was of Scandinavian origin, and scattered across Missouri and Michigan, his father's family was from Wales, and he was from Dakota. They played together for a while in a band called Daddy Warbucks, touring Ramada Inns along the Dakota-Montana border. "My mother used to listen to Jimi Hendrix and shit like that," their son would recall to *FHM*. "She was like a little flower child growing up in the Sixties. A little hippie." His tone had a rare touch of affection, in an interview characteristically hostile to her, as he recognised her own rebellious streak. His grandmother, Betty Kresin, remembered the wilful and passionate way her daughter forced the under-age marriage with Marshall Jnr. into being. When Kresin first refused to give special permission, she told *The Source*, "She threatened me about six months later. 'Okay, if you won't let me get married and go to school, I'll get pregnant and get married.'" It was a typi-cally teenage impulsive ultimatum, in the heat of first love, and at a time when teenage Americans were resisting parents and following sexual desires as never before. Kresin backed down, and in 1972, Debbie and Marshall, Jnr. were married. They lived for a year in his parents' basement in North Dakota. And before that year's end, in Kansas City, Missouri, Marshall Bruce Mathers III was born.

The earliest picture to be made public gives little hint of the conflicts that were to follow. Debbie, now 17 and renamed Mathers-Briggs, is a skinny-armed, T-shirted girl with long, dark, centre-parted hair, her legs folded in a near-lotus position, her mouth in a happy, hopeful grin for the camera. She is holding up baby Marshall, in red, knee-length dungarees. He is looking distractedly at something away from the camera, with big-eyed seriousness. "He always seemed like he was hungry. And always happy," Kresin told *The Source*. "And you know most babies are scream-ing; he wasn't. He was looking around at the world and very happy, it looked like, to be here. I mean, those big blue eyes. He was such a beauti-ful grandson from the beginning." The charismatic blue eyes would stay. And the essentially accepting, contemplative mood Kresin noticed would remain his natural state, whenever stress or public attention were removed. It was the things that happened to him over the next 25 years that mixed that docile intelligence with the violent, vengeful rage which turned Marshall into Eminem.

The first blow came as a consequence of his parents' immature love. "We married so young, it was ridiculous," Marshall Jnr. admitted to the *News Of The World* in a self-serving interview years later, "but I was delighted when your mum became pregnant." Still, passion was quickly spent, and, moving to their own apartment, the young parents soon tired of each other. Mathers-Briggs claimed – though it has never been proven – that her husband was drunk and used drugs, and was even with her best friend as she gave birth to Marshall. Marshall Jnr. said these were all lies. Even the manner of their inevitable split is disputed. Mathers-Briggs said he walked out, one more in a generation of absconding fathers. Marshall Jnr. painted a tragic picture of coming back to their apartment one day to find it emptied like the *Marie Celeste*, of driving round town for weeks, on the apparently impossible task of finding his family. He claimed the eventual divorce was done through lawyers, that he had no way of track-ing down the son he loved. So in 1975, he remarried, and moved on.

Marshall's memories, though, leave no doubt that his father was at least partly lying, or of the wound his absence inflicted. Marshall was about six months old when, for whatever reason, his father moved to California. He was too young to remember having a father at all. But Kresin recalls his childish efforts to communicate with him, anyway. "Marshall used to colour pretty little pictures and give them to me," she told *The Source*. "He'd say, 'Grandmom, can you give these to my Daddy?'" She passed them on to a relative she was sure had stayed in touch with Marshall Jnr. In his early teens, Marshall would send letters, too. All came back marked "Return to Sender". The most painful proof that his father had simply chosen to ignore him came when he would visit Marshall Jnr.'s aunt's house as a child. The adult Marshall recalled the scene to *The Source* with crystal exactness, and emotions that were still raw and live. "I was always over there, and he would call there. I would be on the floor colouring. I remember!" he exclaimed, as if still childishly desperate for someone to believe him. "I would be there just listening. He would call there and talk to them, and never ask to talk to me."

"I think a lot of anger came because he was raised by his mother – no father image or figure was there," Kresin considered recently, to the *Tonight* TV programme. "I once asked him why he was so angry with me," Mathers-Briggs told the *Mail On Sunday*. "He said it was because he didn't have a dad. I tried to explain to him that I left his father because he was abusive" – partially clearing one mystery. *"When you see my Dad, tell him I slit his throat in this dream I had,"* Marshall declared himself in 'My Name Is', the single that announced him as Eminem to the world. But his father was never seriously mentioned again in his work. And in that *Source* interview, his memories of hurt had to be squeezed from him. All he wanted to say, and kept saying, was "Fuck him!" It was his father who had done him the simplest, most damaging wrong, by removing himself from his life. The cost of such abandonment to many children is helplessness and compensatory aggressive anger, a sense of loss and lack of self-esteem. Marshall would exhibit all these traits as he grew up, a typical child, in this way, of his times. Most of all, though, what his father left behind was a hole in his head, which could not be filled. So, in interviews and art, he sealed that wound over, ignored it as best he could, and moved on. His mother was a very different matter.

"Me and my mother have never gotten along from the cradle," he told *NME* in 1999. That mother was a 17-year-old girl when she was left with him. The consequence-blind teenage gamble she had taken with her life, by marrying his father and having him, had already failed. And in the end, all the evidence suggests she did not raise him well. But they were stuck with each other. More than anything, that explains why the dammed fury he kept for his father was not as strong as the hot, active hate he would come to have for his mother; why, by the time he was making records as Eminem, childish love had collapsed into a vindictive state of war.

Everything his parents said after he was famous is tainted by a tone of self-justification, after he attacked them in lyrics and print. But even his father admitted that, in the time he knew Mathers-Briggs, "She was great with you – you were always clean and well-fed and well-dressed, and I couldn't fault her for that." "I am gullible and loving," Mathers-Briggs said of herself, in the *Mail On Sunday*. "As a child Marshall was never spanked, and I never raised my voice to him. The real problem is not that he had a hard time, but that he resents I sheltered him so much from the real world. I love him so much that if he asked me to jump in front of a train for him, I would. I was an over-protective mother who gave him everything he wanted and more." The strained exasperation she felt having to raise this insecure child on her own, barely an adult herself was, though, more realistically described on the *Tonight* programme. "I did the best I could – it was just him and me," she sighed. "Anything Marshall wanted, I would try and get for him. I got kicked out of stores because he'd be like the spoiled brat, lying in the aisle, arms and legs spread open."

Marshall's neediness only grew, though, as a direct result of his mother's actions. In one of his most touching early interviews, quoted in his mother's eventual, infamous suit against him for defamation, he described the difficulty of his childhood, with none of the bravado of later accounts.

"Was your home life ever stable?" the interviewer asked.

"Not really," he replied. "I was an only child for 12 years. When I was little, my mother never had a job, so we used to always stay with my family. We would stay until we got kicked out. Some of the relatives stayed in Kansas City, some in Detroit, so we just kept going back and forth. I guess we were freeloaders, so to speak. Whenever we would come back to Detroit, we would stay with my grandmother. Finally, my mother ended up meeting some dude and shit, so we got a house on the east side of Detroit when I was 12 years old." A little later, he expressed how that made him feel, in a tone of forlorn sadness for himself. "If you're going somewhere constantly and the scenery is changing around," he said, "it makes you feel real nervous and shit, especially being so little. I mean, fuck it, now it's done and over with . . ."

In another early interview, to *Spin*, he gave more concrete details, this time with a dutiful attempt to understand his mother. "I was born in Kansas City, then when I was five we moved to a real bad part of Detroit. I was getting beat up a lot, so we moved back to K.C., then back to Detroit again when I was 11. My mother couldn't afford to raise me, but then she had my little brother" – his half-brother, Nathan – "so when we moved back to Michigan, we were just staying wherever we could, with my grandmother or whatever family would put us up. I know my mother tried to do the best she could, but I was bounced around so much – it seemed like we moved every two or three months, I'd go to, like, six different schools in one year. We were on welfare, and my mom never ever worked."

By the time he talked to *NME* a little later, he had told the story enough times to start to resent what it meant, and be certain who was to blame. "My mother never had a job," he re-emphasised, "so . . . in Kansas City when I was a kid we stayed with my aunts, my uncles, and when they got fed up with us – not really with me, but my mother, she can't get along with no one – they would kick us out. That's how we ended up in Detroit."

His mother's response came in the *Mail On Sunday*. "Obviously, I became over-protective," she said. "I was single, he was my only son. Years later, he abused me because he changed school so many times. Yet the truth is whenever he had a problem at school, he came home and demanded to move. And I gave in to him."

Such private, partially remembered conversations between relatives now in bitter dispute can't be checked for accuracy now. But Mathers-Briggs' reason for their moves at least tallies with Marshall's memory of fleeing Detroit's bullies as a child for Kansas City. Records entered into court during the libel trial about her raising of him – taken with his albums, the most public inquiry into a mother's duties in American history – meanwhile confirmed that Marshall attended five elementary schools in four cities as a child. While not quite as erratic an education as he remembered, it was obviously deeply destabilising, for a boy already feeling abandoned by one parent. As he said, the scenery kept changing. It must have been hard to feel trust in the world.

Instead, it was in these first nomad years that he was forced to turn inwards, and start to nurture an artist's mind. He became absorbed in TV, and comic-books. The latter was a traditional source of inspiration for poor black rappers, especially the superhero genre, with its garish, primal fantasies of impotent, misunderstood striplings with enormous, secret strengths – his D12 bandmate Kuniva would note that "being a rapper in high school was like being one of the X-Men, like being a mutant with hidden powers." Marshall gained so much from comics that drawing them was his first artistic ambition, a daring one for someone from a background with such limited horizons. He would later turn up in superhero costume in videos, and joined the superhero (and rap) tradition of "secret identity" aliases. He gained his first aged five – Eminem, from his initials, and the M'n'M sweets he loved. But puny Marshall Mathers remained his real self.

The wounded, self-protectively sealed nature of that boy was agreed on by him and his mother. "He was a really talented boy," she told the *Mail On Sunday*. "He was very artistic but he was a very shy child. He was too shy. He was a loner and he never wanted to pal up with people." In that sad, court-quoted interview, he gave more reasons why. "It was real difficult making friends when I was growing up, because we used to bounce from house to house and move so much. It wasn't until I was 12 years old that we finally stayed in one spot. In school, when I was little, I was one of them shy kids, and it was hard for me to make friends. Just as soon as I would start getting close to friends, we would have to leave."

"I was the distant kid," he added to a website. "You know, real distant. The friends I did have knew me well, but I didn't have a lot of friends." *"Drugs is what they used to say I was on/ They say I never knew which way I was goin',"* he rapped bitterly of how others saw him then, on 'Brain Damage'. *"Wore spectacles with taped frames and a freckled nose/ A corny-lookin' white boy, scrawny . . ."* The enduring nature of this hurt was confirmed when Brian Grazer, the producer of his movie *8 Mile*, met him last year. "He was very humble," Grazer said, surprised. "He talked about his roots in a way that made me feel . . . damage."

Mathers-Briggs' own state of mind in these first years of Marshall's life, as she moved through her twenties, can only be inferred. Relying on the regularly removed charity of relatives, unable or unwilling to work, it must have been a harried, directionless existence. The freedom and wilfulness of the "hippie chick" days in which Marshall was conceived are rarely to be found in accounts of her raising him. Her own descriptions of her motherly technique in interviews are meanwhile unmistakably idealised, self-justifying in the most transparent way. But when she relates actual altercations with her child – in a flailing tantrum on a supermarket floor, shouting at her for his father's absence, asking to leave schools where he was constantly bullied, failing to make friends – they sound pulled from still strong, specific memories. And they suggest a mother who found her son hard to understand, and found bringing him up too much to handle, more than once.

The only way in which she did continue down the old wild path on which she conceived her son was sexually. "My daughter had a lot of boyfriends," Kresin told the *Sydney Sun-Herald*. "Debbie is not the best mother." There's nothing to criticise in such a young girl staying sexually active and searching for a partner. But Marshall's memories suggest she hardly screened him from the changing cast of men with which his father was replaced.

"The worst place was an apartment in a big house in Detroit that had five families living in different rooms," he said in *Bliss*. "My Mom's boyfriend's friends would all come over and go crazy. It was horrible."

The welfare-based poverty in which they lived also made Marshall – already too visible, for such a shy boy, as the permanent new kid in class – cringe as a child.

"People used to find things about me to make fun of," he told *Bliss*. "My hair, the way I dressed – anything. Sometimes my mother used to send me to school in these blue pyjamas. I'll never forget them. I used to roll them up in the summertime and say they were shorts. I used to get beaten up after school because of that."

It was during his first period on the East Side of Detroit, from the age of five, as he struggled to survive in a series of elementary schools, that this violent intimidation became another factor in alienating the attitude of a child who had begun so happily. He was chased and beaten by gangs, other children, local drunks and addicts. "I was always getting jumped, dog," he told the *Guardian*. "On the way to school, at school, on the way back from school. I was always getting fucked with. I was puny, timid. Fuckwithable."

"Marshall's an itty-bitty thing who wouldn't stand a chance in a fight," his mother helpfully confirmed to the *Mail On Sunday*, when his own reputation as some kind of violent bad boy was at its height.

This terrifying childhood reached its savage nadir in the events described in 'Brain Damage', the afternoon when, aged 10, he had his head smashed into that snowbank in Dort Elementary's playground, by

12-year-old De Angelo Bailey. The song is a dark fantasia of Franken-steinian brain operations, naked school nurses and superheroic, broom-wielding vengeance on bullies. But its atmosphere of resented, relentless fear, and the events at its core, are truthful.

"One guy used to beat my ass every day," he told *FHM*. "I was in the fourth grade and he was a sixth-grader [eighth-grader in the song, typical of his life's slurred imprecision]. Everybody was afraid of him. I was never the type to kiss ass, so he used to beat me instead."

Marshall names Bailey in 'Brain Damage', remembering him as a fat black kid with a boxer father. He recounts being shoved daily into lockers by the bully, having his lunchroom seat, orange juice and chocolate milk stolen, the pathetic, helpless sufferings of a little boy. Then one day, Bailey came up behind him as he was pissing in the school urinal, hammering his face into the cold enamel till his nose was broken, and he was dripping blood, then choking him by the throat, ignoring Marshall's begging, just looking him in the eye and saying, "You're gonna die, honkey." From there the song enters pure fantasy, with the school principal walking in, and helping in the beating, the whole verse seeming like a death-dream, a nightmare of what could have happened with another minute or two of being held down, bruised and cut. Really, 'Brain Damage' conflated Bailey's two worst attacks.

"Everything in the song is true," Marshall told *Rolling Stone*. "He beat the shit out of me. Pissed all over myself. But that's not how I got really fucked up."

By some accounts, the assault that followed on Dort's playground was the fourth by Bailey on his victim. Whether Marshall even went to that school, or was attacked at playtime or a weekend, may also be in dispute. But what happened to him there is not. He insulted a friend of Bailey's, in response to which, he told *Rolling Stone*, the bully "came running from across the yard and hit me so hard into this snowbank that I blacked out."

"He was the one we used to pick on," the adult Bailey, married with children, happily confirmed to the magazine. "There was a bunch of us that used to mess with him. You know, bully-type things. We was having fun. Sometimes he'd fight back – depend on what mood he'd be in. Yeah, we flipped him right on his head at recess. When we didn't see him moving we took off running. We lied and said he slipped on the ice."

'Brain Damage' picks up the story just after the attack: *". . . Made it home, later that same day / Started reading a comic and suddenly everything became grey/ I couldn't even see what I was tryin' to read/ I went deaf, and my left ear started to bleed."*

His mother's reaction in the song – screaming, *"What, are you on drugs?"*, complaining he's bleeding on the carpet, then hitting him with the remote control till his brain falls out of his skull – is another fantastic riff which may start with a germ of truth. But his attempt to sit and read a comic after getting back from such a brutal assault, trying to quietly carry on as if nothing had happened, gives an undeniable insight into the suppressed way he lived his life at 10. And the clinically chilling description of his symptoms' onset tells how it felt as that life almost ended. Sight then sound remorselessly shutting down, and blood dribbling from his ear, like any child he must have felt confusion and helpless panic, like this day of fear would never end. Taken to the hospital by his mother for a brain scan, he collapsed into a coma. He had suffered a cerebral haemorrhage, and did not fully regain consciousness for five days. "I remember waking up and saying, 'I can spell elephant,'" he told *Rolling Stone*.

Even that was not the end of his ordeal. "It was a living nightmare," his mother recalled to *Tonight*. "The doctors gave up on him in a couple of months, and they wanted to institutionalise Marshall. They told me they didn't think there would be anything else they could do, besides keeping him on a lot of seizure medicines. I decided, 'I'm taking him home. I will work with him, I know he'll bounce back.' And he did. It took several months, and a lot of hard work." "He had to relearn how to do simple things like speak and eat," she added to the *Mail On Sunday*, "and one of the side-effects from the head injury, I believe, was his behavioural problems."

No one has ever denied Mathers-Briggs did at least this much for her son. And the seriousness of his injury, so early in his life, was as grave as she said. He was lucky to survive a cerebral haemorrhage with his faculties intact. The tone and title of 'Brain Damage' gave his mature reaction to this pivotal incident. Everyone thought he was some kind of mental cripple as he grew up anyway, a weird kid who didn't fit, someone to hit. So the song grimly revelled in sickness, claimed he really hadn't come back from the hospital quite right. *"It's probably brain damage . . . I got brain damage,"* he murmured at its fade. The truth is, no one can know how such a bloody mauling of his brain, and the reconstruction of its functions when so young, affected him. Maybe this was when one of the synaptic triggers for the utterly unprecedented lyrical flow with which as an adult he would tear apart Bailey and other enemies was set. If so, it was still hard to be grateful.

"De Angelo Bailey – I'll never forget that kid," Marshall laughed ruefully in *Rolling Stone*. "That motherfucker nearly killed me . . ."

"Hey, you have his phone number?" the unrepentant one-time thug cheerily asked the magazine.

It was soon after this that Marshall and his mother retreated to the relative safety of Kansas City. When their options there ran out again, and they returned to the Detroit area, Marshall was, as near as can be gathered from his own subtly conflicting accounts, 11. The teenage years ahead of him would just intensify the fears and frustrations he had already suffered. But, living for the first couple of years in his grandmother's suburban trailer, he also experienced something like stability for the first time. Starting seventh grade at Lincoln Junior High in 1986, aged 12, he even had enough confidence to make friends.

"It was in seventh grade that I started making friends," he confirmed to Howard Stern. "I didn't really start opening up until eighth grade, going into ninth. I didn't want to leave the school when we moved to Detroit on the East Side, so it was like two miles for me to walk to school. My choice boiled down to if I wanted to stay at Lincoln and keep the same friends, or start over at a new school."

He chose the long walk, showing the importance of these tentative social roots to him, and a degree of independent, determined freedom from his mother's choices not evident before. But as an adult, even Lincoln was not remembered with affection. He was still scrawny and funny-looking, not let near the "cool" kids on the small round tables of Lincoln's modest lunchroom. He barely raised a ripple when he was at the school, still staying mostly inside his simmering head. But it was here, as in other areas of his teenage life, that anger at how he was being treated at last began to bubble up.

"I was kinda nerdy, man," he told *The Source*. "I used to try and dress hip-hop, and my hair was all fucked up. I think my first year of ninth grade, I had a fuckin' mullet or something until I started to rock the fade. It'd be all shaved on the sides and the back, and my hair used to be spiked up, like a flat-top." He was a quietly surly, reluctant student too, the boy who would grow up to update Pink Floyd's *"We don't need no education"* chant on D12's 'Revelation'. "I was kind of a smart-ass," he told a website. "Teachers always gave me shit 'cos I never went to school. Then when I did show up, they would fuck with me. They'd be like, 'Oh, Mr. Mathers decided to join us today.'" This was standard teacher sarcasm, of course, not exactly undeserved. But eventually, one educator went far enough to lodge himself in Marshall's brain, doubting him with such scorn that the memory became a spur, an irritant he could scratch only by proving him wrong.

"There was this teacher," he told *The Source*, "he once singled me out and told me I wasn't gonna be shit. Everybody in class laughed. I don't even remember why he said that. But it stands out in my head . . . it really hurt my feelings, and I was thinking that it shouldn't. Here's this guy I didn't give a fuck about saying this, but it hurt."

He was still rapping about the incident on 'Revelation', written when he was 28. Added to the crushing weight on his self-esteem of an absent father, erratic home life, obvious poverty, and constant street beatings he was too weak to do anything about, he was wide open to be bruised by such words. But these aspects were also coalescing into the fury that turned him into an artist, the need to prove himself and strike back, or else vanish. "I run on vengeance," he said in his most revealing interview, and these were the years when he stored up his fuel.

When his mother left Warren for Detroit's East Side, probably when Marshall was 13, and probably following a boyfriend, a further, vital kind of violent friction entered his life. Living in a black neighbourhood, and making black friends, while still crossing 8 Mile into Warren for school every day, was like trying to blithely pass the Berlin Wall. Marshall and his friends attempted to ignore their city's racial blockade. But others coldly enforced it. "I'm colour-blind – it wasn't an issue," Mathers-Briggs told *Rolling Stone* of being among three white families on their block. "But the younger people in the area gave us trouble. Marshall got jumped a lot."

"Most of the time it was relatively cool," he considered generously to *Spin*, "but I would get beat up sometimes when I'd walk around the neighbourhood and kids didn't know me. One day I got jumped by, like, six dudes, for no reason."

Worse than that was the second time his young, vulnerable life was almost finished, as he walked back from a friend's one afternoon through 8 Mile's Bel-Air mall, aged 16 (15, in one version). "All these black dudes rode by in a car, flippin' me off," he told *Rolling Stone*. "I flipped them off back, they drove away, and I didn't think nothin' of it." But they'd parked, and were coming for him. "One dude came up, hit me in the face and knocked me down," Marshall continued. "Then he pulled out a gun. I ran right out my shoes, dog. I thought that's what they wanted." He was crying as he ran, he admitted to *Spin*. "I was 15 years old and I didn't know how to handle that shit." But they kept after him, stripping him of his clothes and holding the gun to him. Only a white trucker who stopped, got out and pointed his own pistol scattered the attackers. The trucker drove him the short distance home. "He came in wearing just his socks and underwear," his mother remembered. "They had taken his jogging suit off him, taken his boombox. They would have taken him out too." Walking the same way the next day, Marshall found his trainers where he had abandoned them. "That's how I knew it was racial," he said. The same year, he was shot at by a black gang member. He didn't know if the bullet was to frighten, or kill.

Living in a white minority, victimised and twice almost murdered by blacks, Marshall could be excused for starting to feel racist himself. The tribal nature of city hostility works that way everywhere, more so in America, and more so still in Detroit's huddled, severed communities. But, crucially for his future career, he took the opposite view. He had, after all, also seen white bikers point guns at his black friend Proof, taunting him for daring to enter Warren, when Marshall lived there. They had shot at them right outside his mother's door, when Marshall challenged them. In this way, his wandering early life had at last done him good. He had walked between white and black America so often, his feet had smeared the borderline. He saw both sides with double-vision, from inside and out. He knew too much to be racist. Instead, his Detroit days made him hair-trigger sensitive to racism, from whatever skin colour, from then on.

At home, his life was becoming more complicated, too. In 1986, his half-brother Nathan was born. "Marshall was 13 when I became pregnant," Mathers-Briggs remembered to the *Mail On Sunday*. "He was delighted." For once, their memories tally. Nathan brought out in Marshall a need to give the parental love he had felt deprived of himself. "I think parenthood comes naturally to me," he told *Spin*, after he'd had his daughter Hailie. "My little brother was born when I was 11 years old [still carefully lying about his age at this point], so I pretty much raised him from the cradle." The two boys would remain devoted to each other.

Two years later, a more disruptive addition to the household arrived, one that would ripple through all his life and music, inspiring songs, violent rages, near-jail, marriage and helpless love. "I have always loved kids," Mathers-Briggs recalled of the newcomer's route in to the *Mail On Sunday*, "and fostered four. The house was always full of waifs and strays. One of those troubled souls was Kim Scott, who moved in with us when she was 12. Marshall was about 15, and she lied about her age, saying she was the same. They got together and that was it. Chaos reigned."

Kim and her twin sister had had their own difficult histories, frequently being sent for stays at the local children's home, frequently escaping from it. By whatever means, she was out the day she met Marshall. He was spending his morning as he often did by then, dodging out of school with a friend once they knew the friend's mother was working, cranking up the friend's stereo to hear the latest raps. Kim was visiting the friend's sister. "I had a red kangol," Marshall said, still able to picture every detail of the moment for *The Source*, 14 years later. "I was jumping on the coffee table, singing along to an LL song. I was really into it. I kinda saw her come in the doorway out the corner of my eye. I just kept going. Showing off. She watched until I finished the song, and then my friend's sister introduced us."

They rowed and wrestled like brother and sister at first, but soon became inseparable and, after a few years, lovers. Mathers-Briggs' account of the start of what remains Marshall's only serious relationship, one so consuming and exhausting he seems to have nothing left for another, and which stoked such furies he rapped about strangling Kim, sounds truthful.

"He went through a lot with Kim," she told the *Sydney Sun-Herald*. "A lot of his anger came from that. I could tell they were getting too chummy. Kim was jealous of Marshall and his friends and anyone who took attention away from her, including me. There was a lot of chaos in the house."

"Until then, Marshall was a normal, happy boy," she added to the *Mail On Sunday*. "She changed him, she wound him up, and they had the most terrible rows. I had to break up the cursing between them. The girl thrives on confrontation. But Marshall was never violent towards her. He may rap about raping and murdering her, but he has never laid a finger on her. When they had a row he took it out on his car, he would come screaming home and punch the car. I've never seen a vehicle with so many dents in it."

"I've been very betrayed by Kim," she revealed to *Tonight*, sadly, when her relationship with her son had fractured. "There are a lot of things that have happened that Marshall's not even aware of."

His home was now a pressure cooker of conflicting, escalating insecurities and needs, an emotional war-zone. Mathers-Briggs' habit of serial fostering, despite subsisting on Welfare, when added to her early pregnancy with Marshall, suggests a classic woman's attempted short cut to affection and fulfilment. As boyfriends passed briefly through her life, surely children would love her? It says more about her vulnerabilities and desires than any of her words. With the children's home habitué and confrontation-addicted Kim now also under her roof, the atmosphere of neediness must have been intense. It's hard to tell who in the apartment had the lowest self-esteem. But as Kim sided with Marshall against his mother, when not angrily arguing with him, the unhealthiness of the manipulations for control which seemed to fill the two young women's days together, till anger and spite became the norm, can only have added to the teenage boy's misery, and his later music's misogyny.

Mathers-Briggs meanwhile continued to change addresses, this time, according to Marshall, one step ahead of unpaid rent. He hid their Welfare food when friends visited, still ashamed of his poverty. And, around the time Kim arrived, when he was 15, he claimed financial need made his jobless mother force him out to work. He had just failed Lincoln's ninth grade for the third time, anyway. But he saw the abrupt end of his schooling as part of yet another pattern of parental abuse.

"As soon as I turned 15," he told *Rolling Stone*, "my mother was like, 'Get a fucking job and help me with these bills or your ass is out.' Then she would fucking kick me out anyway." His mother denied it to the magazine. "A friend told me, 'Debbie, he's saying this stuff for publicity.' He was always well-provided for." But he stuck to his story, adding angry details to *Rap Pages*. "I would end up getting kicked out like every fucking day, literally just for nothing. Sometimes it was for coming in late, hanging out on the streets with my friends. My mother felt like I was too young to be running the streets. That would be her excuses."

His description of her own daily life was withering. "It was a complicated thing, 'cos my mother was taking a lot of drugs, so she would be in and out of different mood swings. My mother would take three or four naps a day and just get up and start running around the house stomping – 'This house is a goddamned mess' – and start throwing shit, breaking dishes and stuff, 'You get out, motherfucker, you get out and never . . .' blah, blah, blah. I would end up sleeping over a friend's house for a while and shit like that."

When his mother sued him over these comments and others, he became more specific, admitting that the drugs he meant were the prescription anti-depressants Valium and Vicatin. She gave her own version of her usage in the *Mail On Sunday*. "Marshall has accused me of being addicted to prescription pills," she declared. "Well, back in 1990 I was run over by a drunk driver. I had to eat baby food as I couldn't swallow, and during that time I was on medication. It wasn't pill-popping and, whatever he says, I brought Marshall up in an alcohol, drug and smoke-free zone." Still, her regular use of anti-depressants was not disputed in court; whatever she was doing to her son, her own life still seems to have been unhappy and shapeless. As to his evictions, his grandmother confirmed that he regularly appeared at her door in Warren at night, sighing, "Grandma, she kicked me out again." Kresin added that sometimes her daughter would abuse her, too. "She would get mad at me, and punish me by keeping him away from me and my son, Marshall's Uncle Ronnie. They were best friends and really close, and she would keep them from each other."

To *Rap Pages*, Marshall added tired details of his situation: "I had one factory job sweeping floors a mile from home. Doing good. My mother used to keep all of my cheques and give me like 40 bucks outta each cheque, and I made over 140 bucks. My mother would keep the hundred and pay the phone bill or the light bill. That's how I was able to stay. I ended up getting kicked out and staying at my boy's house, three miles away, so I ended up losing that job."

It was to *NME*, though, that he revealed the full scale of his resentment and hurt at this latest round of changing backdrops to his life, and the screaming matches soundtracking them. "I had to stay with friends for two months at a time," he complained. "I would bounce from house to house. It was shitty. I had a lot of friends who I would stay with and their parents were always cooler than my mother. I would tape my mother throwing me out and play them to my friends' parents just to show them how crazy she is. I'd stay at Proof's house and his mother did not care what we did as long as we were safe. My friends' parents liked me!" he suddenly pleaded, like he needed witnesses to prove he wasn't worthless. "They liked me! I was a likeable person, it was just me and my mother did not get along." He shook his head to himself. "It was not my fault. It was not my fault."

In this mood of introspection, he considered the whole nature of his teenage life. "You only realise how bad it was later. I look back now, dog, and I lived a crazy-assed life. I mean, getting kicked out all the time, having no money, getting jumped all the time. I failed ninth grade three times and then left school. I was a fuck-up." Then he reconsidered his earlier excusing of himself, with the diffidence and wish for fairness he would never quite bury, even at his most outrageous: "But it wasn't entirely my fault."

In the midst of all this turmoil, in a place where many teenagers would go wildly astray, Marshall was spoken to by Detroit's police only twice. The first time was for standing up for his mother, another clue that things were not always poisonous between them, but sometimes loyal and loving. In his early teens a woman on their block was threatening Mathers-Briggs, and jabbing her finger in her face. Marshall jumped between them, shouting, "You're not hurting my Mom !" The woman's husband then attacked him with a baseball bat, which Marshall took off him as they wrestled to the ground. That was when the police arrived to drag Marshall away. But enough neighbours had witnessed the scuffle for his innocence to be proved.

Two more crucial incidents, though, combined at the end of his adolescence to ruin it further, and to cripple his love for his mother for good. In 1991, when he was 19, his Uncle Ronnie – son of Kresin, and brother of Mathers-Briggs – killed himself after a girl rejected him. The apparent trigger for his death cannot have helped Marshall's increasingly defensive, hostile attitude to women, as they ruled and warred in his home. But Ronnie dying at all was the worst.

"The two were just six weeks apart and were more like brothers," Mathers-Briggs told the *Mail On Sunday*. "They did everything together. But when they were about 16, Marshall got into rap, and Ronnie liked Bon Jovi. They fell out and didn't speak for two years. When Ronnie killed himself, Marshall was devastated."

"I don't know whether it takes balls or a fucking coward to kill themselves," Marshall, who would later toy with suicide himself, as would his wife, wondered to *Rolling Stone*. "I ain't figured it all out yet. With my uncle, I just wish I could have talked to him before he did it to find out what the fuck was really on his mind." At the time, he was simply wrecked. "I didn't talk for days," he told Q. "I couldn't even go to the funeral." His uncle's name was one of the tattoos of key people in his life with which he would later ink his body.

Ronnie's suicide then burst to the surface again, during another fierce row between his sister and nephew. "I wish it was you who died,"

Mathers-Briggs screamed, "and Ronnie was still here!" It's not an unknown thing for a mother to wish on an adolescent son when at snapping point; she needn't mean it for more than the second she says it, and we don't know the provocation. Her own upset at her brother's death should also be remembered. But for Marshall, emotionally fragile and already resentful, something broke with those words. "It got quiet," he remembered to *The Source*. "I could see in my friends' faces. Even they kinda looked at me like, 'Damn, that's fucked up.'" He focused on his mother's furious sentence with the same intensity as he had that Lincoln teacher's dismissal of his hopes. He would not forget, or forgive. "She said that," he said this year, then paused. "So I'm gonna be as dead to her as I can get."

No one has said when this happened. But, with friends round, and after he and Ronnie were 19, it cannot have been far from the night of his twentieth birthday. He had his second brush with the law then, and it was very different from his first. His mother called the police to accuse him of assault and battery. The once-puny Marshall had been lifting weights since he was 17, after coming so close to violent death the year before. In photos of him with his mother as an adult, he towers above her, with muscular arms. The thought of him attacking her is not pleasant. But perhaps, like her savage words to him, it just shows how oppressive their life together had become. Both had now been driven to lash out without restraint. Their future lives would move towards open battle.

Ronnie had done one more pivotal thing for his nephew, while he was still alive. Mathers-Briggs might remember their musical differences. All Marshall knew was that his uncle left him the gift which let him hang on to sanity, without which his life would have shaken apart. Age 11, Ronnie played him his first rap record.

3

THE WHITE NEGRO

"The first hip-hop shit I ever heard was that song 'Reckless' from the *Breakin'* soundtrack," Marshall told *Spin* in 1999. "My cousin played me the tape when I was, like, 9. Then there was this mixed school I went to in fifth grade, one with lots of Asian and black kids, and everybody was into breakdancing. They always had the latest rap tapes – the Fat Boys, L.L. Cool J's *Radio*. I thought it was the most incredible shit I'd ever heard."

The element of calculation in Marshall's first public appearances as Eminem is underscored in that statement's inaccuracies. He certainly could have been nine when the early hip-hop exploitation movie *Breakin'* (*Breakdance* in the UK) came out in 1984, if he'd been born in 1974. As we know, though, he was born two years earlier. The mental readjustment of each key event of his life into different parts of his youth every time a question was asked in his hundreds of early interviews, so that the odd deception would hold, must have done strange things to his mind. All the time he was Eminem to the world, he had to think as if he really was two years younger. Calling Uncle Ronnie his cousin shows how mutable his floating, fractious family unit could become in his head, too, thanks to such initial, contradictory recountings.

At any rate, Marshall was not a precocious little boy when hip-hop first seized him, but nearing adolescence, with its extra dose of frustrated anger. The music's almost mystical answering of every need in his insecure young life was remembered in one of his most nakedly autobiographical verses, in D12's 2000 rap, 'Revelation'. After dismissing his mother for failing to raise him, he spits: *"Full of crazy rage, an angry teenager/ nothing could change me back/ gangsta-rap had me acting like a maniac/ I was boostin', so influenced by rap, I used it/ as an excuse to do shit/ no one could tell me nothin'/ hip-hop over-whelmed me, to the point where it had me in a whole 'nother realm/ it was like isolatin' myself was healthy/ it felt like we was on welfare but wealthy/ compelled me to excel in school and failed me, expelled me . . ."* The sense that he had been transformed by rap, changed into a more furious, powerful, criminal (*boostin'*) boy than he had ever been before, flows through the verse. Probably there's an element of play, too, with credulous critics' belief that rap fans dumbly do whatever rap records say. But the idea that it was *"an excuse to do shit"*, to act positively for himself at last, is no joke. And the feeling of being *"overwhelmed . . . in a whole 'nother realm . . . on welfare but wealthy"*, rapped in a tone of fervent transport, suggests gospel transcendence: that gangsta-rap's gritty street tales lifted him out of his poverty-stricken, unhappy existence, into something better.

He remembered that sensation again when *Newsweek* suggested his own raps were harmful. "I don't think music can make you kill or rape someone, any more than a movie is going to make you do something you know is wrong," he said, "but music can give you strength. It can make a 15-year-old kid, who is being picked on by everyone and made to feel worthless, throw his middle finger up and say, 'Fuck you, you don't know who I am.' It can help make them respect their individuality, which is what music did for me. If people take anything from my music, it should be motivation to know that anything is possible, as long as you keep workin' at it and don't back down. I didn't have nothin' going for me . . . school, home . . . until I found something I loved, which was music, and that changed everything."

Of course, rap didn't strike him like that all at once. After the first rush of Ice-T's 'Reckless', and with Uncle Ronnie continuing to be his musical mentor, it was the fearless, taunting, street-wise raps of Queens' L.L. Cool J which convinced him the music was for him. The attitude alone must have been a wistful fantasy, for a skinny boy preyed on so often by bullies he loathed, but couldn't beat. "When L.L. first came out with 'I'm Bad', I wanted to do it, to rhyme," he remembered. "Standing in front of the mirror, I wanted to be like L.L." He would wear shades, too, lost in his superhero secret identity. And, in pursuit of this dream life, he became studious, in a way he never managed at school. "When my son first got into rap as a teenager," his mother remembered to the *Mail On Sunday* with a sigh, "he would wake me at 5 am to ask me what words rhymed with what. I bought him a dictionary, and it all went downhill from there." The capacious vocabulary this high school drop-out would go on to flex on records shows how deeply he absorbed that gift. His life with his mother was part of the reason. "We were so fuckin' poor," he told

Kerrang. "My mother used to do so much fucked-up shit to me, I couldn't wait to get the fuck out of that house and just . . . *do* something. Even my mother used to laugh at me about this rap shit. She'd hear me upstairs, I'd have two radios set up – one playing the beat, and the other one recording me rapping over it. She'd be going, 'I don't know why you're wasting your time with that – you can't rap.' Thanks, ma!" *"It was like isolatin' myself was healthy,"* as he rapped on 'Revelation'; he was reading, listening and recording round the clock, abstracting himself from the futile, bored adolescent life he could have had. Instead of fading away on a street corner once his pressure cooker home flung him outside, becoming a petty criminal in a city with nothing for the young, rap had shown him a route out.

The records he heard as he moved through his teens replaced the education he'd abandoned at Lincoln. LA's N.W.A. (Niggas With Attitude) and Miami's 2 Live Crew were among his favourites in the late Eighties. While the latter specialised in obscene, juvenile, sexist sex songs, without balance or apology – handy training for Eminem's misogyny – they became best known for police and government attempts to censor them. These culminated in the 1987 arrest of a female shop assistant for selling one of their records, a 1990 Federal court ruling that their single 'As Nasty As We Wanna Be' was illegally obscene, and a contrasting jury trial finding 2 Live Crew themselves innocent of obscenity.

N.W.A. meanwhile provided a more skilful and complex lesson in what rap could say, and how easily it could appal figures of power and authority. Guided by ambitious producer Andre Young (aka Dr. Dre), and including main rappers O-Shea Jackson (Ice Cube) and Eric Wright (Easy-E, who also financed the group, initially with money from drug-dealing), N.W.A. pushed rap's rebel appeal to the limit. On their début album *Straight Outta Compton* (1988), they replaced the more literary, distanced super-pimp persona of original West Coast gangsta-rapper and Marshall inspiration Ice-T with more lurid, exaggerated evocations of LA's violent street life. Brightened by Dre's bouncing, Seventies P-Funk sampling beats, they ranged between the poles of their first hit 'Express Yourself', Cube's ode to rap's inspiring of individualism, and the infamous anti-LAPD rebel song 'Fuck Tha Police'. It was the latter which made the FBI fire off a threat to N.W.A.'s Ruthless Records, and police departments across America loathe them. Though their "gangsta" image was mostly a contrivance, intended to sell records to Compton's thousands of real Bloods and Crips (whom Dre especially had studiously avoided in real life), the American Establishment easily confused art and reality, and overreacted accordingly.

Eminem would exploit, and suffer from, exactly that vein of lazy thinking. He would also, to his humble amazement, find that Dre, ten years after his teenage hero-worship, wanted to be his producer. Most important of all, perhaps, was N.W.A.'s tapping of an eager white audience for their gritty fantasias of black life, until suburban white kids became gangsta-rap's main market, and the music's gunplay and misogyny grew still more cartoonish, to reflect these outsiders' expectations.

Marshall experienced this shift from a uniquely clear-eyed perspective: as a white boy partly from the suburbs, and partly from black ghetto streets like the ones N.W.A. eulogised. He was hearing a powerful fantasy and his grinding, inescapable reality, all at once. But what he responded to most was simple. In a home, neighbourhood and hormone-addled body that made him feel cramped and trapped, N.W.A. showed him how to scream with rage: fuck tha police, and everything else. Analysing his own audience later, he described the sensation. "My attitude attracts a lot of kids, especially white kids from the suburbs," he told *NME*. "When someone comes along and goes against the grain and just truly doesn't give a fuck, they wanna be that person. 'Cos I know when I was younger and the Beastie Boys came out they seemed like they didn't give a fuck, and when N.W.A. came out they *really* didn't give a fuck. The whole attitude attracts people." The Eminem anthem 'The Real Slim Shady' would imagine, and try to inspire, an army of such listeners. But he did so with such feeling because in 1988, aged 15, he was one of them himself, "putting on the sunglasses and looking in the mirror and lip-synching," as he remembered, "wanting to be Dr. Dre, to be Ice Cube".

Marshall would follow Dre and Cube out of N.W.A., into their solo work of the early Nineties. Dre's *The Chronic* (1992), and his production on *Doggystyle* (1993) by Snoop Doggy Dogg, his first protégé, finessed Marshall's favoured gangsta-rap into still more fantastic scenarios of super-pimp wealth, sex and violence, with complicating, residual touches of ghetto reality. Cube, meanwhile, a more talented rapper, kept a closer connection to the melting social situation on his home Compton streets, one of the few locations to make Detroit look good. But on his masterpiece, *The Predator* (1992), he, too, demonstrated that great rappers could turn themselves into fictional creatures on record, superheroic aliases with which to do their dirty work. In his private life, Cube was an essentially law-abiding musician. But as the Predator, he took on all the anger, paranoia and violence of South Central LA's black population, slipping inside Rodney King's body as the batons came down, then reappearing to gun down racist cops, till he literally exploded, laying waste whole city blocks when cornered, a lyrical thermonuclear device. This was the lineage from which Slim Shady emerged.

The final black rapper to rivet Marshall was in some ways the closest to him. Tupac Shakur (aka 2Pac) was Eminem's predecessor as the top star on their label, Interscope. His 1996 drive-by shooting in Las Vegas by unknown assailants martyred him and, among black Americans, made him perhaps the most revered rapper of all. Album titles like *Me Against The World* (1995) – at the time, Marshall's favourite hip-hop LP – suggested the mournful mix of deep paranoia, egotism, death wish and hurt which characterised much of Tupac's work. But of more relevance to Marshall were the elements of social radicalism, low self-esteem and painful parental relations which he and Tupac shared.

The gangsta trappings for which Tupac became famous – trumpeted Crip affiliations, shoot-outs with cops, bragging after he was shot once, seeming to invite that second, fatal attempt, and jail-time for a rape conviction – were as much willed wish-fulfilment for him as they would have been for Marshall. Though he had lived in ghetto conditions as a child, Tupac was educated and intelligent, a trained actor, and not really tough; like the adult Marshall, the muscles he flaunted were those of a pumped-up, essentially mild-mannered stripling. He lacked Eminem's ironically distancing wit, and pop instinct for truly overground hits (despite sometimes using Dre himself). But where the two men met was in the matter of mothers and fathers. Tupac never knew his father, either; even his mother did not know the man's name for sure, and his only father-figure (and possible real father), Legs, appeared briefly in his teens, only to die of a crack-caused heart attack. It left Tupac feeling "unmanly", insecurely angry, always with something to prove. *"Seeing Daddy's semen full of crazy demons . . ."*, he would rap, cursed and crazed by fatherlessness, as Eminem would slit his dad's throat *"in this dream I had"*; both felt emasculated, and could be stupidly macho. Both were products of an absentee-father America.

Tupac's mother Afeni, meanwhile, was an ex-Black Panther, who mostly raised him alone, and would eventually become a crack addict. She called him her "Black Prince", and filled him with revolutionary consciousness, which his records reflected. But, as poverty kept them on the move, he, like Marshall, found his sense of self a fragile, cracking thing. "I remember crying all the time," he said. "My major thing growing up was I couldn't fit in. Because I was from everywhere." It could have been Marshall speaking. Shared knowledge of family breakdown would be among his strong bridges to black rap fans.

The differences between them were as acute, and revealing. As a politicised black man, Tupac could plunge straight into the racial realities of America as he saw them, directly and seriously preaching change from his first record. White boy Marshall, almost equally radical, in part from listening to rappers like Tupac, would mask his views on race and his country at first, adopting a more cartoonish, satirical persona. As a white rapper, he had no "people" he could feel a need to address. With no vacancy for a "White Prince", rap's new ruler would have to start as Court Jester.

Then, there was Tupac's attitude to women. Though his mother worked for a while, her long-time crack addiction, and raising of him in shifting locations including homeless shelters, do not compare favourably to Mathers-Briggs' "abuses". But, though Tupac could sometimes conform to gangsta-rap's thuggishly misogynist standards in music and life, his first hit, 'Brenda's Got A Baby', showed woman-hating was not mandatory for a mother's boy. *"We all came from a woman, got a name from a woman . . ."*, he reminded, as he *"gave a holler to my sisters on welfare"*. His later 'Dear Mama' was similarly sympathetic. But Eminem, an equally angry young man, would offer no such forgiveness. Denied race as a playground for his rage, he would spitefully attack women in his raps. Tupac's unlikely white replacement would not worry about *"sisters"*. Only himself.

One more element was needed to make Marshall decide to be a rapper. He might put shades on his nose, look in the mirror, and imagine he was L.L. Cool J. But the face looking back at him was too pale to ever convince. It took The Beastie Boys' *Licensed To Ill* (1986) to reassure him that needn't matter.

"When I first heard them, I didn't know they were white," he told *Newsweek*. "I just thought it was the craziest shit I had ever heard. Then I saw the video and saw that they were white, and I went, 'Wow.' I thought, 'Hey, I can do this.'"

"I was like, 'This shit is so dope !'" he added to *Spin*. "That's when I decided I wanted to rap."

The Beastie Boys had grown up further from Marshall's world than

Tupac or Dre. The three of them were all upper-middle class Jewish New Yorkers (continuing a bond between black and Jewish American music, with Jews as the bridge to WASPs, which stretched back to Cab Calloway hearing his jazz howl first in the wails of Harlem synagogue cantors, and which has been constant since). But the brattish, loudly obnoxious personas The Beastie Boys adopted were anyway ideal inspiration for Marshall, 14 when he heard them. Layered with ear-splittingly dense rock production by Rick Rubin, the Beasties' obvious rap skills and adolescently sexist and violent poses, on record, and in tours replete with caged go-go girls and court appearances for minor acts of aggression, were almost a blueprint for Eminem. That it was all just a joke and an excuse for teenagers to let off steam, to "not give a fuck", was certainly a lesson he learned. Their biggest hit, 'Fight For Your Right', meanwhile, could have been written for him at 14, when *"living at home is such a drag"*, and *"Ma looks in and says 'WHAT'S THAT NOISE?'"*, till you *"get chucked out"*. Eminem would repeat such songs of valueless teen rebellion and, not bothering with the Beasties' faked stupidity, better them. But the important thing was that these successful white rappers existed at all.

Having found role models he could aspire to, Marshall then had his dreams dashed by a man who would in some ways be his nemesis. Vanilla Ice, whose 'Ice Ice Baby' (1990) was the first US rap number one, was almost a parody of the racism in the American music industry. His records were mediocre, about nothing in particular. But, with his white skin, sculpted cheekbones, and stormtrooper square-cut blond hair, he could not have looked more aggressively Aryan. It was assumed rap had found its Elvis, its commercial messiah to suck in white masses otherwise scared of black music, in Nineties America's segregated pop nation. His first album duly sold 18 million. To add to the insult of each sale to far better black rappers, listeners not only clearly bought him in such unprecedented numbers because he was white, but were not bothered that he looked like a Nazi. In fact, this deliberate styling must have been a selling point. Though Vanilla Ice vanished as swiftly as he had appeared (after being allegedly dangled off a 15th floor balcony by infamous Death Row label boss and Dre associate Suge Knight, over disputed credits for his black songwriter), his spectre would rise to haunt Eminem's early success. "Vanilla Twice," critics would sneer. Ice himself would reappear to taunt this rival white face. He, like Eminem, had as a boy been a genuine hip-hop fan. But, sucked into the mainstream music machine, encouraged to fake a gangsta past while being as Caucasian as Pat Boone, his success a pure product of racist avarice, he made the idea of white rappers again seem an offensive joke. Watching in Detroit, Marshall was mortified.

"That crushed me," he told *Newsweek*, of first hearing 'Ice Ice Baby'. At first, I felt like I didn't want to rap any more. I was so mad, because he was making it real hard for me. But then 3rd Bass restored some credibility, and I realised that it really depends on the individual. Vanilla Ice was just fake. 3rd Bass was real."

New York Jews like the Beasties, 3rd Bass were the last white rappers of substance before Eminem. Their *Cactus Album* (1991) was a more media-literate, serious and sly work than *Licensed To Ill*, addressing hip-hop culture from their own position, not impersonating blacks like the Beasties and Ice. 'Product of the Environment' in particular addressed the racial loneliness and pitfalls of Marshall's decision to rap, but also indicated why he might survive. *"His reward was almost a bullet in the chest,"* as MC Serch rapped of his early days. *". . . 'Cos I'm a product of the environment/ there it is, black and white."* But as he recalled an early performance, the tone was almost of a vision, of race ceasing to matter, of rapping skill and true street knowledge saving him: *"Never had static, 'cos everybody knew me/ . . . I'm protected and respected for my own self/ 'cos of talent, no shame or nothin' else/ In a time of tension, racially fenced in/ I came off, and all the others blessed me."*

The teenage Marshall must have ached for such acceptance. The journey he had started by listening to such records so reverently, though, and by choosing to make hip-hop his life, was unavoidably one of racial transgression, with its history of hostility and risk. Norman Mailer's epochal essay *The White Negro* (1957) had first sketched the opportunities and dangers that becoming lost in black culture could give to whites: once jazz (rap's first ancestor) had entered white society as "a communication of art because it said, 'I feel this, and now you do too' ", Mailer's hipster "White Negroes" swapped middle-class repression for the swifter, riskier, nerve-end reactions of life on the edge, where poor black Americans had to live. Shrugging off restraint, they would value "the naked truths of what each observer feels at each instance of his existence", a prophetic definition of rap's uncensored, individual's art. The essay's predictions were erupting in underground America as Mailer wrote, in the musical miscegenation of rock'n'roll, as poor white Southerners like Jerry Lee Lewis and Elvis Presley learned from the black musicians around them. But somehow, as everyone in Nineties Detroit could attest, America's racial walls had never truly tumbled. So rap had to breach them again.

The cover of Ice-T's *Home Invasion* LP (1993) showed the music's intent. It pictured a white suburban teenage boy with Iceberg Slim and Malcolm X books by his side, headphones clamped to his ears as he listened to Ices T and Cube and imagined a scantily clad white woman, maybe his mother, grabbed roughly from behind by one darkly masked man, while another coldly slaughtered a white man, maybe his father. It was many white parents' worst nightmare, the explicit truth of what Elvis, and Little Richard, and Louis Armstrong had threatened, the reason, Ice-T knew, that gangsta-rap was condemned in America. Like jazz, it was another ghetto "communication of art", of ideas of violent rage, rebellion and injustice. It too said, to unprotected white ears in their neighbourhoods, "I feel this, and now you do too".

Home Invasion could also have been drawn from life in Marshall's bedroom. When he achieved stardom as Eminem, and his background of gangsta-rap addiction was revealed, he seemed to be the living proof of the cover's prophecy, the first fruit of gangsta-rap's demon seed in white youth. The difference, though, and the reason it would be Marshall who took the white rap crown, was that he was not solely some slumming suburban kid. He was also a true product of ghetto streets, a "White Negro" almost from birth. Beaten up and taunted by black neighbours, a white boy struggling for acceptance in a black medium, he was as much a victim, and creation, of the racist barriers erected by whites generations before as anyone. He did not cross the tracks to become a rapper, as the likes of Jerry Lee Lewis had done to learn rock. The tracks crossed in him. He was a new kind of white American, the end-result of the experiment Norman Mailer first noted. And to strike out and succeed, to top the rap records he loved, he would first have to face down concerted black racist contempt – to be treated like a minority.

He was helped by one of his closest friends, future D12 MC Proof (real name, Deshaun Holton). The two met when both were 15 (13 in some stories; but Eminem stuck ruthlessly to his false age back then, and 15 fits other facts better). Proof was idly sitting on a brick wall outside his mostly black school, Osbourne High, when a white boy unusually walked towards him, and handed out a flyer. "They was for a talent show he was doing," Proof told *Spin*. "He said he was a rapper." Immediately, they traded rhymes. When both matched "first place" with "birthday" (which takes some doing), they recognised kindred spirits. Soon, Proof was introducing Marshall to a would-be producer who lived round the corner, Kon Artis (aka Denaun Porter). Kon remembered the day in a way which made clear the exceptional steps Marshall was taking. "Motherfucker came to my door, and I'm like, 'Hmmm, what the fuck? White boy at my door!'" he drawled to *Spin*. But it was Proof and Marshall who kept the closest bond. Blasting out his stereo "as soon as my Mom would leave to play bingo", staying with Proof's mother when his own home overheated, Marshall continued his rap education with his friend. "Basically, we checked everything," Proof told icast.com. "No matter if it was wack, we would know, because we were bright. Every tape that was out, we bought it. He had a tape collection that was incredible. I had the vinyl, and he had all the tapes."

It was around this time, aged 15, that Marshall took serious steps to be a rapper himself. When not annoying his mother with his primitive twin-radio recording set-up, he was, he told *Spin*, "picking up a pencil and like getting busy and shit. I started, you know, getting better and better. Then I was like, 'Yo, I want to do this.'" Proof gave him the first opportunity to test himself, at Osbourne High. "Listen, I'll tell you this," he said to icast.com. "I went to a black dominated high school, and I used to sneak him in there into the lunchroom. And they'd be like, 'We want to battle you.' 'No, you can't battle me, why don't you battle the white boy first?' And everybody would be like, 'I'll kill him.' Then Em would come out and kill the whole lunchroom, which was a black dominated school and would be looking like, 'Damn!' It was like *White Men Can't Jump*."

Other encounters, though, were more traumatic. "When you're a little kid, you don't see colour," Marshall considered to *Spin*, "and the fact that my friends were black never crossed my mind. It never became an issue until I was a teenager, and started to rap. Then I'd notice that a lot of motherfuckers always had my back, but somebody always had to say to them, 'Why you have to stick up for the white boy?' I'd hang out on the corner where kids would be rhyming, and when I tried to get in there, I'd get dissed. A little colour issue developed, and as I got old enough to hit the clubs, it got really bad. I wasn't that dope yet, but I knew I could rhyme, so I'd get on the open mics and shit, and a couple of times I was booed off the stage." One incident in particular lodged in his mind. "I remember I used to go to this place called the Rhythm Kitchen way back in the day," he said. "I was probably 16 or 17. The first time I grabbed the mic, I got booed before I even said anything. As I started to rap, the boos just got louder and louder, until I just got off the mic."

When it happened again, at another venue, it terrified him. "The first time I grabbed the mic at The Shelter [a Detroit MCs' hangout], I got dissed. I only said, like, three words, and I was already gettin' booed as soon as the mic was handed to me. I was like, 'This is fucked.' I started getting scared, like, 'Is this gonna happen? What the fuck is gonna happen? Am I gonna make it or not?'"

Many would have quit after one of those nights. For a teenager with self-esteem which was already battered, getting on stage must have been bruising enough. For jeering crowds to let him know he was not wanted in the places he most craved acceptance, sometimes before he could say a word, must have crushed him. The obsessive love of hip-hop he expressed in 'Revelation', the sense that only it could save his desperate life, must have had something to do with him picking himself up. But it was also true, as his subsequent career proved, that the beatings, insults and disappointments of his early days did not leave him shaking and weak. Instead, they toughened him, fed him aggressive resentment and rage, determined him not to be broken. The pressure of those early open mics only intensified his will to succeed. And the racist nature of the taunts, like the racist assaults he had suffered, did not make him stupidly racist back. Instead, it made him despise all racism, with a black rapper's force.

He gave his most thoughtful account of his resentments to *Spin*. "In the beginning," he recalled, "the majority of my shows were for all-black crowds, and people would always say, 'You're pretty dope for a white boy,' and I'd take it as a compliment. Then, as I got older, I started to think, 'What the fuck does that mean?' Nobody asks to be born, nobody has a choice of what colour they'll be. I had to work up to a certain level before people would even look past my colour; a lot of motherfuckers would just sit with their arms folded and be like, 'All right, what is this?' I did see where the people dissing me were coming from. But, it's like, anything that happened in the past between black and white, I can't speak on it, because I wasn't there. I don't feel like me being born the colour I am makes me any less of a person."

That diffident, defensive last sentence could have come straight from the mouth of one of Martin Luther King's black marchers, 40 years before. The weird racial inversion of Marshall's America was proven by the outlandish thing he said next. "There was a while," he admitted bravely, "when I was feeling like, 'Damn, if I'd just been born black, I would not have to go through all this shit.' I'm not ignorant – I know how it must be when a black person goes to get a regular job in society. But music, in general, is supposed to be universal. If I'm a white 16-year-old and I stand in front of the mirror and lip-synch every day like I'm Krayzie Bone – who's to say that because I'm a certain colour I shouldn't be doing that? And if I've got a right to buy his music and make him rich, who's to say that I then don't have the right to rap myself?"

He was less considered, but as truthful to *NME*. "People say I'm offensive. Know what I find offensive? People always dwelling on me being a white rapper, a white this, a white that. That shit makes me sick to my stomach. It's not like it's a huge fucking secret! I wake up in the morning, look in the mirror, and see I'm white, thank you! It doesn't make what I do any less valid. I've lived just as hard a life as anyone in America. I've been to all-white schools, all-black schools, mixed schools." He paused, to make his most meaningful point. "I've seen it from every angle, and I've always been poor. I've always been poor."

It was at another Detroit venue that the tide at last turned for Marshall, and racist contempt changed to respect. The Hip-Hop Shop, on 7 Mile, was the rap record-selling property of hip-hop clothing entrepreneur Maurice Malone. Proof would become an account executive for the company's fashion wing, before D12 claimed all his time. But on the Saturday afternoon which let Marshall know his dreams of rap success might yet succeed, Proof was in charge of the Shop's first open-mic session. Another future D12 member, Head, was the house DJ. He remembered how Marshall rose to the challenge of a full-scale rap battle – a gruelling baptism with no rock equivalent, in which contestants duelled vicious rhymes about each other till one fell, with the crowd's roar as judge and jury; an artistic adaptation of the street's rough logic. "I seen Em take this motherfucker out in like five, six lines," Head told *Spin*. "It was an open-mic battle, the first one we did. Three hundred people, lines out the door. It was a ruthless, cut-throat battle. And he won it."

Marshall told his version of events to msn.com. "The first time I ever got respect was when I grabbed the mic at The Hip-Hop Shop. I had said some shit and people was quiet at first, then cheers and applause, and it got louder and louder. That was the spot I started going to every Saturday. They would have official announcement battles every couple of months, and I kept winning them." Of his change in fortune, he considered: "I think it was something a little different about me. I started growing up, and I just got better. At 15 or 16, I was wack. But at 18, 19, I started learning, this is how I should sound on the mic. Learning how to battle, practising freestyle. That was what I was known for in Detroit, in the underground, for a couple of years."

Of his Detroit contemporaries, Kid Rock, the white, rap-influenced, porn-minded, long-haired rocker who was the first to gain national success, was his only significant idol. Marshall would haunt his record signings, and beg him to battle. "I was 15 at the time, and he was a couple years older," he told *Spin*. "He used to always kind of laugh it off and say, 'Battle me in record sales.' He saw a little bit more about the record industry than I did. That's probably what I would have told somebody." He paused, and considered. "No, I don't think that's what I would have told somebody. Back then, I was all about battling."

The Hip-Hop Shop's hothouse forged bonds with Detroit rappers closer to home anyway. It was Proof's idea for himself, Marshall, DJ Head, Kon Artis, Kuniva, Bizarre and Bugs, all regulars at the Shop and like-minded friends, to join forces in 1995, in a rap super-group of local unknowns. Proof gave them their name, D12, for Dirty Dozen – each of the six who rapped would have two aliases. It would be a little while before Slim Shady made himself known to Marshall/Eminem, making the concept concrete. But the group were soon working on rhymes. "We was gonna do this Western song where we were all outlaws, like the Dirty Dozen," Marshall recalled for *Spin*. He squinted to remember its lyrics. "I said something like, *'I ride rails to cover wide trails / Slide nails to a killer inside jail, denied bail / Tell him I'm-a break him out tonight / And we gonna unite / So be ready for a gunfight.'* Some shit like that."

This fascinating attempt at 19th-century frontier rap, written in the heart of the inner city, was only scuppered when a trip to the video shop revealed *The Dirty Dozen* was a war movie. Peckinpah's weirdly moral *The Wild Bunch* might have been closer to their intentions. But their style, at least, stayed constant from the start. "It was to be disgusting," Proof explained. "To piss people off, raise eyebrows," Marshall added, to make "raw, ridiculous shit for the underground kids who like it vulgar." D12 would perform regularly around Detroit, before anyone else had heard of Eminem. They would all keep each other's hopes up, and remain loyal in ways neither failure nor success spoiled.

Marshall's Hip-Hop Shop battles also attracted another admirer who would be invaluable to his future career. "I heard him in a battle with 50 other MCs," said Paul Rosenberg. "He took them all by himself." Rosenberg was another white kid obsessed with rap, the same age as Marshall. But, visiting from deep in the suburbs, he had no wish to perform. He just wanted to enter the music business. He went on to law school, and a law firm in New York. But he kept in touch with Marshall. When the time came, he would become his lawyer and manager, another part of the band that helped take him to the top.

Two more men completed Marshall's rap education. The pair have stayed in the shadows on almost every occasion his story has been told, while Dre and the rest have been analysed and applauded. There is good reason for this. If anyone in his life fits the profile of record business Svengalis, it is Jeff and Marky Bass. They are the uncomfortable complication in the idea that Eminem and Slim Shady were wholly made by Marshall Mathers' driven genius.

"I got with this little production company in Detroit, Web Entertainment [the Bass Brothers' business]," was how Marshall remembered it to elamentz.com. "They were like, um . . . they were like these guys . . . well, I was rapping on a local radio station when I was like 15 years old, and I used to rap on the air and shit every Friday night with this thing called open mic. These guys with Web Entertainment, I guess they heard me in their car rhyming on the radio. They called in to the station one night, and we were talking to them and shit like that and they was like, you know, why don't you come through, blah, blah, blah. We got together, we got down, and then we been working together ever since. Since I was like 16 years old, we been working. But I didn't have what it took until I was 20, 21."

The Bass Brothers were local successes, producing national stars including George Clinton, The Red Hot Chilli Peppers, and Detroit girl Madonna. But by 1987, they were looking to break into the burgeoning rap scene. Marky Bass recalled to the *Detroit News* what happened after he heard Marshall rapping on the radio, as he drove through Detroit, this way. "He was doing an open mic, and I called over to the radio station. I think the DJ was Lisa Lisa, and I said, 'Lisa, have this kid call me.' He called me up and we talked for a minute. Then, at 4 o'clock in the morning, he showed up at my studio. And that was the start of grooming him for about three or four years. He had incredible skills, lyrically and rhythmically. He had focus, he knew exactly what he wanted to do. And with our experience as producers and his as a hip-hop head, we kinda put it together and created a project. Actually, we raised him since he was, like, 15."

The Bass Brothers signed him to Web Entertainment right then. As The Rolling Stones were to their first, moulding manager Andrew Loog Oldham, and as Elvis Presley was to his label boss/father-figure, Sam Phillips, so Marshall Mathers was just the white raw material the Brothers had been searching for. It was the same year Marshall left school, and the same year his mother threatened to turn him out for good if he didn't get a job. So, as his obsession with rap and the pressures of home cost him his conventional schooling, and he started a series of hopeless jobs, his contract with Web, signed so young, must have seemed a promise to cling to. He was not a nobody. He had signed on the dotted line, to be an artist. While the teenage Marshall struggled in the daytime, the Brothers would "raise" Eminem at night.

"He was amazing at that age," Marky sighed to the *Sydney Sun-Herald*. "He combined a lot of triple-tongue stuff with some of the best rhyming I'd ever heard. We stayed in the studio every day for five years. We worked hard on getting him to the point where he is now. There was a lot of grooming and technique. We didn't want to throw Em out as just another rapper."

Marky's comments in the press about Marshall being in the studio "every day" may have been exaggerated. No one else remembers his teenage years that way, and all parties had other, paying jobs to attend. Nor did Marshall ever credit the Brothers with "raising" him. But the seriousness of their joint venture was clear in that contract, and the slow care with which it was realised. And Marky Bass told the truth about one other thing. Marshall Mathers was not ready to become Eminem in his teens. The vicious goblin of Slim Shady, after all, had not yet visited him even once. He had some living to do before the venom and vengeance which would make him special really soiled his insides. He had to get through his early twenties. That was when his already gruelling life crashed to rock bottom.

4

CRACKING UP

Marshall and Kim still lived in his mother's home, on and off. Though the love between Mathers-Briggs and her son had been shattered by brutal words and acts when he was 20, and she and Kim loathed each other, Marshall still depended on her. "Right up until he was 26 I took care of his finances – he didn't have a bank account – and his car insurance," she told the *Mail On Sunday*. "When he got a job as a chef, who taught him to cook? Me. When he fell out with his friends, who resolved it? Me." The inability of the three to survive separately, the resented holds and conditional favours of such lives must have drained them all.

That job, meanwhile, was as short-order cook at Gilbert's Lodge. His ability to stick at it for years while, in his co-worker and sometime lover Jennifer Yezvack's memory, changing clothes the moment each shift was over, to go to friends' homes or clubs to rap, shows a quietly serious ambition at odds with his later "don't give a fuck" image. He wasn't afraid of work, whenever he saw it was needed. No rap star-approved ghetto short-cuts, no drug-dealing or gunplay, would shake his life. Instead, he cooked meatloaf and burgers, out of sight in a family diner, saying little, seeming likeable, and unexceptional, like at school, as he plotted his escape. "He was a good worker," his manager Pete Karagiaouris told *Rolling Stone*. "But he'd be in the back rapping all the orders, and sometimes I had to tell him to tone it down. Music was always the most important thing to him." Yezvack thinks he enjoyed his time there. "Well, he kept coming back. He got fired, quit, came back. Over a period of – God – five years? He must have liked it a little bit. The people are pretty good here, the owner works with them. I think that's why we're all here. So I think he liked it. And once Hailie was born, Kim wasn't working much at all. So he had to work for that."

Kim's pregnancy in 1996, with the baby they'd name Hailie Jade

Mathers, was perhaps the most crucial event in Marshall's life. It threw more pressure on his shoulders to earn money, to make something of himself. It gave him the chance to explore the paternal instincts he'd shown with his half-brother Nathan, to do better than his own vanished father and hated mother. And it heated up his always combative relationship with Kim, until love here, as with his mother, seemed to melt into mutual loathing.

Some around her felt that way already. "When she got pregnant, she went back home to her mother and wouldn't let Marshall see her or the baby," Betty Kresin said to the *Sydney Sun-Herald*. "Finally her step-father met him with a gun and said, 'If you ever come round here again, I'll shoot you.' Two years later, they got married. Kim only did it for the money. I tried to tell him."

"I'm the wrong person to ask about Kim," Yezvack reflects, about the girl she sometimes rivalled for Marshall's affections. "Her and I do not get along. She was just vengeful towards him. She got pregnant at a young age, hardly worked, was dependent, didn't want to be with him, then she did, then she didn't. She'd call here for him, and there'd be drama all the time. He couldn't keep his head straight, because she was always messing with it. And once the baby was born, she used the baby against him all the time. You know, 'You're not going to see your daughter,' and then she'd want money, and then she lived with him for a while. Ooh. Yeah. She's a treat. She did plenty in the past for him to talk about her the way he does on the records, trust me. She's not stable."

When things had soured for good between them, after he and Kim had briefly married, and were about to bitterly divorce, Marshall would find little to like in their time together, either. Asked by the *Detroit Free Press* if Kim had supported him as he struggled to be a rapper, he replied: "Want me to be honest? It was off and on. When we were younger, she supported everything I did. The older we got, the more reality started to set in. She's one of those people that's down-to-earth, like, 'Hello! You're living in fantasy. These things don't happen with people like us.' I was always the optimist, like, 'Yo, I'm gonna make this happen.' And I just kept busting my ass. To be honest, I really didn't have much support. Nobody in my family, in her family. Just a few friends. And just myself."

The Kim of his records was treated still less sympathetically, immortalised in 1997's 'Bonnie & Clyde' and 'Kim' only as a lyrical punching bag, the helpless victim of a fantasised screaming jag, slashed throat and strangulation, before her warm corpse was dragged to the lake and dumped. 'Bonnie & Clyde' was written when she was keeping Hailie from him, and he felt homicidal towards her, an indication of how the baby intensified their feelings. He even put Hailie on the record, to show who he truly loved then.

Marshall's songs made Kim infamous. But she said almost nothing to counter them. There is little to go on about her and what she meant to him, apart from others' hostile opinions. Inspect one of the few published photos of them together, and she's a slightly chubby-faced, blonde girl, as tall as Marshall, with lurid, glossy lipstick, and a smile for the camera that doesn't reach her eyes. Marshall's eyes, by contrast, look passionately intense and, as the media circle, he is holding her arm, unobtrusively but firmly. It's reminiscent of famous photos of John Lennon protecting Yoko Ono from a baying paparazzi pack in 1969. Clearly, something in Kim inspired much more than hate, in the dozen years they sparred and screamed at each other. Others who she attacked verbally, or who she made Marshall turn against, may have felt she was bad for him. But Marshall kept coming back for more. Someone who was "good" for him cannot have been to his taste. In his resentful, raging relationship with the world, perhaps he needed someone to fight with, and for. Before he placed Hailie beside him for 'Bonnie & Clyde', he and the uncontrollable children's home refugee Kim had been the inseparable outlaws. Even after he'd written that song, he and others agreed she was the love of his life.

"This is what I love about Em," Proof, who'd known them from the beginning, told *Rolling Stone*. "One time we came home and Kim had thrown all his clothes on the lawn – which was, like, two pairs of pants and some gym shoes. So we stayed at my grandmother's, and Em's like, 'I'm leaving her; I'm never going back.' Next day, he's back with her. The love they got is so genuine, it's ridiculous. He's gonna end up marrying her. But there's always gonna be conflict there."

"Me and Kim been through our dramas and shit," Marshall confessed to *Q*. "But I'd be bald-faced lying if I said I don't love her, or I'm with her because of my daughter. I'm with her because I wanna be with her."

His first, all but forgotten recordings showed that love unashamedly, in a way Slim Shady would hide. His début album *Infinite* was released in 1996, during Kim's pregnancy. It was largely produced by the Bass Brothers, and released by their own Web Entertainment, after a potential deal with a major label subsidiary, Jive Records, evaporated. A subset of

D12, The 5 Elementz – Proof and Kon Artis, who co-produced, plus Thyme and Eye-Kyu – shared some rapping duties, on a record which sold less than its 1,000 pressings, and never escaped its makers' Detroit backyard.

In later interviews, *Infinite* was routinely dismissed, as if it wasn't really an album at all, and Eminem had appeared full-blown three years later, with *The Slim Shady LP*. "*Infinite* was me trying to figure out how I wanted my rap style to be," he told *Rolling Stone*, "how I wanted to sound on the mic and present myself. It was a growing stage. I felt like *Infinite* was like a demo that got pressed up."

"That first album was very different from what he's doing now," his future manager Paul Rosenberg, who Marshall reminded of his existence by sending a copy to his New York law firm, told *Newsweek*. "He was just starting out and he was trying to get airplay, so he made a record that he thought would fit in with what was happening at the time in rap. The songs were a little more upbeat."

"It was right before my daughter was born," Marshall added to *Rolling Stone*, "so having a future for her was all I talked about. It was way hip-hopped out, like Naz or AZ – that rhyme style was real in at the time. I've always been a smartass comedian, and that's why it wasn't a good album."

The Bass Brothers have been careful never to reissue this rare, inferior early work by their protégé. It exists now only as bootlegs ordered and burnt over the Internet, or as fan-transcribed lyrics. But, with most of the same producers and co-rappers as his later, celebrated work, this is certainly Eminem's début album, not a "demo". And it expresses his life back then with the uncensored honesty which would make his name, but without the cynical, snarling filter of Slim. This is a record by the loving, uncertain, ambitious Marshall Mathers his friends, family, teachers and co-workers all remember, in the face of his public image.

Most of *Infinite* is taken up by bragging and battle rhymes, hip-hop standard fare, and Marshall's strongest suit on Detroit's circuit. The title track, the only one thought worthy of inclusion in his hardback book of lyrics, *Angry Blonde*, was actually started at a Hip-Hop Shop open mic. "That was '96," Marshall reminisced, introducing it, "the era of just rhyming for the hell of it. People at one point actually said I sounded like Nas, 'cos I used all these big words. This is show-your-skill type shit." The innocent rolling in vocabulary for its own sake in 'Infinite', like stream-of-consciousness from the dictionary Marshall devoured in his teens, was typical of him then. *"My thesis will smash a stereo to pieces,"* he rapped. *"My a cappella releases plastic masterpieces through telekinesis / And eases you mentally, gently, sentimentally, instrumentally / With entity, dementedly meant to be Infinite."* '313' (Detroit's area phone code), 'Tonight' and 'Open Mic' continued Marshall's defining of himself by dissing rap rivals, sometimes in the supernatural terms which always hovered when he discussed hip-hop, his sacred salvation (*"Invisible like magicians with mystical mic traditions / . . . So feel the force of my spiritual images"*). But 'Infinite' concluded with more modest, nervous thoughts: *"I never packed a tool or acted cool, it wasn't practical / . . . This is for my family . . . / Plus the man who never had a Plan B / Be all you can be, 'cos once you make an instant hit / I'm tense to be tempted when I see the sins my friends commit."* Then the weight of the album became lost in Marshall's hopes and deep fears.

'Never 2 Far', for one, was pitched somewhere between desperation and faith, seemingly drawn from real conversations between Marshall and his friends. At its start, he meets one of them on a Detroit street corner, and they scrabble around for the bus fare, wondering whether to scam the driver, till Marshall snaps. *"You know what, look, I'm sick of taking this damn bus everywhere, man,"* he cries, *" . . . I got a baby on the way, I don't even got a car / . . . I still stay with my moms, 21 and still with my moms / Look hey, we gotta make some hit records or something / You know what I'm saying? 'Cos I'm tired of being broke."* Lying about his age even this early (he was 23), he lays bare the terror of a young, poor man with all his life ahead of him, and no way of knowing if it will improve, if he will ever amount to anything, or even be able to leave his mother's care (uncriticised, here). But the chorus, with more than a touch of Sly Stone's euphoric, community-minded 'Everybody Is A Star' (1970), showed Marshall keeping his head above water, by belief in a hip-hop American Dream: *"No matter wherever you are, you're never too far / From revenue, huh, 'cos you can be king / You can rule the world, you can do anything / It's on you, baby, 'cos you can be a star / . . . A million dollars ain't even that far away, man."*

It takes a special kind of strength to sustain such a vision, while flipping burgers in a Detroit diner, and going home to your mother and a pregnant girlfriend you can't support. Outside America, it might seem delusional. But the song showed Marshall did not mean to dream and bitch his life away, when he knew hard, rapping work could save it: *"Yo, I'm not about to chance it and dismiss handling business / I'm cancelling Christmas to gamble and risk this."* Nor did he feel alone. As would be true when he became famous, and too suspicious of others' motives to make new friends, he had already decided D12 were the comrades to help him on his journey. Again, he used spiritual terms: *"The few that I trust, them's the people that I still got/ . . . we move through into time, my crew's true and divine . . ."*

'It's OK', the second track on *Infinite*, was still more specific and heart-felt. It described the effort of will it took to say its title in Detroit. As Eye-Kyu contributed a numb chorus about sleeplessness and alienation, Marshall set out another version of his dreamland: *"One day I plan to be a family man happily married/ I wanna grow to be so old that I have to be carried/ . . . And have at least a half a million for my baby girl/ It may be early to be planning this stuff/ 'Cos I'm still struggling hard to be the man, and it's tough . . ./ I'm on a quest to seize all, my own label to call/ Way before my baby is able to crawl."* Success would not, it would transpire, stop him struggling, or leave him satisfied. And Hailie would be able to walk by the time he had banked his first million, and set up Shady Records. But otherwise, he followed this early agenda to the letter.

'It's OK' clearly unveiled the iron character his roles as quiet, drifty student and cook, and maddened, car-punching son and boyfriend had concealed. But it also put sweaty flesh on what this intense, unrelieved stage of his life, and the responsibility he felt for those around him, was doing to his head: *"Praying for sleep/ Dreaming with a watering mouth/ Wishing for a better life for my daughter and spouse."* For the first and last time on record without the distance of Slim's sarcasm, he then widened his view beyond his own poverty, to picture the whole ghetto he was trying to escape. He saw *"my little brother"* (either Nathan or his terrorised younger self) trying to learn at school, then racing home through streets infested with crack and children shooting each other for clothes. The boy has asthma, Marshall feels his lungs shutting and blood vessels bursting, as if they're drowning in a sunken city; a feeling a visit to Detroit will give you, as we've seen.

He's finally moved to another religious epiphany, a layer of his thinking he's kept almost secret since, apart from the hip-hop rapture of 'Revelation'. He sees the world as fallen (*"It's been Hell on this Earth since I fell on this Earth"*), and scorns the dope-selling avarice around him: *"the root of all evil."* So Marshall finds a different rock: *"in the midst of this insanity, I found my Christianity/ Through God, and there's a wish he granted me/ He showed me how to cope with the stress/ And hope for the best, instead of mope and depressed."*

His later contempt for TV evangelists on *The Marshall Mathers LP* becomes less clichéd and more serious, in this light. Hip-hop alone had not been enough to sustain him in his struggles. He had prayed to God, too, like any good Midwestern boy, and been answered. His indifference to the usual rap star's materialist bragging once he'd made his millions may also be explained by this forgotten song. In it, battling *"the root of all evil"*, he sounds more like Christ scattering the Temple money-lenders than Puff Daddy, dripping "Ghetto Fabulous" gold and bought women.

It may not be in his interests to emphasise this moral uprightness these days, when the world loves Slim Shady's perceived careless sickness. But the Christianity he "found" in his early twenties was not a passing thing. "He's not a hate-monger, he gets on his knees every night and prays with his daughter," his mother told the *Sydney Sun-Herald* last year. And he's happily told reporters this is true. Like his semi-suburban background, his praying is another neglected facet of his public, evil face.

The most embarrassing of buried secrets on *Infinity*, though, may be 'Searchin'', one of three songs complicating Slim's later, loud misogyny. It's shamelessly sappy, abjectly laying his love at Kim's feet, teenage in its unqualified, fervent adoration. Marshall can't sleep, can't speak, goes weak at the knees at the thought of her, can't think of anything else when he's not with her. This isn't R. Kelly "sex you up" stuff, either, not "one for the ladies". Marshall's lost in love for Kim, ignoring hard hip-hop convention for the sort of lines a doe-eyed high school student might slip to his girl in class: *"The way your lips sparkle and glare in the sun / You got your hair in a bun, no matter what you're wearing you stun."* His more serious hopes, and the relationship's frustrations at the time, are expressed at the end: *"I see you grasping to trust, but my intentions are good / 'Cos I just need you to see how much I'm eager to be / Your man legally wed."* The seeds of 'Kim''s murderous vengeance are in this early, nervously exposed, eventually thwarted need.

In 'Jealousy Woes II', surely about Kim too, those seeds grow. With a woman's voice loudly arguing (the kind of dialogue he'd later drop), he paints a picture of a girlfriend faking kisses, fighting him over money, frisking him for girls' numbers, making him grovel with stony silences, laughing at him when he hurts and cries. But the worm turns, in what would become familiar fashion: *"So I'm a wait for your evacuation / 'Cos every accusation makes me wanna smack your face in."* Eventually, he finds she's been seeing another man, the kind of accusation that would later tear them apart. But the pain she could make this essentially soft boy feel when they were younger, and all he wanted was to be a rapper and married to her,

Eminem – the world's most popular rapper. (LFI)

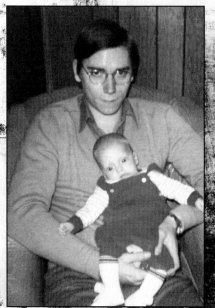

Eminem the innocent. Marshall Bruce Mathers III in happier days, with his father, Marshall Bruce Mathers II (left) and mother, Debbie Mathers-Briggs (right). (WENN)

Eminem aged nine (left), and pre-weight training, stick-armed and picked-on, at 14 (right) (WENN)

Eminem with Kim. "The house was always full of waifs and strays," said Debbie Briggs. "One of those troubled souls was Kim Scott, who moved in with us when she was 12. Marshall was about 15, and she lied about her age, saying she was the same. They got together and that was it. Chaos reigned." (WENN)

Eminem's boyhood home at 8427 Timken, Warren, Detroit, which was sold by his uncle, Todd Nelson, for $40,000. Swiftly auctioned by the purchaser, internet "bids" reached $13 million, before a more sober $75,000 was handed over, in December 2002. (JEFFREY SAUGER)

Eminem with his brother Nathan, aged 13. "I raised him since he was a baby, changing his diapers and feeding him," said Eminem, who in 2001 would take responsibility for Nate as well as his daughter Hailie. (WENN)

Eminem with Debbie and his daughter Hailie at his aunt Tanya's wedding reception, June 5, 1999, shortly before mother and son went to war. (WENN)

Paul Rosenberg, another Detroit white kid obsessed with rap who went on to law school, kept in touch with Marshall. When the time came, he would become Eminem's lawyer and manager, another part of the band that helped take him to the top.
(ERIC MCNATT/RETNA)

Betty Kresin, Eminem's maternal grandmother, who became involved in the ongoing feud between her grandson, his mother and so many others in the family.
(WENN)

Eminem with Kid Rock at the Experience Music Project in Seattle, May 25, 2000. Back in Detroit Marshall would haunt Kid's record signings, and beg him to battle. "I was 15 at the time, and he was a couple years older," he told Spin. "He used to always kind of laugh it off and say, 'Battle me in record sales.'" (LFI)

Home boy. Eminem, proud son of the Motor City, in 1999. (STEVE DOUBLE/RETNA)

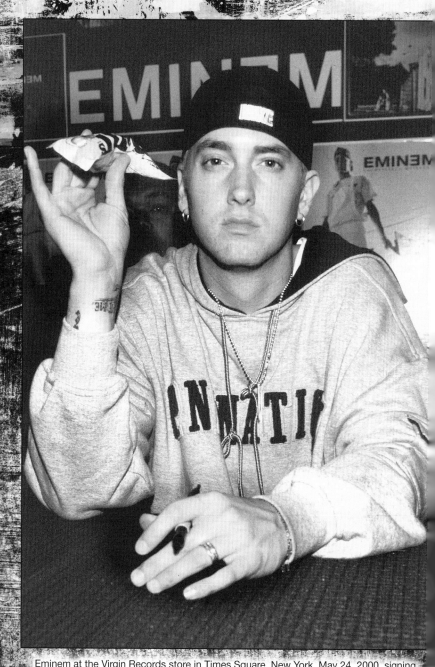

Eminem at the Virgin Records store in Times Square, New York, May 24, 2000, signing copies of *The Marshall Mathers LP,* and swallowing some of the junk food that helped him keep his pasty, poverty-ridden complexion, even as a millionaire. (LFI)

bleeds through this song. He might *"wanna smack your face in"*, in true Slim Shady style but, as would always be the case in real life, he doesn't. Like *Infinite*'s last "female" song, 'Maxine', about a whorish, possibly AIDS-ridden crack addict, the writing is more considered and less obnoxious than later (*"I refrain from getting angry,"* Kon Artis chivalrously tells Maxine; on *The Eminem Show*'s similarly themed, humourless 'Drips', Eminem searches for the *"ho"* to throttle her). Still loving Kim, not yet bitter at her, Marshall at 23 was not a misogynist.

Only one track fully suggested his future persona. 'Backstabber' had been his début single the year before, pressed with the proceeds of an income tax refund. A simple, lurid, pulp comic-book story about chasing a slippery super-villain, its tone was again gauche compared to later. But the Backstabber bore more than a passing likeness to Slim. An escapee from a psychiatric ward like that in *The Real Slim Shady* video, *"he'll stab you with a sword, don't be fooled by his charm . . ./ He has a mean stare but usually cracks jokes."* The narrator this time is a cop, but his arrest methods give a first glimpse of the graphic, sick humour to come: *"He shed his skin, then he promised to come clean/ I took his butcher knife and jabbed it under his spleen/ Cut him at the seam then dragged the fella home/ Beating him over the head with a telephone."* On 'Open Mic', too, Marshall chased enemies *"in a Jason mask"*. *Infinite* might be juvenilia. But his potential was now in place.

The record's complete failure, though, was one of the jolts he needed to force that potential to the surface; and such blows, for the next nightmare year, came thick and fast. "*Infinite*, you know, [the Bass Brothers] lost money on it," Marshall told elamentz.com. "They tried to put out a local tape in Detroit, it sold a little bit, but they didn't really make their money back on it, even. So, then we was gettin' ready to just be like, 'Fuck it.' And then we was like, nah, there's too much there. I was doing too many shows and gettin' too much response."

"When that failed," Paul Rosenberg recalled to *Newsweek*, "he decided to stop trying to fit in and simply make the kind of music he loved. And that's when he started experimenting with the Slim Shady character."

"After that record, every rhyme I wrote got angrier and angrier," Marshall confirmed to *Rolling Stone*. "A lot of it was because of the feedback I got. Motherfuckers was like, 'You're a white boy, what the fuck are you rapping for? Why don't you go into rock'n'roll?' All that type of shit started pissing me off.'"

More concrete factors also helped turn the diffident rapper of *Infinite* into his infamous Mr. Hyde, Slim. Hailie was born on Christmas Day, 1996, after *Infinite*'s hopes had already sunk. Marshall's desperate desire to improve on his own fractured upbringing seemed doomed to sink with it, torpedoed by life in Detroit. "It was a struggle to know that I had a little girl and couldn't afford to raise her," he told *Rolling Stone*. "I'm like, 'Fuck, I can't afford to buy my daughter diapers.' I literally didn't have shit. So when I hit 23 [he most likely means 25, late in 1997], that was like a wake-up point for me. Like, 'I gotta do something now.' That's when I started getting into every single battle in Detroit. Every competition. It was do or die for me." Kim, meanwhile, "had to strip to make money," he told *Newsweek*. He felt like grabbing dollars by any means necessary, too. "I had nothing. I felt like robbing somebody or selling drugs to get myself out of the situation I was in," he recalled to *Q*. The moral high ground he'd taken on *Infinite* was slipping from under his feet.

The places the couple had to live, now they had a dependent, darkened his mood further. "I was working 50-, 60-hour weeks for $6.50 an hour [at Gilbert's Lodge] just to pay the rent," he told *NME*. "And I still couldn't do it. In east Detroit you can get real cheap houses for, like, $200 a month, but once my daughter was born I couldn't meet it. So we were moving every six weeks or so." The similarity to his cashless mother's wanderings when he was a boy, which he so despised her for, must have sickened him. Now he was "changing the scenery" behind his daughter, too, the cycle of poverty keeping him trapped. And when they did stick in one home, it had to be in a crack zone, along 7 Mile. A stray bullet lodged in the wall near Kim's head one evening, as she did the dishes.

More grinding offences followed. "The neighbourhoods we lived in fucking sucked," Kim told *Rolling Stone*. "I went through four CDs and five VCRs in two years." One taunting crack addict was to blame. After his first break-in, he came back a few nights later to make a sandwich, and mark his territory. "He left the peanut butter, jelly, all the shit out and didn't steal nothing," Marshall spat to *Rolling Stone*. "Ain't this about a motherfucking bitch. But then he came back again, and took everything but the couches and beds. The pillows, clothes, silverware – everything. We were fuckin' fucked."

The festering racial tension that had scarred his attempts at a rap career followed him to that house too. "Little kids used to walk down the street going, 'Look at the white baby!'" he remembered to *Spin*. "Everything was, 'white this, white that'. We'd be sitting on our porch, and if you were real quiet, you'd hear, 'Mumble, mumble, white, mumble, mumble, white.' Then I caught this dude breaking into my house for, like, the fifth time, and I was like, 'Yo, fuck this! It's not worth it, I'm outta here!' That day, I wanted to quit rap and get a house in the fucking suburbs. I was arguing with my girl, like, 'Can't you see they don't want us here?' I went through so many changes. I actually stopped writing for about five or six months, and I was about to give everything up. I just couldn't, though. I'd keep going to the clubs and taking the abuse. But I'd come home and put a fist through the wall. If you listen to a Slim Shady record, you're going to hear all that frustration coming out."

It was the thinnest his skin became to his minority status, and the nearest he came to admitting it had an element of choice. He could have snapped under the abuse, gone "back to where he came from", like many a black racial pioneer in his city before him; accepted the white suburban life he'd been half-raised for, and would at least find camouflage in. No wonder he stopped rapping at this moment of crisis. If he retreated from black America, how could he make its music?

But in the end, he carried on. He and his young family moved back with his mother for a while, with the usual crises and screaming. He would later live with friends, while Kim and Hailie stayed behind – an indication, perhaps, of who now riled each other most. And from this tumult, in the summer of 1997, Slim Shady was born to save them all. His genesis was typically unwholesome.

"I was on the pot when I thought of Slim Shady," Marshall happily told *FHM*. "I was taking a shit and it popped in my head. It was because in the Dirty Dozen you have to have an alias. I'm Eminem, but in the Dirty Dozen I'm Slim Shady. I was taking a shit, thought of it, got off the pot, forgot to wipe my ass and went off to tell everybody." "Boom, the name hit me, and right away, I thought of all these words to rhyme with it," was the slightly alternative origin in *Rolling Stone*. "So" – more hygienically – "I wiped my ass, and, ah, called everybody I knew." "I thought of the name and then wrote, *'Slim Shady/ Brain-dead like Jim Brady'*," he recalled in *Angry Blonde*, "and that's when I went with the name."

His Eminem alias was the sort of thing every rapper needed, but never changed who he was, on record or off. This new name was different. Coming when all the simmering problems in his life were reaching boiling point, Slim Shady – plucked perhaps from Shady Lane, near Gilbert's Lodge – set something rolling loose in his head. "The more I started writing and the more I slipped into this Slim Shady character, the more it just started becoming me," he wrote in *Angry Blonde*. "My true feelings were coming out, and I just needed an outlet to dump them in. I needed some type of persona. I needed an excuse to let go of all this rage, this dark humour, the pain, and the happiness." It was as if he had named his sub-conscious, or the rush of uncensored emotions which crash through, for better or worse, on Es (which he'd soon start to hungrily gobble). The way he told it, he had been possessed by himself. In a period of despair, in the crude process of taking a shit, Slim Shady had appeared to set him free.

There would be encouraging hands on his shoulder, when this new Marshall made himself known. To hear Marky Bass tell it to the *Sydney Sun-Herald*, the Bass Brothers had moulded Slim, a product not of a private apparition, but old-fashioned showbiz Svengalis. "His lyrics were a lot tamer when he started out," Marky confided. "He always had his charac-ters and an edge, but it wasn't so much about his life story – and now pretty much everything he is writing about is what goes on in his life. We came up with the idea of shock rap. Things were going a little berserk in Marshall's life, we were getting turned away by labels who didn't want a white rapper, and some of the anger started coming out of him. We said, 'You've got to let this out and ride with it.' His early stuff was accepted within the rap genre and by the critics, he was always clean with his lyrics and his delivery, but the market didn't take to it until it got a little foul-mouthed, a little potty-mouthed. Now, they'll take anything from the kid."

Talking to the *Mail On Sunday*, Mathers-Briggs seemed to confirm the story. "No one should take anything he says seriously," she explained. "He doesn't mean it. He is making money out of negative issues, because he could not make it any other way. When he first started to write filthy lyrics, I asked him why. His answer was the more foul he was, the more people loved him. He didn't make money out of nice things. If he wrote a song about how much he loved his mother and little brother, he'd be laughed at."

Once he became famous as Eminem, Marshall would never be averse to doing what it took to sell records, and the advice of the Basses, still effec-tively his paymasters, must have carried weight with him. But, as even Marky indicated, the emotions that congealed into Marshall's new persona were genuine; Slim was his own creation. "All kinds of shit – not being able to provide for my daughter, my living situation, etc., just started building up so much that I had just had it," he recalled in *Angry Blonde*.

The contrast between Slim and his previous character was shown by the shocked reactions even of his foul-mouthed soulmates in D12, when he rapped Slim's first song for them. It was two freestyle, crazed verses he didn't even bother to name – *"Stole your mother's Acura / wrecked it and sold it back to her,"* was one rhyme he remembered. At its end, Bizarre intoned, "You have now witnessed a white boy on drugs." Proof was still more appalled, warning, "You need to quit talkin' that drug shit." But Slim's malign influence went deeper than Marshall's rap style. His life changed to suit his alias. As he described it in *Angry Blonde*, the decline of his daily existence and the rise of Slim went hand in hand. "[That first song] seemed like it was from out of left field compared to what I usually rapped about," he wrote. "I soon found myself doing things that I normally didn't do. Like getting into drugs and drinkin'. I was reeeaaally fucked up. I was sick of everything. Kim and I had Hailie, my producers FBT [the Basses' pro name] were just about to give up on me, we weren't paying rent to my mom's, and just a whole bunch of other horrible shit was going on."

But now, at last, he had a weapon with which to retaliate. Over the summer of 1997, as his circumstances simply got worse, he wrote three songs which would become the centrepiece not only of the next year's *The Slim Shady EP*, but key tracks on *The Slim Shady LP*, the album which would introduce him to the world. His "first real song", 'Just Don't Give A Fuck', was the one which bottled the essence of his fearlessly, funnily dark new identity best. It was written while he was still living back at his mother's with Kim and Hailie. On record, its introduction by D12 associate Frogger shows the nervous uncertainty everyone around Marshall seemed to feel at his transformation. *"A get your hands in the air, and get to clappin' 'em and like, back and forth because aah, this is . . . what you thought it wasn't,"* he announces, washing his hands of what follows even as he applauds. There's a hacking cough in the background, before Slim Shady roars onto vinyl.

'Just Don't Give A Fuck' is a battle rhyme in essence, but of a ruthless, rude confidence Eminem never managed on *Infinite*. He bundles most other white rappers into touch – Vanilla Ice, Everlast, even the admired 3rd Bass – as well as his Detroit rivals, before admitting *"I'm ill enough to just straight up dis you for no reason."* But the rap's point is to let Slim off the leash, and define him at the start, while burying *Infinite*'s failed Eminem: *"Slim Shady, Eminem was the old initials (Bye-Bye!) / Extortion, snortin', supportin' abortion / Pathological liar, blowin' shit out of proportion / . . .*

*Impulsive thinker, compulsive drinker, addict/ Half animal, half man/ Dumpin'
your dead body inside of a trash can."* By the final verse, Slim's outrageous
thoughts are blending into true moments from Marshall's life, a wrong-
footing technique which would become a trademark; cursing his dishwashing chores at Gilbert's, remembering his quietness at school, he then
imagines he had a Junior High drug habit, and at 13 raped the women's
swim team. What really makes this the "first", fully realised song by
Eminem/Slim, though, is its sneered chorus: *"Screamin' 'Fuck the world'
like Tupac/ I just don't give a FUUUUUCK!"* The rallying cry was irresistible. In the real world, holding down a job to support a baby and girlfriend, Marshall cared too much. But the *"Fuuuuuck!"* he didn't give on
record temporarily trampled all that. It was his first, relished raised finger
to everyone.

'If I Had', by contrast, dropped all bravado, and sank into the troubles
which spawned Slim. A cousin of *Infinite*'s 'It's OK', it jettisoned that
track's artistic distance, for one of hip-hop's most nakedly depressed,
weary songs. Marshall had left his mother's to live with a friend and his
roommates by now. He was still struggling. "I wrote that shit the same
week my car broke down," he remembered in *Angry Blonde*. "My fuckin'
engine blew out and a bunch of fucked up shit was happening, all at the
same time."

"Life . . . by Marshall Mathers," it begins, like a school report, or a teenager's secret diary. It's rapped flatly, almost whined, in Marshall's normal
speaking voice, to a barely varying, downbeat drum track by its EP producer, DJ Head. For the LP, the Basses would spruce it up into a version
that included a descending, looped organ, and a soft female voice. Either
way, it was circular music with no exit, expressing Marshall's true feelings
with no adornment; Slim's existence now letting him be honest as himself,
as well as from behind that dark mask.

What he thought was bleak. Life was a *"big obstacle"*, friends were *"really
your enemies"*, money was, as on 'It's OK', still *"the root of all evil"*; everything was geared to trick and backstab him. *"What is life?"* he wondered.
"I'm tired of life." And, 38 more times, he said *"tired"*, listing the dissatisfac-
tions that drained him. Skinny crackhead friends, drive-by shootings,
minimum wage jobs and petty bosses, DJs playing bad rappers and never
him, his own weakness with drink, *"using plastic silverware . . . not being a
millionaire,"* it all *"tired"* him. He was *"tired of being white trash, broke and
always poor . . . tired of being stared at"* (something which, ironically, would

worsen with success). Slim butted in with a chorus of vengeful fantasy: *"If I had one wish/ I would ask for a big enough ass for the whole world to kiss."* But the overall mood was of rare resignation: *"Just fed up/ That's my word."* It wasn't a song by someone expecting success, or who cared any longer about hip-hop's requirements. It just said poverty had left its writer hopeless and depressed. Bordering self-pity and paranoia, as such feelings do, its shameless self-exposure was one reason he would soon be plucked by Interscope into a new, vastly wealthy life.

'Just The Two Of Us', the *EP* track renamed ''97 Bonnie & Clyde' on the *LP*, was something else again. It was written still later in the summer of 1997, when Marshall and Kim had temporarily split up, and Kim was threatening a restraining order to keep him from Hailie. Both were seeing other people; if the song is to be believed, there was talk of Kim making her new boyfriend and his son Hailie's stepfamily, cutting Marshall out completely. With Kim's stepfather allegedly threatening him too, Marshall's resentment and apparent impotence at Hailie's removal made him lash back with this swiftly infamous song, about the hours after his killing of Kim.

But, unlike its even more notorious 1999 prequel 'Kim', it is not at heart a misogynistic, violent song. As Marshall wrote in *Angry Blonde*, it had begun with his desire to write about himself and his daughter. "But I thought, 'How can I make a song about Hailie?' I didn't want to make the shit corny or nothing, [and] I was also tryin' to piss Kim off." Of the massive invasion of Kim's privacy that resulted, he explained: "At the most I thought it would be talked about in Detroit, but I didn't figure I was going to get a deal and go nationwide with it." Still, to anger Kim in the extreme, he used Hailie as co-vocalist. "I lied to Kim and told her I was taking [Hailie] to Chuck E. Cheese that day," he told *Rolling Stone* of his daughter's participation. "But I took her to the studio. When [Kim] found out, she fucking blew. We had just got back together for a couple of weeks. Then I played her the song, and she bugged the fuck out."

It would not be the last time he'd profess naïve surprise at such outrage from Kim, after a verbal assault. But Hailie's presence on this track, in a half-baby-talk dialogue with Dad when not yet even one, in fact softens the song, leaving its central subject as his love for her, as he'd intended. His fear of being "corny" – which hadn't worried him when he wrote 'Searchin'', and he'd stop fearing again by *The Eminem Show*'s heartfelt 'Hailie's Song' – was, though, also allayed by creepy horror. To dream-like, rippling harps, he quietens Hailie's gurgling queries about why Mama's sleeping in the trunk and smells so bad, why she has *"that little boo-boo on her throat"* (*"it's just a little scratch – it don't hurt"*), and why she won't talk to her child, and wants to *"swim"* into a lake, late at night.

There's a rueful playfulness to his explanations (*"See, honey, there's a place called heaven and there's a place called hell/ A place called prison and a place called jail/ And Da-da's probably on his way to all of 'em, except one"*).

But there's a disturbing, selfish certainty in his attitude, too, which would resurface in future conflicts with Kim and Debbie, as Slim made him suddenly rear up assertively, after years smarting under the two women's thumbs. *"Just me and you, baby, is all we need in this world,"* he murmurs blissfully, not having given his child a choice, and after he's tricked her into helping throw Mama in the lake. In later years, he'd pull not only Hailie but his half-brother Nathan to his side to live, replacing their mothers, quite convinced he was acting for the best. This song shows that pathology's birth, making him sound more like a mad baby-snatching Dad than a murderer, before reaching the closing lines, which were all he really meant to say: *"If you ever need anything, just ASK/ Da-da will be right there . . . I love you, baby."*

A murderous, easy-to-miss twist in the tale, meanwhile, was left dangling. As Kim's rock-weighted legs plunge to the lake's bed, he asks Hailie, *"just help Dad with two more things out the trunk"*. It was Kim's new boyfriend and his son, the prequel would reveal. But at the time, this killing spree's corpses could have been anyone. His mother? Vanilla Ice? Sick Slim Shady left no clues.

'Just Don't Give A Fuck', 'If I Had' and 'Just The Two Of Us' made the 8-track *The Slim Shady EP* a startling step up in quality from *Infinite* when he recorded it, in two weeks, in the winter of 1997. But, as the songs' downbeat nature suggested, this was not a time of creative thrills, but creeping desperation and fear. Slim Shady, and the EP with his name, was part of a last throw of the dice which tumbled through the end of 1997, a gamble which, if Marshall lost it, would condemn him to a dead-end life.

"My daughter was one at the time," he told launch.com. "I couldn't afford to buy her diapers. I didn't have a job. I had job after job and just kept getting fired. I failed ninth grade three times. I was basically going nowhere. When I made *The Slim Shady EP*, I told the production people, 'Yo, if this doesn't work, I'm about to be 23 [25, of course], I gotta quit, get a job, do something.'"

Linked to this feeling of a final chance was an invitation to rap in LA, the mythic home of his gangsta-rap heroes. The offer came from Wendy Day, a white one-time Vice-President of a liquor company who in 1992 had quit, and sunk $500,000 of her money into the Rap Coalition, an organisation intended to combat the often exploited status of young rappers in the record industry. According to one report, she had met Marshall when he and D12, as part of his last-ditch efforts, drove to Miami for an industry seminar, and he gave her an *Infinite* tape; others say it was at a Detroit convention. Either way, *Infinite* convinced her to call Marshall, and invite him to the Rap Coalition-sponsored Rap Olympics, a major battle to be held in South Central LA that October. She'd pay his air fare. The prize for first place would be $500 and a Rolex watch.

Marshall's need to win ratcheted up in the week of the competition. He was still separated from Kim and Hailie. His time living with a friend and other roommates in a cramped apartment had ended when an acquaintance offered cheaper rent, if he and his friend moved across the street. But the acquaintance pocketed their cash, instead of passing it to the building's landlord. "So one day we come home and all our shit's on the fuckin' front lawn," Marshall wrote in *Angry Blonde*. "We never could catch that motherfucker. Till this day, we haven't caught him. It was a real fucked period in my life (no surprise there), and I felt like I had hit 'rock bottom'." He wrote the song of the same name that week, a work even bleaker than 'If I Had', which also made it on to *The Slim Shady LP*. It begins with a dedication to *"all the happy people who have real nice lives/ And who have no idea what it's like to be broke as fuck."* He probably wrote it the night before he flew to LA, when, homeless, he had to break back into the house he'd been evicted from. "I didn't have anywhere else to go," he told *Rolling Stone*. "There was no heat, no water, no electricity. I slept on the floor, woke up, went to LA. I was so pissed."

Homelessness devastates your sense of security and self-esteem, strengths Marshall was already wretchedly short on. But typically, he spent the flight transforming his desperation into iron determination. Now he had to win that $500. So he would. He'd get a record contract, too. He assessed his competition as the plane neared LA, preparing put-downs for the only rapper he thought could challenge him, a boy called Kwest the Mad Lad. He convinced himself that all his hopes came down to what he did that day, in that alien city. Agonising months later, he would be proved right.

It was the 27th of October when he touched down, a Friday. The Rap

Olympics were held in the Proud Bird nightclub, in Inglewood, right by the airport. The British journalist William Hall was there that evening, researching his definitive study of young hopeful South Central rappers, *Westsiders*. Before the first round began, Marshall joined the other competitors milling in nervous clusters, practising their freestyles, psyching themselves up. He was the only white boy in the place. Hall glanced up briefly when "M + M" – he thought – was announced, surprised and disappointed by his colour, then returned to his conversation with an ex-member of the World Class Wreckin' Cru, who once included one Dr. Dre in their ranks. Hall was forced to look up again, by a crescendo of cheers. He realised it was the white boy who was ripping his opponents apart. *"What you need to do,"* came the first words Hall heard, *"is practise your freestyle/ 'Cos you come up missin' more than Snoop Doggy Dogg's police file . . ."* "He's cold," a man next to Hall hollered in approval.

Paul Rosenberg, convinced by *Infinite* to become Marshall's manager, was in the crowd too, willing his friend on. "Oh my God," he told *Rolling Stone*. "There was this black guy sitting next to me in the crowd. After the first round, he yells, 'Just give it to the white boy. It's over. Give it to the white boy.'"

This LA crowd's difference to the racially hostile audiences Marshall had faced down in Detroit was shown when he moved on to the second round. Standing face to face with his new, black opposition, the latter made a snide comment about Marshall's skin, and was greeted with loud boos. Marshall, used to such attacks, deflected it back to destroy this crude opponent. *"Every body in this place I miss you,"* he rapped, *"If you try and turn my facial tissue/ Into a racial issue . . ."* The cheers were for him again.

Marshall kept going, round by round. It was like it was a movie, like it was his destiny to win, as he'd made himself believe it was when he fled his wrecked Detroit life for this night. But in the final, something happened. He faced not Kwest, the obstacle he'd been preparing for, but an unknown. The other rapper walked away when Marshall stepped up to battle him, standing behind a nearby projection screen, destroying the drama of confrontation. Still, Marshall was sure he'd crushed him. "He was garbage," he told Hall afterwards. But somehow the judges disagreed. And suddenly, his chance to change his life had been and gone. "He really looked like he was going to cry," Rosenberg remembered.

"Em was so far ahead of all the competition, it was embarrassing," Dan Geistlinger, then an 18-year-old intern for Dre's home, Interscope

Records, who would be promoted to a top A&R man for what he saw that night, told *NME*. "I think the reason he didn't win was that if he had he would have had to battle the competition MC, this guy called Juice. I don't think he could've handled the humiliation. Em just crushed everyone that night." That was no consolation to an appalled Marshall. "When I lost, I was ready to kill somebody," he told launch.com.

He was sitting with Rosenberg, washed out and angry, when two men walked over. Led by Dan Geistlinger, they both worked for Interscope. They'd been watching him carefully. "He came up to me afterwards and I didn't know he was anybody from anything," Marshall told *The Source*. "He was like, 'Yo, you got a tape or anything?' I was all pissed, like, 'Yeah, here, just take it.'" He shoved them a demo of *The Slim Shady EP*. He thought nothing more of it. Someone else came over and asked him to appear on the local Sway & Tech radio show the next morning, and he did so. Then he flew back to Detroit, almost broken.

He patched things up with Kim. He returned to work at Gilbert's Lodge, intending to work overtime at Christmas, to get a present for Hailie's first birthday. And he held onto one lifeline for a future as a rapper, a promise of a deal from a major label contact. Then, over the last week of December, even these small securities tore apart. He thought he had hit rock bottom earlier that year. But it was now that he smashed into it, and cracked. That week, he thought about killing. Others, for money. Or himself, to get it over with.

First, he lost his job. "That was the lowest I got," he told *NME*. "It was five days before Christmas, which is Hailie's birthday, and I had $40 left. I was a cook and this new chef fired everybody. He told me it was because I hadn't worn my chef's shirt one day. I was like, 'I worked here three years and you're firing me because I didn't wear the right shirt one day?' I almost choked him."

Then, on Christmas Eve, as he recorded 'Rock Bottom', the song he had written when made homeless in October, he was told the man who had promised him a major deal was a fraud, who worked in the label's mail-room. "I didn't know when I wrote it that it was going to come out so sad," he said in *Angry Blonde* of the song consuming him that night. "I had actually meant it to be an uplifting song, but when we were sitting around making the track, Head had a sample that we played over that beat and it was just so sad. I said, 'Fuck it, let's go with this one.'"

'Rock Bottom' wearily reviewed the details of a life that had gotten him down: envy at more successful rappers, disgust at how money corrupted them, and dismay at his own drug-addicted peer group. It described the poverty-stricken enervation that left his daughter short of diapers, as *"yesterday went by so quick/ it seems like it was just today/ My daughter wants to throw the ball but I'm too stressed to play/ Live half my life, and throw the rest away."* Time itself was closing in on him, evaporating as he lacked the energy to use it, the classic inertia of unemployment and drug use. But 'Rock Bottom''s real clue that he had sunk further since the similar 'It's OK' and 'If I Had' was his solution in its last verse. As he shivers in the *"house with no furnace, unfurnished"* where he probably wrote it, he realises he's become *"evil"*, and wants money and fame at any cost. Earlier in the song this closet Christian could *"pray that God answers,"* but by its end, he's resigned himself to *"Hell"*. Having nothing, the careless, solvent safety of others looks like an affront, which he means to snatch away, *"to kill"*: *"My daughter's feet ain't got no shoes or socks on 'em/ And them rings you wearing look like they got a few rocks on 'em."* But before he could turn on the world, and become truly lost, the setbacks which made 'Rock Bottom' too appropriate to bear altered his aim. During a break in taping, he chose instead to kill himself.

"There was this one time when I really felt like I wanted to do something to change my life," he said to music365, remembering those hours in the studio, "whether it would be doing something I regretted, or with rap or whatever. A bunch of other personal shit was happening in my life right about then, and I just thought I wasn't gonna get a deal no matter what, and I just took a fucking bunch of pills. I puked the shit up. I didn't want to have to go to hospital but my fucking stomach hurt so bad. I had a little problem and I just took too many. I don't know if I was necessarily trying to kill myself, I was just really depressed and I kept thinking, more pills, more pills, I just kept takin' 'em. I bet I took 20 pills in the course of two hours, [the painkillers] Tylenol 3s. That's why I like going back and listening to my album, and thinking of what I was feeling back then."

Though he called himself a *"criminal"* in a later song, it was typical that, with murder on his mind, Marshall turned that malevolence on himself. Even after Slim Shady appeared, he was still too soft-hearted to really hurt others, and too painfully aware of his faults to blame strangers. And the purging of his harshest emotions with that half-meant suicide bid did him good. Those hours of depression, gut agonies, and the pills' eventual throwing up, which made sure he lived, really were as bad as it got. It was as if he'd passed a test, or his prayers had been listened to after all. Because in early 1998, his wildest teenage dreams came true, all at once. It was Jeff Bass, William Hall was told, who walked in on Marshall in a Detroit motel, and broke the news.

"We got an appointment with Interscope Records on Monday," Bass said.

"Oh, yeah," Marshall replied.

"Yeah, some doctor . . ."

"Doctor? What are you talking about ?"

"Some guy who calls himself Dr. Dre."

Marshall's stomach twisted again. His mind locked, not daring to believe. He could only keep shouting the same words, for minutes afterwards. "Don't fuckin' lie to me, man. Don't fuckin' lie to me . . ."

5

MY NAME IS

Dr. Dre was in a crisis of his own when Eminem entered his life, a tailspin he might not have pulled out of. Born in 1965 in Compton, one of three children of his single mother, who christened him Andre Young, Dre had been a basically amiable youth, secure inside his lone parent's family in a way Marshall never was. One of his earliest memories was of DJing for his party-loving mother aged four, flipping from one seven-inch single to the next, learning how music flowed. He would sleep with headphones on. And, though he moved between Blood and Crip neighbourhoods in the years when their rivalry turned to mass slaughter, gangsta-rap's future king steered clear of trouble, and stuck to his musical ambitions. Even when he helped create the sound of Niggaz With Attitude in his early twenties, putting Compton's gang culture on the global map, Dre (who had by then awarded himself his doctorate, in homage to basketball great Julius "Dr. J" Erving) was a peaceable young man.

But as N.W.A.'s 1988 LP *Straight Outta Compton* and its successors showered sudden wealth on its makers, along with adoration from young fans like Marshall, the lifelong division in Dre's head between records and reality blurred. He was encouraged in this by the brutal man who became his employer, Marion "Suge" Knight. The most feared and destructive individual in hip-hop, whose throttling hand was only removed from the genre by a 1997 jail-term, the mountainous Knight was an associate of real Compton Bloods. He latched onto Dre as his way into hip-hop's vast market, using protection racket threats to release the Doctor from his old label, Ruthless. Knight then made Dre the production powerhouse behind his Death Row Records. For Dre's solo début, *The Chronic* (1992), Death Row went into partnership with Jimmy Iovine's Time-Warner affiliated Interscope, and over the next few years, all these future players in the Eminem story would be soiled by rumoured association with violence, intimidation, gangsterism or greed.

Dre's own record in this period was brainless and despicable, a far cry from the cuddly figure familiar from later Eminem videos. Most notoriously, in December 1990, while still with N.W.A., he coldly battered the MTV presenter Dee Barnes, at an industry party. He felt Barnes, a friend of his, had disrespected his group and so, in Barnes' own account in Ronin Ro's book *Have Gun Will Travel*, let Knight punch the man she was with, while he took care of the girl. Apparently drunk, Dre, a tall, burly man, grabbed Barnes by her neck and hair, and started smashing her face into a brick wall. As she stumbled to a stairway, he tried to throw her down it. Then he chased her into the Ladies' toilets, grabbed her hair and punched her in the face, beating her till associates hustled him away. Dre denied her charges, in lazily unconvincing terms, but later settled with Barnes out of court. "There's a lot of women that he beat up," Barnes told Ro, "a lot that he smacked around. But I'm the one that fucking pressed charges." Dre eventually admitted to *Rolling Stone*, with something short of remorse: "I was in the wrong, but it's not like I broke the bitch's arm."

For the next few years, Dre's production style, meticulously refitting Seventies funk for the slow-rolling tempo and swirling paranoia of Nineties LA, made him hip-hop's man with the golden touch; *The Chronic* and his protégé Snoop Doggy Dogg's 1993 *Doggystyle* alone made Death Row $113 million. But the criminal company he kept at the label – exactly the people he had so carefully avoided growing up – made his life stagger out of control. In Death Row's bunker-like headquarters, and their offices at Interscope, Knight orchestrated terrifying beatings and, it was even rumoured, rapes of black male underlings and associates. White Interscope executives like Iovine, Ro suggests, turned deaf ears to the screams under their roof, so long as the profits rolled in. And, in his new millionaire's mansion, Dre too partied with Knight's tame Bloods, becoming vacant on spliff and drink while they trashed, set fire to, fought in, fucked in, and turned the stereo up in his exclusive home.

Dre sank further into criminal ways himself. In 1992, he was put under house arrest for breaking record producer Damon Thomas' jaw, after Thomas caught Dre fucking his girlfriend. In 1994, a drunken high-speed car chase with the LAPD ended with Dre – in a symbol of his life – driving over a cliff, and being sentenced to 180 nights at a halfway house, one step away from real jail-time.

Looking back in 2000 for *NME*, Dre was asked if, meeting him now, he would like the wild man he'd been then. "I would like the person but I would hate his ways," he said, taken aback. "The immaturity, the fucking, um, because I was wild, I was a wild kid, man. Obnoxious, wild, careless – I was really obnoxious. You got to realise that when I was 20 years old, I had a house, a Mercedes, a Corvette and a million dollars in the bank. And taking a guy who grew up the way I did, out of Compton and put him in this fucking mansion, you couldn't tell me shit at that time. It was pretty bad, actually, now I think about it. But I got through it. I grew up."

Dre's time in the halfway house helped arrest his self-destructive spiral. So, in 1996, he acrimoniously left Death Row to strike his own deal with Interscope, with his own label, Aftermath. The same year, as Knight faced nine years in jail for leading Tupac and others in beating a man in Vegas the night Tupac was shot dead, and federal agents investigated a drug dealer's investment in Death Row, Iovine's Interscope, too, severed their ties with Knight's label.

Knight's incarceration in 1997 seemed to close this dirty chapter in hip-hop history. But for Dre, a second decline was just beginning. For gangsta-rap's largely voyeuristic, white audiences, after all, beating up women, crashing cars and associating with thugs were positive traits for a performer. Dre was just keeping it "real". So when the previously failure-proof Doctor's next two records, *Dr. Dre Presents The Aftermath* and *The Firm*, revealed his new, positive attitude, they were derided, and flopped. In 1998, Dre had saved his soul, but as a result seemed set to lose his career.

If Marshall's tape had found its way to Interscope and Dre a year earlier in this sordid narrative, things might have been very different. As it was, the menacing influence of Knight, who had corrupted several artists, including Dre, Tupac and even Vanilla Ice, had been removed. Iovine, though still courting controversy with the goth-rock shock tactics of Marilyn Manson, no longer let gun-toting Bloods into his building. And Dre, almost as much as Marshall, was focused on finding a hit. When he heard that white boy's tape, he knew what to do.

The story of just how Dre found his star, when it was first told, had all the supernatural luck and judgement of a Hollywood fable. It was said Dre had been driving through LA, surveying his kingdom, when he happened to hear Marshall's performance on the *Sway & Tech* radio show, the morning after his Rap Olympics failure. Before Marshall could vanish to Detroit, Dre tracked down his hotel room, and phoned him up. In another version, the demo Marshall had handed to Dan Geistlinger in LA fell to the floor of Iovine's garage, where it lay till Dre saw it, and somehow knew he should place it in a tape deck.

The reality was more prosaic, of course. It was Geistlinger's attendance at the Rap Olympics, doing the spadework the likes of Dre and Iovine had no time for, which made a fortune for all concerned. *The Slim Shady EP* demo made its way from him to Iovine, who played it to Dre. Even when telling this true tale, Dre couldn't resist the grand gesture. "In my entire career in the music industry," he reminisced to *Rolling Stone*, "I have never found anything from a demo tape of a CD. When Jimmy played this, I said, 'Find him. Now.'" As the Bass Brothers' phone number was on the cassette, it didn't take Sherlock Holmes.

One other factor may explain the gap between Geistlinger getting the tape in October 1997, and Jeff Bass telling Marshall to pack his bags to meet Dre in LA, four months later. "When we went to Interscope, we worked him as the Marilyn Manson of rap," Marky Bass confided to the *Sydney Sun-Herald*, as he explained how the Basses "came up with the idea of shock rap", and encouraged Marshall's Shady side, because of its commercial appeal.

No doubt such considerations were discussed at length inside the Interscope building, while back in Detroit the object of their calculations contemplated poverty and suicide. The Presley-like potential of a white rapper of such filthy skill was lost on no one, and when Interscope did reveal Eminem to the world, nothing in their campaign would be left to chance. But when Marshall was summoned to LA, his first taste of his dreams was still clean.

"When I met Dre in the Interscope offices, I was awestruck," he told *NME*. "I was such a big fan. He thought I didn't like him! I was like, 'Dog, you're a living legend, how am I supposed to act?'"

The suddenness of it all was remembered by Bizarre. "He was missing from Detroit for three weeks. Nowhere to be found. Then he just up and called out of the blue: 'Yo, man, I just signed with DR. DRE! He's got this fresh condo out here, you got to see it . . .!'"

Marshall was signed to Dre's Interscope subsidiary, Aftermath, soon after his arrival. In rap circles, the question of exactly who was helping whom was soon being asked. "I wouldn't say I was bringing Dre back,"

Marshall would protest to the *Launch* website, once their work together was a success. "I don't think he ever left. 'Phone Tap', on the last album, *The Firm*, was dope to me. Dre basically saved my life; my shit was going nowhere. I was reaching a boiling point, doing a lot of drugs and fucked up shit because I was so depressed. So when I say Dre saved my life, I mean he *literally* saved my life, and I feel like I owe him a lot. Dre took me in and taught me a lot, not just rap-wise, but business-wise. Whatever I can do to return the favour, I'm here."

"I felt I brought something out of Dre that he always had in him," he added to *The Source*. "I just helped bring it out again, and he did the same for me. I learned to do things with my voice that I never thought possible. Before I used to just rap; I was good at rhymin' words. Now, I'm able to rhyme a word with a certain attitude that I didn't have before."

To icast.com, he explained their creative relationship this way: "It's like this – I'm a lyricist and a writer. He makes beats and produces. He has a vision. He can make that come to life. Damn near every Dre beat that I hear, I wanna rap over it. It makes me instantly think of things. We just get together, and in one studio session, we can knock out one or two songs right there. It's like when him and Snoop Dogg first got together. There's a chemistry."

The most crucial thing the former Nigga With Attitude gave Marshall, though, was what he had struggled for since his first public performance, but could never have gained alone: the respect of black rap listeners. "It's some very awkward shit," Dre considered to *Rolling Stone*. "It's like seeing a black guy doing country and western, know what I'm saying? I got a couple of questions from people around me. You know, 'He's got blue eyes, he's a white kid.' But I don't give a fuck if you're purple; if you can kick it, I'm working with you." *The Source*'s Robert Rosario put it plainly: "When I first heard Em, I knew he could hang. The guy keeps getting more respect. But if it wasn't for Dre, there wouldn't be any Eminem – and vice versa."

It was Marshall who was eager to impress, anyway, when the two quickly went to work. "We clicked," he told *NME*. "First day in the studio, we knocked off three songs in six hours. He said he'd never done that but I was anxious to show him what I could do. I loved hip-hop so much, knew and appreciated the history of hip-hop, and I always wanted to have a voice in hip-hop. This is the goal I'd worked towards all my life."

"I was writing like crazy when I got out to Cali," he recalled in *Angry Blonde*. "Especially after I got my deal, so I wasn't tryin' to let it slip." With the work ethic of someone who had toiled at rapping in the night hours between dishwashing jobs, he scribbled lyrics, went to Dre's home studio to record them, then wrote more, junking songs midway when new inspirations came, thriving under the pressure of his one chance to make his hopes come true.

To *Launch*, he revealed how the writing happened: "I collect ideas throughout the week. It might take a while, but I write on a sheet of paper, scattered ideas, words and metaphors. When I have enough ideas, I'll piece the shit together. I do it purposely so that if a rhyme sheet is lost, whoever finds it won't know what it means. Half a sentence will be here . . . a word over here. I start at the corner of the paper. I write in slants." In the studio, he explained, he and Dre guzzled down Es, heating up their energy and emotions, of love and hate. "We get in there, get bugged out, stay in the studio for fuckin' two days," Dre confirmed to *Rolling Stone*. "Then you're dead for three days. Then you wake up, pop the tape in, like, 'Let me see what I've done.'" In this environment, what became *The Slim Shady LP* took 12 days to finish.

The three songs Dre and Marshall completed in their first session included two which went unreleased: 'When Hell Freezes Over', Marshall's first attack on Detroit rivals Insane Clown Posse, and 'Ghost Stories', a gory haunted house tale. 'Role Model', though, was much more important. Its creation started the intuitive, open-minded studio collaborations between whoever was at hand which would become the hallmark of every Eminem album. Dre began it by playing Marshall one of his stockpiled backing tracks, this one with a slow, circular beat, to see what it triggered. Marshall recalled a rhyme that would be right for it which he'd started the night before, finishing two verses and a hook on the spot. Dre associate Mel-Man then rapped, *"Don't you want to grow up to be just like me?"*, the line which became the track's ranted chorus, and gave Marshall the thematic focus to finish it.

The result stated his defence for his lyrical outrages, before anyone had heard them to attack. *"We recordin'?"* he asked as the track began, emphasising its spontaneous feel. But there was a self-consciousness, tight detail, and almost prophetic awareness and outracing of listeners' expectations in each packed line, too, with little precedent in pop. With giddily free association, Marshall moved from attacks on enemies he hadn't made yet, like Hilary Clinton and Lauryn Hill, to a list of crimes so extreme they couldn't be believed, and acts so self-destructive he could never have survived. A corpse himself one minute, killing O.J. Simpson's wife the next, referencing Warner Brothers cartoons and *Psycho II* for cultural context, the song's genital wart-pussed, brain damaged, hallucinating Shady could never really be confused with the "role model" of its title. The climax was a chorus of acid irony: *"Now follow me and do exactly what you see/ Don't you wanna grow up to be just like me!"* In a deeper trap for the literal-minded, he even declared himself fictional: *"How the fuck can I be white, I don't even exist."* Add comically schizoid dialogues between multiple Marshalls – yelling *"Bitch!"*, *"Hi!"* and *"Fuck you!"* to himself from stage left – and bubbling sound effects suggesting the man we heard was a drowning suicide, and the musically simple result boiled with contradictory life. It also showed startling, full-blown confidence. Marshall had walked into Dre's house looking like a starry-eyed, anonymous apprentice. But after all he had been through to get there, he made sure he took the mic like a master. In one song, half-written right there, he outrapped almost everyone hip-hop's most famed producer had ever worked with.

Although Marshall makes no mention of it in *Angry Blonde*'s reminiscence of that first session, legend has it a still more definitive Eminem track was recorded that day: 'My Name Is'.

Heard on the radio for the first time, when it became the single that brought him worldwide fame, this would make every record around it sound like it was in slow motion, and at least two fewer dimensions than Marshall's hyperkinetic, sensurround, emotionally seesawing head-space. It was "knocked out in about an hour," he breezily informed *Rolling Stone*. But that belies the result, which sounds like a perfect partnership between Dre's famous studio perfectionism and Marshall's suddenly bottomless, instinctive creative well.

On *The Slim Shady LP*, it comes after the first of the 'Public Service Announcements' which would introduce all his subsequent records, too: a portentous, Fifties style disclaimer by Jeff Bass warning the album's contents are "totally fucked" and "not necessarily the views of anyone"; furthermore, that children shouldn't listen to it with "laces in their shoes". However, "Slim Shady is not responsible for your actions." After a minute, you can hear Marshall whispering this legal nonsense in the announcer's ear. Asked if he has anything else to say, his first words on his first album to be heard outside Detroit are: "Yeah. Don't do drugs."

Then, there's a second of old-school scratching. And Marshall's message to the planet blasts in: *"HI! My name is . . . my name is . . . my name is . . . Slim Shady."* Dre's production, often over-emphasised in accounts of Marshall's career, earns its reputation with what follows. Rumbling beats and a child-like, toytown-tinny sort of Stax organ riff create the momentum and viral catchiness of that repeated, calling-card chorus. The production then alters for every packed, narrative verse, sometimes peeling back to what sounds like just a slowing heartbeat, other times adding eerie, outer space effects.

But the track's real trick is to extend 'Role Model''s multi-voiced experiment, till the first-time listener might have wondered just how many radio stations he was receiving from the ether, or some more appalling source. Where Marvin Gaye once spent weeks constantly layering his own voice to create a sonic bed of spiritual balm on 1971's *What's Going On*, 'My Name Is' saw Marshall and Dre do the same, to suggest a maniac's multiple identities ricocheting round a padded cell. The first Slim you hear lasts just four words, *"Hi – my name is . . .",* that are heckled on every off-beat – *"Who?", "What?"* – before the answer arrives, faint and buzzing with faraway, ominous static: *"Slim Shady".* While this dialogue plays out, a third Slim is noisily clearing his throat and asking for the class's attention, *"for one second",* like some beaten-before-he-starts Lincoln teacher, if not for his next words: *"Hi kids! Do you like violence? Want to get fucked up worse than my life is?" "Uh-huh !"* chirps a helium-voiced tot. Where are we, and with whom, and to what place will he take us? These questions had rarely troubled regulars to chart radio stations or record stores in years. Within Dre's solid sonic structure, the answer was a flowing, fast journey around Marshall Mathers' mind.

He'd only just introduced himself, but already he was pouring his heart out, about people in his life we'd never met. *"99 per cent of my life I was lied to,"* he began one verse, *"I just found out my Mom does more drugs than I do."* Another section finished: *"and by the way, when you see my Dad, yeah, tell him I slit his throat in this dream I had."* When his life started to be scalpelled open in interviews, these infamous lines would be the instruments. His mother would enter the debate with a lawsuit. It was the surely deliberate start of his anonymous, awful life becoming a public soap opera, the script for which was made available on his records. His vengeance on Mathers-

Briggs' destabilising of his youth was to cast her as a white trash Joan Collins, a villainous super-bitch. It was a role she would find hard to shake. His further criticism that she couldn't breast-feed him as *"you ain't got no tits"* was a bit harsh.

Indications of Marshall's own instability were inserted as casually (*"Since age 12, I've felt like I'm someone else"*). But these downbeat passages were off-set by stories of stapling English teachers' balls to their desks, and running over friendly ETs. With its jaunty tune, it was dubbed a novelty record. The novelty in 1999's chart was its inspiration, unflagging for four-and-a-half minutes. The one downside for its creator was when Labi Siffre, writer of 'I Got The', sampled for 'My Name Is''s rhythm track, took deep exception to a lyric about raping a lesbian, among other soon-to-be familiar offences. With Interscope pressure to get radio play, too, Marshall considerably toned down his first mass market missive.

Dre produced only one other significant track on *The Slim Shady LP*. 'Guilty Conscience' would be the follow-up single to 'My Name Is', and would cause much more controversy. Dre came up with the idea of a duet with Marshall, first called 'Night'n'Day', in which the pair would trade opposing views. Returning from the gym, where they worked out and talked in between the album's draining sessions, Marshall wrote the lyrics, as usual, in a day. It was a more cinematic track than anything he had attempted before, presenting three scenarios, argued over in the protag-onists' heads by an angelic conscience (Dre) and devilish tempter (Slim). The moral dilemmas were the robbing of a liquor store by a depressed young man trying to support his kids; the drugging of a 15-year-old girl at a party by a 21-year-old man as they make out, so she'll forget him fucking her; and the murder of a man's wife and lover when he discovers them both in bed.

They were all potentially queasy situations. But more slick production from Dre, the pair's keen sparring, and the tales' linking by a Sixties TV-style, moralising narrator and evocative, radio play sound effects created a highly enjoyable, visually suggestive track. It also turned Dre into another supporting character in Slim's rapidly expanding rep company, as a grumpy foil to his live-wire young charge, a persona developed in future videos. Marshall memorably ran rings round his mentor's high-minded pronouncements this time by suddenly smirking: *"You gonna take advice from somebody who slapped DEE BARNES?"*

"Dre lately had been on the positive tip," he recalled to *Launch*, "trying to clean up his image and shit. I'm at the stage where I don't give a fuck. At the end of the song, I felt I was losing the battle, so I felt I had to take pokes at him. And I remembered when he slapped Dee Barnes. I didn't tell him I was going to say it. He fell over in his chair laughing, so I guess it was all good. But I was thinking the whole time, 'What is he going to say?' "

The more serious hostile response, though, came from those critics who were repulsed by the climax of the rape verse, in which Slim argues: *"Yo, look at her bush, does it got hair? (Uh-huh)/ Fuck this bitch right here on the spot bare."* 'Guilty Conscience' 's light, fictional tone was the lines' main defence, as would be the case throughout *The Slim Shady LP*, generally less savage and misogynistic than its successors. Another strong track, 'As The World Turns', seems typical of his attitude at the time. Though in it he intends to rape a trailer park blonde, and ends up fucking her to death with his *"go-go gadget dick"*, in between she knocks him through a plate-glass window and bites off his leg, a castratingly, sexually voracious match for all he attempts. As the song includes autobiographical school single combat with a fat female bully he also needs magic powers to beat, he seems to have been more worried by women than they had to be of him, at this stage. Still, in interviews he responded aggressively to 'Guilty Conscience' 's critics.

"Why can't people see that records can be more like movies?" he asked the *LA Times*. "The only difference between some of my raps and movies is that they aren't on a screen. I'm put on a blast for 'Guilty Conscience', but the idea came from *Animal House*, which is a movie that everyone thinks is funny and wonderful. Dre and I were talking about doing a song about what's on somebody's mind when they are thinking of doing something bad, and I remembered *Animal House*, where the girl passes out and the guy was about to rape her. He had a devil on one shoulder and the angel on the other saying, 'Don't do it.' So we did the same thing, only in a little more graphic detail."

To *City Detroit* he gave a less convincing, but more interesting explanation. "My reaction is suck my fucking ass, you little prick," he informed a particular critic. "These people are just ignorant to the music, and they don't understand. They do not understand that damn near every song that I do has a message to it. All I was trying to show was that it seems that nowadays everybody's got a good half and an evil half to 'em, and it seems like the way America is now, nowadays the bad half always rules. Evil always rules in your conscience, and that's how crime happens, that's how everything happens."

The remainder of *The Slim Shady LP* fell into two distinct halves. 'Brain Damage', 'If I Had', ''97 Bonnie & Clyde' and 'Rock Bottom', the spartan, mostly Bass-produced tracks from his already swiftly receding period of hopelessness and self-pity the previous year – which, curiously, had helped secure him his deal – were retained from the *EP* and the sessions just after it. They gave an undertow of loss and misery to the more confident, funny California tracks (like the bad trip routine, 'My Fault'). It was the Slim-defining cousins of 'My Name Is' and 'Just Don't Give A Fuck' that domi-nated the album, though, a sequence including 'Still Don't Give A Fuck' that sounded like a single unstoppable gush, a notepad of Tourette's psycho-sis, written with the good humour of someone quite sane. Slim might say he was born in an earthquake and would die by lightning, first cousin to the Stones' crossfire-hurricane-spawned Jumpin' Jack Flash. But the smirk and wink of a word addict saying the unsayable (that he shot up schoolyards, for instance) only because it made life more amusing, and because he knew they were just words anyway, were never far from such demonic jive. 'I'm Shady' was one track in which he explicitly separated jokes from truth. He expected such discernment from his listeners, too.

"On my album, I've got my happy songs, crazy songs, serious songs," he explained to *Launch*. "There are songs like, 'Okay, I've slit my wrist 90 million times, I cut my own fucking head off, but this is how I really feel,'" he expanded to *City Detroit*. "It's not rocket science here. It's so clear when I'm joking and when I'm serious. 'If I Had' and 'Rock Bottom', those are a couple of the serious songs. I made those songs so people could really see what I went through. A lot of the album represents my serious side. But even in the joking songs, there's a lot of truth. Like if I say I wanted to slit my father's throat – that's true feelings. 'Rock Bottom' or 'If I Had', those are my two most serious songs. All jokes aside."

The album had one further unusual strength. In a hip-hop genre where extra-musical efforts were usually limited to lame spliffed-up "skits" between tracks, *The Slim Shady LP* presented a cohesive, populated world. Slim Shady was its crazed king. But Debbie, Kim, Hailie, Dre and put-upon Marshall were locked inside too. Other characters were introduced, like Ken Kaniff from Connecticut, a sleazy-voiced, snickering gay man who obsessively love-hates Eminem, Paul Rosenberg ("Em, the album . . . can you tone it down a little bit?"), and the Public Service Announcer. All would be retained for future records. A dramatist's mind, as well as a satirist's, had been at work. Interscope's Jimmy Iovine was one who noticed. "He has an incredible ability to tell stories," he told the *LA Times*, "and if he keeps working that muscle, he could write movies, anything. He's got wit and imagination. He could write the Marx Brothers' *A Day At The Races*, if he ever wanted to."

The Slim Shady LP was everything its backers had hoped it would be. Now, they went slickly to work to ensure their investment's return. Marshall was a willing partner in their schemes. He wrote 'Still Don't Give A Fuck' on the advice of Paul Rosenberg, effectively composing a sequel to order. He toned down his lyrics when asked, too, on 'My Name Is' and others, as Rosenberg admitted to the *LA Times*. "Have there been times when we had to change stuff [because of Interscope]? Yes. Em understands that he wants the stores to stock his records or he won't be heard, so he'll do what it takes for the most part, unless the complaint is just ridiculous." A "clean" version of the album was even prepared, and released, allegedly as a sop to potential obscenity trials. Marshall claimed embarrassment, but let it happen.

As 1998 wound down, Interscope put their secret new star to work. He went out on rap's prestigious Lyricist Lounge tour, and a radio-unplayable track from the album, 'Just Don't Give A Fuck', was selectively released as a single. Marshall naïvely spilled the strategy at work to elamentz.com.

"The Lyricist Lounge tour? My production company hooked it, I guess . . . I don't really know. All I know is Interscope Records came to me and was like, 'You're doing the tour.' The single that's coming out, it's mostly for the Lyricist Lounge. They're like pressing up vinyl and shit to give out. You know, to get the buzz going. What they're trying to do is elevate the underground buzz. Then they're gonna drop the second single, probably right before the album. And then, um . . . the second single is gonna be called, 'My Name Is'. It's a song that Dr. Dre produced."

There was a genuine "buzz" on Marshall by this time, anyway, from those who had heard *The Slim Shady EP*, or his stray verses on indie singles like Shabaam Sahdeeq's '5 Star Generals' (recorded for cash and forgotten about in his unsigned days, and suddenly selling), or seen him battle (he had even been on a Lyricist Lounge tour before). But the shift from underground to mass market, with credibility intact, was now fine-tuned. A subtly controversial sleeve for the album was prepared. On its front,

Marshall and little Hailie stared thoughtfully from a pier's edge towards the water, under an ominous moon. "Kim"'s feet could be seen sticking out from a nearby car boot. On the back, a blue-lit, bare-chested Marshall shut his eyes and held his head, a picture of pretty-boy angst. For the record's release, hundreds of interviews were arranged, along with mind-frying, demographic-bridging tours, playing to rock then rap audiences the same day, leaving no listener immune. Marshall would not complain, till he collapsed. He had worked hard at cooking meatloaf. He would work hard at this.

The true secret to *The Slim Shady LP*'s mass acceptance, though, was much simpler: 'My Name Is', and its video.

Marshall had made one previous video, in 1998, for 'Just Don't Give A Fuck'. Mostly black-and-white, with uncensored lyrics, it was cheaply shot, for "underground buzz". It tried to make him a threatening B-boy, emphasising his muscular arms, and surrounding him with women shorter than he was. Marshall scowled for the cameras, punched an old woman, and moved like a slasher movie killer. But the images were generic and incoherent, and Marshall was listless and unconvincing, detracting from his song. He looked like just another Detroit thug.

'My Name Is''s video bore more personal touches. "The thing of it is that, with the videos, people produce them and that," Jennifer Yezvack reveals to me, "but I'm telling you – those are his ideas. He's out there! He's very imaginative. He's creative. He's an artist."

The clip is the opposite of 'Just Don't Give A Fuck', with a depth foreign to MTV, but a top kids' TV show's sense of controlled chaos, colour and glee that was addictive to its viewers. Starting in the living room of a sweaty, stereotypical white trash couple – him a fat pig in a vest cracking nuts, her a slutty tramp in a slip swigging whiskey – as they settle down for an afternoon's mutual loathing and sappily bad TV, their hopeless channel-hopping stops at *'The Slim Shady Show – Starring Marshall Mathers'*.

The first Marshall we see is a bespectacled nerd, waving outside a picture-book Fifties suburban house, a straight white American ideal version of his Warren trailer. A hurled newspaper almost swats him in the face. A little nonplussed at this hostility, he gamely keeps smiling. Marshall Mathers did wear glasses at school, and was once that geeky and peaceable. But *The Slim Shady Show* could hardly stop with him.

The channels hop again, along with the song's bouncing beats, but now

Marshall/Shady's on all of them, in a casual deconstruction of the clip's medium, and a garish introduction to Shady's head. He's a golf swing-practising showbiz pro, a ventriloquist's dummy, Marilyn Manson and President Clinton, in a variety of bad suits and wigs. The scene keeps switching too, even the film stock does, as the variety of scenarios Marshall packs into each verse becomes visually explicit: he's falling drunk out of his car on *America's Most Wanted*, being hurled out of a club by indignant strippers, and fervently moralising from the President's podium, till we see his pants are down, and a Lewinsky-alike pops up guiltily wiping her lips, and trots off at *Benny Hill* speed (far from the last time he'd pull the President's pants down in his work).

Like his album, though, what was most impressive and electric about the clip was the persona it kept defining, the many moods of Slim Shady it shoved at you. The jump in performance skill and personal revelation from the anonymous 'Just Don't Give A Fuck' was total. No longer just a moody bad boy, everything he did with his body looked original, the Lincoln class clown and sarcastic Gilbert's Lodge cook merging with the snickering D12 filth merchant and snarling Shady, and adding to the confident, quick-witted Marshall Mathers Californian success had turned him into. Whether in a straitjacket (again, not for the last time in his video career) being inspected by Dre, or in a dream-zone with "Mom" – her hip whorishly cocked outside a white trash shack – or just as his smartly tracksuited self, he used his eyes and mouth for maximum, exaggerated expression, and moved his arms and hands in far more interesting shapes than the B-boy semaphor he'd started with. His eyes were charismatic black holes on the screen, too, however funny he was being. For someone who would prove a stilted stage performer, he had mastered this second medium right at the start. He had also stayed true to his roots, and made a social point, in his allotted four minutes. The white trash couple are shown coming alive as they watch him, not just slobs, but roaring and bonding, over someone as unashamed as them.

There was one more striking alteration in this second video. Marshall Mathers had always been a brunette. This new creature's hair was dyed platinum blond.

The only drawback of the video as an introduction to Eminem was that it necessarily used the "clean version" of 'My Name Is' (with scared substitutions of many of his best lines – the one about slitting his Dad's throat changed to the nonsensical *"if you see my Dad/ ask him if he bought a porno mag, and saw my ad,"* for instance). But that made it all the more perfect for MTV, who slapped it on heavy rotation to an almost unheard of extent for such a new act. "They jumped on the video before the video was even done, when they got the rough draft," Marshall told *?*. "It's like, 'Finish it up. We wanna play it right away.' So two days, three days later, they were screening it. And MTV is what made radio jump on it." Interscope again cemented in all possible demographics, giving the station a clip in which Dre and Missy Elliott sang this new rapper's praises. Advertising time was also bought to screen 'My Name Is' during Howard Stern's prime-time TV show.

'My Name Is' and *The Slim Shady LP* both finally reached American stores on February 23, 1999. The appetite for what Eminem had to offer was far greater than anyone had expected, even after such careful cultivation. With first-week sales of 280,000, the album entered the *Billboard* pop chart at number two. It would become the R&B number one as well, the sort of double-header in which Elvis once specialised. In March, 'My Name Is' was a UK hit too, as was *The Slim Shady LP*, released there on April 10. By the end of that month, the album had sold two million in America.

Reviews were hardly relevant in such a frenzy. Critics anyway mostly saw him as amusing, if unmistakably talented, the rock press adding immediate if muted distaste at his woman-beating words. *Rolling Stone* compared him to comedians Rodney Dangerfield and Pee-Wee Herman, as well as helium-voiced rappers like the Beasties' Ad-Rock and Cypress Hill's B-Real; noting "the bitch-bashing gets tired fast", and, insightfully, the loneliness of his white voice on the record ("he has hardly any homies"), it judged him to "earn his buzz as a bona fide rap star". *NME*'s Steven Wells led a still less serious British response, calling him a "Wonda-Wigga" and "squeaky motherfucker", with a "comedy album" ideal "if you're retarded, stoned or 12." He then wondered why "all the women on this end up raped, battered or slaughtered white meat", fondly imagining the day "a tuff lezzer is going to twat you between those baby-blue eyes." 'As The World Turns' already imagined something similar, of course, drawn from Marshall's life. But it was a sign of conflicts to come.

Somewhere among this, Marshall Mathers, the anonymous, abused boy from Detroit who a year before had seen only emptiness in a life he toyed with ending, disappeared. For the world at large, at least, that identity was no longer important. It was like Clark Kent, a boring front for the man who really mattered. From now on, except for a few in Detroit who knew the real Marshall he remained in his heart, he would be Eminem.

In a spare moment, he considered his position. "I dealt with a lot of shit coming up, a lot of shit," he told *Rolling Stone*. "When it's like that, you learn to live day by day. When all this happened, I took a deep breath. Just like: 'I did it.'"

6

AFTERMATH

Eminem had jumped from rock bottom to the top in 12 months. But if he thought he had at last reached a place of stability, he was wrong. Sudden wealth and fame was not a plateau where he could catch his breath and reflect. It would prove more like rocketing through the Bends, being spat from his old submerged life into more rarefied air, where bubbles in the brain made your actions, and those around you, dangerous and strange.

Rise, a journalist for elamentz.com, watched the journey begin when Interscope introduced him to Eminem in August 1998. A cog in the record company's chanceless hype machine, Rise was told the rapper was "the next big thing", six months before his LP's release. But the white boy in a grimy baseball cap he met standing outside an Ol' Dirty Bastard show on LA's Sunset Boulevard "looked more like he should be delivering pizzas," Rise recalled in his eventual piece. "All I can think of is, 'This guy raps with Dre?' Not because he is white" – oh, no – "but I guess I just imagined more of an . . . image." Instead, this boy was still a styleless, hopeless outsider, despite his record deal. He despaired of getting into the show to the Detroit friends and disappointed, dagger-glaring girls with him. "Yo, man, I ain't got no pull around here to get into this shit," he explained, embarrassed even to be trying. "These fuckin' guys don't know who I am. I ain't nobody! Fuck it, let's just go . . ."

A week later, the man whose interviews would one day be doled out like diamonds casually took Rise to Tijuana in a cheesy white rented convertible. "Yo, are you about to do a real interview for real?" he excitedly asked. "Set it off then . . ."

After using the tape for quickfire comic impersonations (including *South Park*'s Cartman, a minor influence, he'd later admit), he settled into serious responses, about his race ("anything that has to do with colour, it's like, next question"), influences ("my daughter"), and wanting to be famous.

"Would I sound right saying no?" he answered wisely, knowing how ingratitude would play to those in the life he'd just escaped. "Famous is not really the term I'm looking for. I want to be respected. I want to be looked at past the colour. But fame if it comes with it, I'm gonna take it, 'cos you know, fame ain't gonna feed my daughter. Fame, money, yeah. That shit's gonna feed my daughter." Looking across to his oblivious subject as he drove, the interviewer started to believe the hype, observing: "You could tell it was his time to shine. Not because he was owed it, but because he wanted it so badly and had worked so hard for it."

September, and Rise caught Eminem on the Lyricist Lounge tour. Outside, street pluggers handing out *Slim Shady LP* samplers were sneered at by rap fans, for skin reasons ("Vanilla Twice"). Then Eminem's performance was delayed when bouncers wouldn't let him in. He was blocked from the VIP lounge even when he left the stage, protesting vainly, "I'm Eminem. I just performed . . ." He was barred twice more that night, unrecognised by anyone, still seemingly expecting no better. He and *LP* guest rapper Royce Da 5-9 joked on the street outside about one day being stars, with fans and limos.

In December, at his own gig, he still struggled for recognition. The idea that a skinny white guy could be a hip-hop star still made bouncers laugh, as he again pleaded, "I *am* Eminem. I am headlining the show." In the queue, though, even before 'My Name Is' reached MTV, girls were starting to scream: "Oh my god . . . he looks like such a babe. He looks like a fucking superstar!" Inside, fans sang and jumped to unreleased album tracks they already knew by heart.

By February, at his record release party, Eminem was entering unchallenged, past rows of fans wanting his autograph. A limo awaited him. He had moved from one side of the rope to the other, and now looked out of celebrity's looking glass. His own shut out self six months before could have stared him in the face.

In April, a *Rolling Stone* cover story offered more insights on the changes he was going through. It picked up where elamentz.com left off, just after 'My Name Is' hit, with Eminem and a posse of 17 piling into a vast white limo, to ferry them to three distinct shows he'd play in New York that night. They were all in clubs booked before he was famous, sweatboxes where he was close enough to touch. A black hip-hop audience gave him their familiar frosty indifference, before his four-song set broke them down. Manhattan models and fashionistas enjoyed him in the small hours.

But it was the night's first set, at an all-ages show, that showed the distance 'My Name Is' had dragged him from his hard-won Detroit rap roots. Shut-out teenage girls screamed his name as he entered. Inside, they lapped up his filthiest raps. When one young girl shouted, "I love you," he said it back and bent to hug her, only to be kissed on the lips, and the girl next to her to yank his head away and kiss him hard on the mouth. Other girls tore at his pants, one gleefully screaming, "I touched his dick!" He seemed to relish it on stage. But when a teenage girl pulled her shirt down and shouted, "I want to fuck you!" as his limo eased away afterwards, he showed his ambivalence to this strange temptation. "I want to fuck you, too," he murmured. "But I won't."

"That actually makes me feel kind of sick," he'd mention to *NME*. "Some girl will be telling me how fine I am and trying to sit on my lap and I'll be thinking, 'If I was just me and I didn't have all of this fame, you wouldn't look at me twice. You wouldn't look at me once.' People wonder why my lyrics are so misogynistic and violent towards women. But my opinion of girls is not very high right now."

More revealing still was when *Rolling Stone* followed Eminem back to the home town where he'd always been dismissed. "I like living in Detroit," he said loyally. "My little girl is here." But everywhere he went, there was now a chill. At Gilbert's Lodge, only owner Pete Karagiaouris seemed interested to see him, mildly asking, "Coming in to buy the place?" One waitress waltzed up to say she never saw him on MTV. For 20 minutes, as he sat in a booth at the place where he'd laboured loyally most of his working life, he wasn't served. Instead he seethed over the waitress's slight, stardom seemingly no shield to him here. To *NME*, he later described the hurt the diner's staff made him feel. "I go back there now and pull up in a limo just for the spite of it," he tried to brag, "hop out, go to the bar, drop a couple of hundred dollars for a tip and throw it in their faces. They took me for a joke, but the joke's on them." But he couldn't keep up the cocky front. "When I go back, it's not to flaunt," he admitted. "I go back to try to be cool with people and see how they're doing. I went in there the other night to see my old manager. But he couldn't look me in the eye." He broke off and thought about this. "It's funny. It's very funny."

"This is his reality," Paul Rosenberg sighed, watching his client with *Rolling Stone*. "He came from this. And after everything is over, this is the reality he has to go back to."

The group moved on to Eminem's latest Detroit residence, a mobile home in a St. Clair trailer park. It had been taken over from his mother, who had left for Kansas City as soon as he got his deal, and the means to make her payments. Inside were the few things he owned, after his life of poverty and being thieved from: a few CDs (2Pac, Snoop Dogg, Luther Vandross, Esthero, Mase and Babyface); photos of him and Dre, one signed ("Thanks for the support, asshole!"), and one of Hailie; *The Slim Shady EP*'s artwork; a seat for Hailie; a TV. And, on the wall, a list of "Commitments for Parents", including this: "I will give my child space to grow, dream, succeed and sometimes fail." It was a mantra he must have felt his mother never read.

The little time he'd have left in this modest home for young parents was clear anyway even as he walked through the trailer park with *Rolling Stone*. In the month *The Slim Shady LP*'s two-millionth sale was recorded, he found an eviction notice stuck to his door. He'd forgotten his payments, while on his sell-out tour. "Don't worry, we took care of that one," Rosenberg advised. The realities of arrears and evictions, so central to his Detroit life, were no longer his concern. As the notice was casually crumpled, the message so many American stars had discovered before him seemed clear: you can't go home again.

"From the day after we shot that 'My Name Is' video, I remember shit just moving so fast," he'd look back to *The Source* a year later. "Like, I went from being home all the time to never seeing my girl, to being out on the road, to bitches throwing themselves at me. Shit was like a movie," he considered in wonder, "the shit you see in movies." The fictional world he'd created for *The Slim Shady LP* had almost instantly dropped out of his control, consuming chunks of his real life he wanted to keep. "I wish I could come off-stage and turn off the lights that flash over my head saying 'Slim Shady' and 'Eminem'," he'd admit to *Muzik* in 2000, only two years after Slim had saved him. "I wanna turn that shit off and just be Marshall Mathers again."

"It's something bigger than he ever expected, the pressures he has to go through," Jeff Bass explained to *City Detroit*. "Just because he's doing so well, he's from Detroit, and the media keeps pointing out he's a white rapper, it's very intense. You're talking about going from making pizzas to being almost a household name. You can't prepare yourself for any-thing like this. He has to put a hat on and a hood, 'cos as soon as someone sees his blond hair they know who that is. But," he backtracked, "he's got his age and his experience on his side because he's been doing music so long. He has no problems with it; he rolls with the punches."

That wasn't how it seemed. Eminem was experiencing a new kind of alienation, opposite and yet the same as when he'd locked himself in his teenage bedroom. "I don't trust nobody now because anybody I meet is meeting me as Eminem," he told the *LA Times*. "They don't know me as Marshall Mathers, and I don't know if they are hanging with me 'cos they like me or because I'm a celebrity or because they think they can get something from me." The sudden pressure swiftly forced him from the trailer park. "Once I hit MTV everybody was coming up to me and talking about it," he explained to *Hip-Hop Connection*. "People that knew me for the longest were starstruck, the kids in the neighbourhood were knocking on the door all day. It got to the point where I was like, 'I've been here all my fucking life, what is different about me now?' Before I could walk down the street and nobody said shit. Now it's ridiculous." Even his anger had to be checked, his assertive street instincts reined in. "One of the main things that's really fucked up is when people piss you off, you can't hit them in the face," he complained to icast.com. "When somebody disrespects you on a street level, you want to do something to retaliate. But you got to learn to control your temper and you got to take the 'Fuck yous' and 'You sucks!' " Sighed Proof, sitting next to him: "The way it used to be, we was the bully busters." A 6' 8" bodyguard, Byron Williams, was brought in to discourage those who might show a lack of respect.

As fame denatured him, even the bad old Detroit days began to look good. "My life wasn't always depressed and dark," he decided to tell the *LA Times*. "I still tend to miss certain things, like running in the streets and hanging out. The good things were just being young and buying the hottest new albums. We didn't have money. But it was always liveable."

The most disorientating change of all was the dollars in his pocket, in part from songs like 'Rock Bottom', written when he was destitute. He was too knowledgeable of hip-hop's history, and the ghetto superstars who'd ended up penniless, not to be wary of his wealth. As his "money is the root of all evil" sermons on *Infinite* had shown, he was never materialistic anyway. "He never had money, so he doesn't know what the hell to do with it, and he's scared to spend it," Paul Rosenberg told the *LA Times*. "His idea of splurging is spending $500 or $600 at Nike Town."

Eminem meanwhile recognised that, now he was rich, he would have to stay that way. To be desperately poor now he'd tasted the security of wealth, to be dragged back through the looking glass and dumped on the sidewalk, would destroy him. "I don't think I'd be able to go back to a regular lifestyle," he admitted to *Melody Maker*. "I think I'd do something really fucking crazy if I did. It worries me. To be honest, I think about it a lot, and I'm being really, really careful with my money. I think about the future more than anything." So, counter to the rash Slim Shady myth the public was swallowing by the million, he spent with the prudence of a suburban civil servant; or, more relevantly, a responsible family man. He bought and refitted a big new house for his wife and daughter, "way out in the suburbs, away from everything", trailer parks just a bad dream. "I'm putting some money aside so my daughter gets an education, and grows up in a decent area," he added. He had bought stocks and bonds, too, and just two cars. And Interscope had donated his own label, Shady Records (his first signing, he indicated, would be an MC Proof).

But the single real thrill he seemed to get from his instant millions was much more personal. "When my daughter was born," he told *NME*, "I was so scared I wouldn't be able to raise her and support her as a father should. Her first two Christmases, we had nothing, but this last Christmas, when she turned three she had so many fucking presents under the tree. She kept opening them saying, 'This one's for me, too?' My daughter wasn't born with a silver spoon in her mouth. But she's got one now. I can't stop myself from spoiling her."

The intense Interscope schedule that helped pay for Hailie's presents, though, also made such moments depressingly rare. The company put Eminem on a tour so intensive, he couldn't even talk to his daughter when she called. The non-stop dates started in January and peaked in June, when he'd play an afternoon slot on rock's high-profile Warped tour (alongside the likes of Blink 182), drive hours to perform nights in hip-hop clubs, then drive on to catch up with the Warped roadshow. He still professed to love the shows, for reasons rooted in class. "I like to go out and earn crowds," he told icast.com, "because it makes me feel like I'm working for my money. I want to be in touch with the crowds and talk to people, keep eye contact, and try to see what they're feeling. These are the people that's buying my records, they're paying my way."

NME saw 15,000 greet him ecstatically on Warped's second date, in Dallas, where his first hero Ice-T watched approvingly from the wings. When he was photographed in front of a chain-link fence that afternoon, the young white fans' faces pressed behind him looked proud and happy, a fresh army awaiting his lead. On a flying visit to London in April, a one-off gig at the tiny Subterranea, reported at 20 minutes, left many booing and feeling cheated, but a five-page PR itinerary meant every second on British soil helped sales anyway. Journalists who met him then found him generally affable, and eager for stimulation. He was amused and un-bothered by the stiff formality of his Kensington hotel, for instance, on his first trip outside America. He seemed obsessed with sex on this endless time away from Kim, and bragged he was getting plenty; but still muttered about them both being loyal, claiming: "I believe in sticking with the girl who's been with me from day one, before all this fame."

To keep up with the tour treadmill's grinding pace needed more than sex, though, and it was the drink and drugs interviewers observed him guzzling that should have triggered alarm in his aides. Bacardi was downed with abandon, and his limo slowed to take wraps of Es through its window, *Rolling Stone* seeing three downed in a night. On May 9, at San Francisco's Fillmore, the wheels inevitably started to whirr from his control. He was reported to have dived off the stage towards a heckler, fists flying, with his bodyguard and security in pursuit, before the heckler was ejected, and order restored. To *FHM*, Eminem gave a rougher account, claiming he'd stopped his show when he saw kids at the front fighting, jumping on them when they ignored him. "I got pulled down in the middle of it and these kids were stomping on me, and then my boys came running, beating the shit out of everybody. I thought I was gonna get arrested that night." The same day, he reportedly punched out a man who challenged him in Haight-Ashbury, and incensed local DJ Sista Tamu so much with a freestyle about slapping a pregnant "bitch" that she snapped his CD on air.

Two months later in New England, near the end of the Warped tour, the crash he'd been hurtling towards all year arrived on cue. It was the second section of his life he termed a "crack-up", excessive success now shattering him as failure had. Sprinting onto the stage, he skidded in a pool of liquid, and fell 10 feet to the venue floor. He cracked ribs. It could have been his head. "It was insane," he admitted to the *LA Times*. "I knew I had to slow it down. The fall was like a reminder." In 2000, he confessed to *Star*: "Last year, I was a little bit gone. There are quite a few things people ask me about that I don't remember. Marshall Mathers stops when the booze kicks in. Then I become Slim Shady."

Critical fire also crackled around his ears during 1999, with a heat that would only get worse. Washington rock censorship pressure group PMRC (Parent's Music Resource Center) was among his attackers. But it was a full-page crisis column by *Billboard*'s then-editor Timothy White that caused the biggest stir. He accused Eminem of "making money by exploiting the world's misery", and tied 'Guilty Conscience''s imagined date-rape to real equivalents. Eminem's defence was built in to *The Slim Shady LP*, on 'Role Model' and 'Still Don't Give A Fuck', and he had already explained 'Guilty Conscience' even more. But to interviewers who repeated the accusation, he justified himself in fresh ways.

"The older people are getting it confused," he told *Launch*, "tending to take my shit too literal. I don't care, it's funny to me, because if I say my brain fell out of my skull, and they believe it, what's wrong with them? The younger people have a sense of humour, and can determine right from wrong. I only get flack from the white-collar motherfuckers, who don't know about hip-hop anyway." To *Consumable Online*, he added: "Maybe I am the first person to say this shit to this extreme, but all I do is say what's on my motherfucking mind, man. Hip-hop is hip-hop, and it's always been like this." His most impassioned response came to *Select*, right after that Subterranea show, as he considered the influence of earlier demonised rappers like N.W.A. on himself. "I listened to it all, but I never went out and shot nobody. I just did dumb shit like getting into fights, because the music made me feel something. If your music makes you feel something, you doin' your job."

The real life melodrama he had leeched and magnified for his bestselling music meanwhile carried on its course. On June 14, back in his birthplace of St. Joseph, Missouri, he and Kim finally married. It was kept a secret till the *Detroit News* discovered documents later that year. "A big part of it is females buy 80 per cent of Marshall's records," Kim explained, in a rare interview. "Lots of girls are fans, and he's good looking. They think they stand a chance."

Mathers-Briggs, now living in Missouri, attended the ceremony, of course. But this blissful interlude for Eminem's fractured family could not last. When the truce with his mother broke, he would claim she had been exploiting his name ever since his fame started, beginning with that St. Clair trailer home.

"When I got my record deal I took it over – just to give me somewhere to stay," he told *FHM*. "Next thing, my mother's selling the trailer on the Internet, advertising it as 'Slim Shady's Trailer'. And in the paper, she's saying if you buy this trailer Slim Shady will personally come round and autograph the walls. My mother's crazy. While I was on tour she was taking posters that I'd left, signing fake autographs on them and selling them to the kids in the neighbourhood. My mother came backstage at a show in Kansas City and she was saying to the kids, 'If you want a picture with my son it's $20.' And I didn't know anything about it until this little girl came up and said, 'Can I have my picture taken 'cos I've paid my $20?' My mother's a snake."

To *Consumable Online*, he detailed the numb remains of their relationship: "I talk to her every now and again, but as little as I can. She's got my little brother, so when I do talk to her, it's really to talk to him. I really don't have much reason to talk to my mother. My mother's done so much fucked up shit to me that it's like, now that I don't have to talk to her, I ain't gonna."

On September 17, his mother struck back, with the lawsuit that would finish their harsh life together. The mobile home was again at issue, the sort of financial wrangle domestic breakdowns so often fixate on. The late payments had not been fixed as she would have liked, as she alleged Eminem's failed promise to "at a minimum, help his mother" with its mortgage and rent had led to her and Nathan's eviction, and its repossession (which seemed to ignore her living in Kansas City when he was responsible for it). She claimed damages for "loss of her mobile home; harm to credit rating and associated detrimental consequences; humiliation, embarrassment and many sleepless nights; loss of and/or diminished self-esteem; and other damages and injuries to be determined through discovery and trial." More notoriously, she sued for the content of his interviews with *Rolling Stone*, *Rap Pages*, *The Source* and the Howard Stern TV show, as well as the claim in 'My Name Is' that *"I just found out my Mom does more drugs than I do."* Stating she had been characterised as a drug abuser, unstable and, amusingly, lawsuit-happy, her suit added she had sustained "physical and psychological injury and damages", including "damage to Plaintiff's reputation in the community at large and among her family, friends and peers; emotional distress and loss of or diminished self-esteem; humiliation, mortification and embarrassment; and sleeplessness and anxiety"; and that this distress had been intended by Eminem, whose conduct was "extreme, outrageous and of such character as not to be tolerated by a civilised society" (she would not be the last to make that claim), and "for an ulterior motive and purpose".

And the requested bill for this behaviour? $10 million.

To the *Tonight* TV show's Trevor McDonald, Mathers-Briggs would later claim to be "in shock" when her son told her the papers had been served on him. "I sat there and thought, 'This is not happening.' My lawyer was supposed to send a letter warning him to stop being so demeaning and say if he didn't stop the lawyer would hit him with a lawsuit. I walked up to my lawyer and he said, 'This is a wake-up call.'"

Whatever the truth of that, Eminem's initial response came in Rosenberg's careful, legal language: "Eminem's life is reflected in his music. Everything he said can be verified as true. The truth is an absolute defence in a case of defamation. The lawsuit does not come as a surprise to Eminem. His mother has been threatening to sue him since the success of his single 'My Name Is'. It is merely the result of a life-long strained relationship between him and his mother. Regardless, it is still painful to be sued by your mother and therefore the lawsuit will only be responded to through legal channels."

Of course, Eminem couldn't leave it at that. To the *LA Times*, he hedged: "I have to be careful about what I say about my mother, because I'm sure her lawyers are looking. How does it feel? It feels like shit. How would you feel? One thing I can tell you is that every single word I said about my mother and my upbringing was true." To *Muzik*, he added: "She doesn't have a leg to stand on. I would love it to go to court, I want it televised. I want people to see what type of person she is and what my life has been like." To *NME*: "She's always been out to get me, and now she knows I have money, she won't leave me alone. I know that's not a nice thing to say about your mother, but unfortunately it's true." To *Q*, he freestyled a rap hoping to settle things in court. Otherwise? "I'll slit the bitch's throat."

Also to *Q*, he described the finality of his severance from his mother, after the last straw of her suing him. "I speak the truth. I've got no reason to fabricate my past, no reason to lie. There will be no reconciliation. I've tried, I'll say that. I can't comment further." All he admitted regretting losing was access to Nathan. "I raised him since he was a baby, changing his diapers and feeding him. It's gonna be hard."

But he had already suffered a worse loss that year. On May 21, D12 member Bugz (aka Karnail Pitts), 21, had been expected to perform as part of Eminem's tour, in Grand Rapids, Michigan. He never arrived. That afternoon, while he was with a friend and the friend's cousin at Detroit's

Belle Isle Park, a man shot the cousin with a high-powered water pistol, to her rage. A fierce argument ended with Bugz jumping in to help his friend in a fistfight with the man. A friend of the man then pulled a rifle from their car, and shot Bugz three times at close range, including bullets in the chest and neck. The pair then ran him over, to make sure. Snarled in Detroit traffic, an ambulance arrived too late to save him. When his fellow rappers found out the next morning, Federation Records' Rico Shelton told *Rolling Stone*, "Hearts were dropping. I've never seen so many sad faces. Everybody knew him; he was part of Detroit." Said Proof: "It just makes you look at life more serious." Remembering his friend to *Muzik*, with the variants in detail customary in this story, Eminem spoke softly. "He got shot in the face twice, then run over by a car. It was over some stupid shit. He wetted this girl with a water gun and these dudes came over and got their revenge." It was the sort of pointless end he could have come to himself, and as a youth, at the Bel-Air mall and other places where pistols were pointed at him, almost had. In so many ways, success had come just in time. D12, too, weren't going to let their chance slip. Bugz was soon replaced by Swift (aka Ondre Moore, 23), and they proceeded with recordings of their own.

Interscope meanwhile continued to push *The Slim Shady LP*, as 1999 ran down. In August, 'Guilty Conscience' was released as a single, making number five in the UK, and 25 in the States (his biggest home hit yet). The very popular video, dramatising the song's three controversial scenarios, used stop-motion special effects to help create a new side to Shady's visual persona. While Dre lumbered around the song's tempted characters with the sluggishness of his raps, Eminem blinked and buzzed with manic energy, a super-speed blond irritant barely in control of a body being jerked by unseen hands. Dre shook him like a rag doll when he mentioned Dee Barnes, but just made him flap faster, till the Doctor threw in the towel. A fourth video, for 'Role Model', would chuck bustling, 'My Name Is'-style business at a track finally too draggily downbeat to come out as a single. Only daring digs at the Catholic church (Father Eminem not only hearing a sultry teenage girl's confession, but beckoning a young boy to his bed), and another fresh batch of acting styles from the rapper (from subtly intense sociopath to wide-eyed stooge) were worth watching.

September saw him win the first of what would become incessant music industry awards, at the Video Music bash by his friends at MTV, where 'My Name Is' (Best Male Video and Best Direction) and 'Guilty

Conscience' (Breakthrough Video, whatever that meant) came first. It was appropriate his painstaking videos should be gaining as much attention as his music (which would win two Grammys in February 2000, for Rap Solo Performance ['My Name Is'] and Rap Album). But fresh tracks, and the product-placement of old ones, also kept his momentum up as 1999 turned into 2000. Dre and Eminem duetted again on the *Wild Wild West* soundtrack's 'Bad Guys Always Die', while the Schwarzenegger dud *End Of Days* and MTV's *Celebrity Death Match* were seeded with *Slim Shady LP* cuts; Eminem meanwhile guest-rapped on indie 12-inches (some recorded before his success), and major releases from Missy Elliott's *Da Real World* to the late Notorious B.I.G.'s *Born Again*. Quality stayed conspicuously high, as if he couldn't let a single listener start to doubt he was here to stay.

His most high-profile new work, though, again emphasised his bond with Dre to the public. *2001*, released in November 1999, was the Doctor's first LP since the string of flops that had preceded him meeting Shady. Now, his reputation was restored. It reached number four in the UK and two in the US. If anyone doubted Eminem's part in this renaissance, they only had to listen to the album. It had more of the room-filling pop boom of *Slim Shady* than *The Chronic*'s squealing funk, and Dre's raps, poised between realism at his millionaire, near middle-aged family life and gun-wielding threats to pretenders to his throne, were unusually sharp. But there was also a languor to the record, and dull thuggishness to its many guest raps – until Shady walked in the door and, for a precious few minutes, electroshocked it to life.

'What's The Difference' was his first intervention. "Stop the beat!" he woozily lurches. "Dre, I wanna tell you this shit right now, while this fuckin' weed is in me – I love you, dog!" Everyone heard before, including Snoop Dogg, suddenly sounded anonymous, drowned out by this helium-voiced fool. And Eminem didn't just praise the boss. He made the track another part of his expanding world, a footnote to 'Bonnie & Clyde' – observing, when he and Dre sentimentally swap offers to off each other's enemies that, if he really wanted to kill Kim, afterwards he'd stick her body not in the boot, but the front seat, then add shades and wave her dead arm as he drove her rotting corpse from Detroit to California, where he'd dump her in front of a police station, and pull away with a screech. Like a novelist's famous characters appearing in other books' backgrounds, it was a satisfying, controlled cameo.

'Forgot About Dre' was still more impressive, with Eminem again injecting the addictive element. His rap was an unbroken but perfectly articulated stream of words with a racing, staccato beat, effortlessly increasing in speed as his anger increased, till he sounded like a tape flapping free of its machine. The virtuoso technique was a shocking advance on his own LP. And again, he added to his ongoing tale as much as Dre's, telling Hailie she would now have to live with the Doc, as Dad was *"crazy"*.

'Forgot About Dre' was *2001*'s second single, reaching number seven in the UK in May 2000 (25 in the US). That month, Dre travelled with Eminem to Britain, to duet on all their collaborations at the Brixton Academy, to a sold out, racially mixed crowd. The dream ticket of the two together was plain again.

But the excitement that month was more immediate. Eminem's buffeting by fame during the past year had not slowed his artistry at all. In December, he had started work on *Slim Shady*'s sequel. And, as he and the world still reeled from their first contact, this fresh blast was about to be unleashed.

7

PUBLIC ENEMY

The Marshall Mathers LP was recorded in 20-hour, sometimes drug-fuelled sessions, in a two-month creative binge, nearly matching its predecessor's 14-day birth. Holed away with Dre and the Bass Brothers in LA, the law-suits, family feuds and condemnations of the previous year could not touch Eminem. Reporters who watched him in the studio caught a rare glimpse of the personal control which had helped pull him from his old, incoherent life: the mature real man, Marshall Mathers, who allowed his unhinged artistic alter ego Slim to flourish. Asked about his work in these months, he was unusually forthcoming, describing alternating rhythms of icy perfectionism and druggy mental derangement. It was a good explana-tion for the seemingly free-styled and amorphous, yet somehow precise and pointed behemoth *The Marshall Mathers LP* would become.

"I'm focused when I'm recording," Eminem told the website music365. "I slip into the zone. I don't like to talk a lot. I like to stick to myself and get my thoughts together, think how I'm gonna map out each song. Each song is fairly easy to write. I record vocals on one day and take the tape home to listen to them overnight. Then I do more vocals the next day. I always do my vocals twice. I might have the skeleton down, the vocals and the beat, for two months before I think of the finishing touches to put on it, like sound effects, or if I want the beat to drop out right here. I take my time on my shit that way."

As the May release date neared *The Source* found him listening to a play-back of 'Shit On You' (a D12 collaboration eventually held back for their 2001 début, *Devil's Night*), Dre nodding silently as his alleged protégé snapped off a list of delicate changes to a raptly listening engineer. "We're going to sit back and listen to everything, listen to what I feel is missing on the album, if there's anything missing," he explained. "I want every song to be perfect."

But at other moments, he revealed a more intuitive, if equally self-conscious method of creation. "I also got a studio in Detroit," he told music365, "that I can go to if it's the middle of the night and I want to lay some shit down. I can't help when the ideas come. Most of this shit comes either when I'm laying in bed waiting to sleep, or if people are talking. If they say something, a lot of the time I'll hear the way they've put words together, and they'll be talking to me and I won't even be listening to them because the last thing they said gave me an idea. I sit there with a blank stare and people think I'm on drugs constantly. I do that to my girl a lot. She'll be talking to me and I'll be like, 'Uh-huh, uh-huh.' I'll be looking off and she'll say, 'You're not even listening!' 'Yeah, I am!' 'Repeat what I said!' 'I don't know what the fuck you said!' "

It was a distanced demeanour his Detroit schoolmates would have recognised, the almost autistic withdrawal of a mind constantly ticking at a depth mundane distractions could not touch. And now, he had unlimited access to instant shortcuts to that state, as he explained to *Muzik*: "For those who are curious about my methods in the studio, it goes a little like this. If I'm writing rhymes I smoke weed or take Tylenol, or muscle relaxants, something to get the stories rolling. Or I take Ecstasy."

"A couple of the songs on the new record were written on X," he confirmed to music365 – at almost the same time as Dre too, and, more ambiguously, Missy Elliott bragged of the influence of European rave's "love" drug. It had reached the US rap community a decade late and, judging by their music, seemingly stripped of its pacifying, loved-up powers, if not its hotwire route to raw feelings. "Somebody will just be looking at me wrong," Eminem continued, "and I'll just flip a table over, like, 'What the fuck are you staring at?' If you're in a good mood you love everybody, but if you're in a bad mood and you got shit on your mind, you're gonna break down. The hardest shit I've fucked with is X and 'shrooms."

The wearing intensity of the hours, the sheer unwavering commitment to this phase of his artistic life, as if he knew that now were the months that mattered, the time that would prove his talent and establish his career, or leave him sliding back into the gutter, recall the legendary creative peaks of other musicians: Bob Dylan's acid-heated mid-Sixties records and tours, or the intuitive, night-long small-hours sessions of Elvis Presley in 1969/70, recording whole albums on an evening's whim; or, more pertinently, Eminem's idol Tupac Shakur, who can be seen in studio home movies eagerly speeding from one track to the next, not even bothering to name them, expressing himself with such gushing force that even his murder could not stop the release of seemingly endless new albums, an undead flipped finger to his enemies.

Eminem, Dre, the Bass Brothers and their collaborators – principally bassist and keyboardist Mike Elizondo, keyboardist Tommy Coster Jnr., drum programmer DJ Head, and Dre co-producer Mel-Man – similarly seemed to thrive in the studio air. Eminem confessed to being a "studio rat", happier when in the isolation bubble of writing and recording than anywhere else. Most of the key tracks on *The Marshall Mathers LP* cohered only thanks to the constant availability of musicians and technicians over such long, free-flowing sessions. "Every time we're fucking around in the studio we seem to come up with the dopest shit," Eminem commented in *Angry Blonde*. 'Marshall Mathers' came from Jeff Bass's casual strumming of an acoustic guitar, 'Criminal' began with Eminem hearing Bass picking out an off-kilter piano line in the studio next door. Between them, the songs helped forge the album's thematic core.

Such unrelenting work was also beating Eminem's own rapping and studio techniques into shape. As he explained in *Angry Blonde*: "The more I learned about music, the more comfortable I felt behind the microphone and the more I could slip into character. It got to a point where I wasn't just worried about getting the rhyme out and sayin' it, I was worried about my pronunciation, about saying shit with authority, or even sometimes saying it softly. I learned to play with my voice. I made it do more things that I didn't really know it could do. After *The Slim Shady LP* and Dr. Dre's *Chronic* album [*2001*], I had simply had more experience behind the mic."

But such technical advances only mattered because what Eminem wrote about had also expanded. Where *The Slim Shady LP* had been often playful in intent, its sequel eagerly fed on the anger he felt at his notoriety – the way fans who once didn't know he existed now hounded him in his own home, while critics dissected and recoiled at his words.

A defining feature of Nineties fame was the manner in which it warped almost everyone it touched. The bleached, weird features of Michael Jackson were the most awful warning of how far success could remove you from common humanity, but everything about modern celebrity crept in that direction. Stardom had become a universal dream, but the few who attained it found themselves unable to leave their dream homes without phalanxes of bodyguards obscuring the view, unable to eat, drink or sleep safely with anyone not breathing the same rarefied air. Even in Britain's more cynical, less hothouse atmosphere, previously well-balanced, mature people like Pulp's Jarvis Cocker felt themselves scorched by the skin-stripping intrusion that fame had become.

Many Nineties rappers obscured the problem either by rapping primarily about how great they and the trappings of their wealth were – a continuation of Run-DMC's gold chain-wearing Eighties materialism – or by bringing as many of their street posses with them as they could, pretending, effectively, that nothing had changed. "Keeping it real" was a phrase religiously toasted by nearly all the decade's hip-hop stars, with goblets of the finest champagne, in videos showing them in hot-tubs full of compliant, bikini-bulging models. The real gangstas and bloodshed in the highest echelons of black showbiz, often associated with Dre's one-time partner "Suge" Knight, completed the unappetising picture of rap's dishonest response to fame. It was a vision Eminem wearily dismissed, on the new album's 'Marshall Mathers': *"And amidst all this Crist-poppin' and wrist-watches/ I just sit back and watch and just get nauseous/ And walk around with an empty bottle of Remy Martin . . ."*

Instead of colluding with his fame Eminem, alone among his contemporaries, used his new album to go to war with every aspect of stardom. He used intrusions on his private life to feed aggressive assertions of undimmed individuality – even as, on tracks like the soon to be infamous 'Kim', he destroyed whole new tranches of his privacy, scorched-earthing what might have been fuel for his enemies into energy for himself.

The smallest attack on him over the previous, wrenching year triggered hysterical lyrical overreactions, nuclear verbal force. At least one critic, *NME*'s Sylvia Patterson, thought he had lost himself in the useless self-obsession also typical of today's famous. But Eminem's mind was far too lively to stop there. Although he regularly claimed once *The Marshall Mathers LP* was out that it was all about answering "the critics", and showing people "the real me", he was also drawn into far more important controversies in his year of fame. He had watched his label-mate and fellow young white American rebel Marilyn Manson have his name opportunistically associated by the authorities with April 1999's Columbine High School shootings (in which two students in Colorado killed 15). Typically, he saw through this hypocrisy, with a force which at once made him a political threat to an American Establishment that consistently scapegoated pop for the nation's deeper ills.

Eminem's first Columbine reference on the new album was secreted in the speedily written (even by his standards) 'I'm Back': *"I take seven kids from Columbine, stand 'em all in line/ Add an AK-47, a revolver, a nine/ A Mack-11 and it oughta solve the problem of mine/ And that's a whole school of bullies shot up all at one time."* As the LP's release date loomed, it was these lines that Interscope put most pressure on Eminem to change, fearful of attacks from the parents of Columbine's victims. Simultaneously, they were squeezing him for a "lead-off single" to boost their 2000 profits. Typically, these two impositions only focused his resentment, at both his paymasters and mainstream America's deluded sensibilities. 'The Way I Am', written in Kim's parents' home after a month of fruitless, itinerant hotel room scribbling, addressed both frustrations in a hoarse, furious voice, over a nagging, claustrophobic keyboard loop. Snarling at how fame had changed his life (*"But I can't take a shit in the bathroom/ Without someone standin' by it"*) and commercial demands (*"Let's stop with the fables/ I'm not gonna be able to top a 'My Name Is'"*), he depth-charged this enforced bit of hit-writing with a still clearer, less apologetic Columbine reference: *"When a dude's gettin' bullied and shoots up his school/ And they blame it on Marilyn . . . and the heroin/ Where were the parents at/ Middle America, NOW it's a tragedy/ NOW it's so sad to see, an upper-class city/ Havin' this happenin'."*

"My whole thing was, what is the big fuckin' deal," he expanded, in *Angry Blonde.* "Why is that topic so touchy as opposed to, say, a four-year-old kid drowning? Why isn't that considered a huge tragedy? People die in the city all the time. People get shot, people get stabbed, raped, mugged, killed, and all kinds of shit. What is the big deal with Columbine that makes it separate from any other tragedy in America?"

In an interview with *The Face* later that year, his status as an enemy of the state was reinforced. "Parents should have more responsibility," he declared, asked about Columbine again. "Those parents just didn't pay attention to their fucking kids. That kid's getting bullied every day . . . I guarantee you, he's coming home, punching some walls. And the parents aren't talking to that kid. Okay – innocent kids died. But those other kids got pushed to the fucking limit. And nobody saw it from their side. Growing up in school, I was bullied a lot. And I know what it's like to feel you want to kill somebody."

To music365, he reflected more widely: "My shit was real political, but people didn't see it like that, they thought I was just being an asshole. I look at the way I came up and the things I was around and the places I was raised, and I figure, that shit made me what I am. So if people perceive me to be an asshole, the way I live made me an asshole, what I been through has made me an asshole." Lest there be any doubt, in discussing 'Criminal' with *Muzik*, he called himself a "political rapper": "I'm taking stabs at crooked motherfuckers in the system. When someone says kids look up to me, I'm like, 'Our President smokes weed and is getting his dick sucked and is fucking lying about it. So don't tell me shit, I'm not the fucking President, I'm a rapper and I don't want to be a role model.' I'll tell a kid, 'Look up to me as someone who's come from nothing and now has everything. Don't look up to me for being violent and doing drugs. Don't be like me.'"

'The Real Slim Shady', the eventual "lead-off single", turned this politicised counter-blast at his detractors into a hall of mirrors from which no one escaped. Its genesis showed Eminem's unapologetic skill, when he chose, at the old-fashioned, hit-making side of pop. It started with a hook he had stored up for a while. That came to life after hours of exhausting experimentation one Friday ended with Coster Jnr. finally finding the keyboard notes the track would begin with. Dre then added beats. The next morning, they met Interscope executives, who expected to hear the album-finishing hit they'd requested. 'The Way I Am', they judged, was "not the first song". Eminem, at this stage of proceedings the industrious professional musician, not the "fuck you" rebel, promised he'd offer a completed 'Slim Shady' that Monday. Recent comments by Will Smith dissing the obscenity of stars like Eminem, and Christina Aguilera's public mention of his marriage on MTV was typically petty fuel, as he blazed through the lyrics in a weekend. "I came in on Monday, recorded it, and was done. Interscope, obviously, was satisfied," he noted proudly, in *Angry Blonde*. But 'The Real Slim Shady''s power as a pop hit, on permanent MTV rotation from its moment of release, went far deeper than a good hook and inter-celeb bitching.

The video, which added so much to the single's impact, returned to the uplifting, disarmingly funny style of 'My Name Is', again emphasising Eminem's comedic skill and charm. Beginning in a *One Flew Over The Cuckoo's Nest*-resembling, nurse-ruled mental ward, where he was joined by D12, he leaned into the screen to put over his points, moving his hands like a hip-hop conductor. In an interlude at a Grammy ceremony peopled by stars including the real Fred Durst, and Eminem in the roles of a ditzy

Britney Spears, a smarmy reporter, and himself, looking quizzical, the good humour was infectious. With lyrical digs at not only Britney, Will Smith, the Grammys, and Aguilera (no doubt regretting her MTV indiscretion after she was charged in the song with giving Durst head, and Eminem the clap), but gay marriage, bestiality on children's TV, feminists who fancied him, Tommy Lee beating Pamela Anderson, and Eminem's murder of Dre (the Doc's scared face is hilariously "Missing" on the back of a milk carton Em places in his fridge), the impossibility of offence at this concoction was remarkable.

One reason was that, whichever flank you tried to attack it on, Eminem was already there to meet you. Sexual explicitness? *"Yeah, I probably got a couple of screws up in my head loose/ But no worse than what's goin' on in your parents' bedrooms."* Intolerance of every sort? *"I'm like a head trip to listen to, 'cos I'm only givin' you/ Things you joke about with your friends inside your living room/ The only difference is I got the balls to say it in front of y'all."*

When you brought the whole album home, this self-consciousness spread everywhere: on 'Who Knew', in which Eminem proclaimed himself blameless if millions wanted to buy and agree with his thoughts, even if some of them self-mutilated, or shot up their school; 'Steve Berman', in which his own label boss disowned him (*"Tower Records just told me to shove this record up my ass. Do you know what that feels like?"*); 'The Way I Am''s ju-jitsu flooring of his critics (*"I am whatever you say I am. If I wasn't, then why would I say I am?"*); and the fan love-hate of 'Stan'.

But 'The Real Slim Shady' disarmed potential enemies, and became Eminem's true anthem for more positive reasons. When its scattershot points were collected, it was about individuality, in a way at once personal and universal. There was no "real" Slim Shady, of course; he was just another, obnoxious layer of disguise Marshall Mathers had placed between himself and the world. But the frustration Slim/Eminem/Marshall felt at the hypocrisies and persecutions shackling him as he just tried to be true to himself were as real as could be, and spoke to people who would never have to worry about seating at the Grammys.

In its video form especially, what 'Slim Shady' most resembled was the MTV breakthrough of that first bleached-blond, white youth icon of the Nineties: 'Feels Like Teen Spirit' by Kurt Cobain's Nirvana. But where that video disrupted MTV's bland consumer parade by presenting mainstream teenagers as faceless, robotic cheerleaders, 'Slim' was more assertively subversive. It showed a secret production line cranking out and clothing blank-faced Eminems by the dozen; in another sequence, Eminem raps from a room filled with nodding lookalikes, clones he's only slightly more authentic than: *"And there's a million of us just like me . . . And just might be the next best thing but not quite me!"*

As he would on 'Stan', he was taunting fans who lost their own identities in idolising his. But in 'The Real Slim Shady''s climactic lines, he also imagines a true army undermining America by petty acts of rebellion, detectable only in their hearts: teenagers spitting on fast food during serving jobs designed to deaden them, or swerving senselessly round parking lots, blasting music offensively loud for the sake of it, venting fury that can't be coherently released at lives they don't know how to change. The video shows a few of them, white kids clumsily acting out their Eminem moves outside the mall. They're the lost young men Marshall Mathers would be among if music hadn't saved him. And what 'The Real Slim Shady' offers to the millions he left behind is a happy, knowing song to holler along to when it comes on the radio, to go *"circling, screaming, 'I don't give a fuck!' "* to. It finishes with a response to its opening request for *"the real Slim Shady"* to *"please stand up"*. *"Fuck it, let's all stand up,"* Eminem murmurs as it fades, Spartacus speaking to his rebel army of slaves.

But there was another side to *The Marshall Mathers LP*, and to Eminem when he made it, which was far more difficult to defend. Though there were still some stray moments where he imagined himself insane, or impotent, or retarded, or deformed from his mother's alleged drug use, or killed for his unshuttable mouth, the vulnerable autobiographical sections of *The Slim Shady LP* which had balanced its humour and rage were mostly absent. Instead, the violent fury of his imagination was turned outwards, at the enemies he now perceived to be circling him. When, as on those Columbine-baiting tracks, he traded blows with censors and officials, from parents to the President, he maintained a laser-sighted aim and class-based logic more intelligent than his detractors. But when he focused on individuals he wanted to batter and bruise, he revealed a more thuggish side. His new targets were not the bullies, absent father or black racists that had abused him before he was famous. That intimidating world of straight, violent males that had damaged him so much was left alone. Instead, he concentrated on verbally beating up, raping and strangling women, with a side-order of threats to effeminate gay men. If you were physically weaker than him, Slim Shady was going to get you.

"If a critic calls me a bigot, a misogynist pig or homophobe I'm gonna be that," he tried to explain to *Muzik*. "If your perception of me is fucked up, I'm gonna be fucked up. If your perception of me is that I'm a decent guy, I'm gonna show you a decent guy. It's sarcasm which is too extreme to be funny. It's me backlashing at people who take everything literally." This ceding of moral and artistic control to a bunch of critics he felt unable to ignore was damaging and limp enough. But the obsessions thrown up by his "backlashing" made matters worse. Mock-encouragement to *"slap bitches"* in the otherwise innocuous 'Drug Ballad' added to a misogynistic slate also including 'Who Knew' (where he rapped, *"rape shit"*, and mentioned his wife being *"Fucked up after I beat her fuckin' ass every night, Ike"* – a reference to pop's première wife-beater, Ike Turner), the wife-murdering prequel to ''97 Bonnie & Clyde', 'Kim', and the unequivocal 'Kill You', of which he bragged in *Angry Blonde*: "The whole hook is basically beating up women . . . then at the end of the song I say, 'I'm just kidding ladies, you know I love you' . . . like you can say whatever you want so long as you say you're joking at the end. Which is cool 'cos that's what I do."

It's true that it's hard to stay offended at 'Who Knew' and 'Kill You', as both skid between flashing signposts telling you baiting the naïve is their intent (*"You probably think I'm in your tape deck now/ I'm in the backseat of your truck with duct tape . . ."*), defending his art in the context of American reality (*"You want me to fix up lyrics while the President gets his dick sucked?"*), and verbal swerves too giddy to do anything but laugh at (*"Just bend over and take it like a slut, okay, Ma?"*). 'Kill You''s references to *The Texas Chainsaw Massacre*, *Psycho*'s Norman Bates and O.J. Simpson, especially, make it a sort of woman-culling Americana pageant. But even as he slaps you round the head with your stupidity in getting wound up by a bunch of words, and triggers more useful, challenging thought than any politically correct liberal mantra, the chorus keeps coming: *"Bitch, I'ma KILL you!"* And when you do get to 'Kim', near the LP's end, you know he's not just joking, and that real misogyny is in this brilliant record, and him.

His memory of writing it tells you so much. It was the very first song he recorded for the album, after he had finished *Slim Shady*, at the end of 1998. He and Kim were separated, and he spent an afternoon alone watching a romantic film at the cinema. It made him want to write a love song, to flush out all his feelings of frustration at the split. But he balked at being sentimental on record. Instead, when he began work in the studio that day, buzzing on Es, he decided, he wrote in *Angry Blonde*, to "scream". "The mood I wanted to capture was that of an argument that me and her would have," he added.

Those must have been frightening times for his wife, if that's true. Where ''97 Bonnie & Clyde' depicted the aftermath of Kim's imagined murder, and managed to be quite funny and tender in depicting him explaining what had happened to his daughter, 'Kim' is the opposite. In a raw-throated, barely relenting scream, Eminem enacts the pained emotions which, he said, meant that "at that time" he "actually wanted" to murder his wife. It's the most queasy and questionable of all his tracks to date. Its scenario: Eminem has already butchered the man the then-estranged Kim was allegedly seeing, and his four-year-old son. While taking her to the lake in the boot of his car, his moods swing psychotically (*"I SWEAR TO GOD I HATE YOU/ OH MY GOD I LOVE YOU"*), but never stray for more than seconds from uncheckable anger, even as his voice hardly wavers from its grating roar. Near the end, it's true, it does touch the distancing effect of, as he suggested to music365, "some movie shit". When Kim makes a run for freedom, only to be chased down, slit in the gurgling throat, and dragged through the undergrowth, the sound effects make you imagine a cheesy slasher flick, more than a real woman's fear. What's more disturbing is the nature of "an argument that me and her would have": the way his voice obliterates her feeble interjections (rapped by Eminem, too, in a weaker, scared scream), just as his multi-million selling songs about them have crushed her version of their lives together.

"You never would've thought, but I played it for her once we started talking again," he wrote in *Angry Blonde*. "I asked her to tell me what she thought of it. I remember my dumb-ass saying, 'I know this is a fucked up song, but it shows how much I care about you. To even think about you this much. To even put you on a song like this.'" It's unfortunate but fitting that this is the classic line taken by real wife-beaters and their victims – that he "cares" enough to hit her. And the despicable bullying of such actions sweats from 'Kim''s corners: *"Quit crying, bitch, why do you always make me shout at you?/ . . . Am I too loud for you? Too bad, bitch, you're gonna finally hear me out this time."* The last verse's climax – *"NOW BLEED, BITCH, BLEED! BLEEEEED!"* – really gilds the lily.

There are hundreds of precedents for such violent misogyny in rock: The Rolling Stones' 'Under My Thumb' and rape fantasy 'Midnight

Rambler', Bob Dylan's vituperative put-downs to exes, and Saint John Lennon's *"I'd rather see you dead, little girl, than to be with another man"* in The Beatles' 'Run For Your Life', all no doubt in the record collections of baby-boomer detractors of Eminem like Bill Clinton, spring easily to mind. The stabbings, shootings and beatings between men and women which litter the lyrics in pop's primal root, country blues, are no better. The pervasive misogyny of hip-hop – largely the product of insecure black men from ghetto communities where few fathers are present, and "bitches" and "hos" are routinely demonised – hardly needs mentioning. The Geto Boys' 'Murder Avenue' (1993), for instance, made me far more uneasy than 'Kim' when it came out, with its relished, seedy fantasy of breaking into a woman's apartment, grabbing her from the shower and wrestling with her wet body before stabbing her over and over.

And lest we forget, the these days mild-mannered Dr. Dre really, brutally beat up Dee Barnes, while Tupac was among hip-hoppers with a real sex crime conviction. Eminem, by contrast, claimed, "I'm not mad. I leave my anger in the studio." Anecdotally, the girl I know who's suffered the most male violence didn't find Eminem's attitudes unusual, and preferred to hear them in the open. But neither did she think they were anything other than classically woman-hating. Even his biggest female fans of my acquaintance would rather not listen to 'Kim'. And, in a period of peace with his wife, once *Marshall Mathers* was out, Eminem himself admitted: "I just don't listen to the song any more."

When *The Marshall Mathers LP* was released on May 23, 2000 in the US, and May 30 in the UK, the public's phenomenal reaction anyway briefly crushed all complaints. It sold 1.76 million in its first week, breaking the all-time record for a solo artist, set, ironically, the week before by Britney Spears. It topped the US pop charts for eight weeks, and the R&B charts for four. 'The Real Slim Shady' and its addictive video was the key that unlocked popular success on a scale *The Slim Shady LP* never touched. It was played with a regularity far heavier than Heavy Rotation on MTV, and reached number four in the US, his biggest hit there. On July 2, it became Eminem's first UK number one. "The Home Secretary should ban sales of records like this," a Tory MP, Julian Brazier, predictably declared.

Critics hardly seemed to count during such commercial carnage. But for the most part, despite Eminem's paranoid hate of them, they found the LP's quality, with all its unpleasantness, inarguable. *NME* called its maker "misanthropy's smartest mouthpiece". In "storytelling of breathtaking skill and dexterity, Marshall Mathers turns the torchlight on the deepest malignancy at the heart of our rotten society: rank, festering hypocrisy . . . And we have the audacity to slag *him* off?" To *Rolling Stone*, it was "a car-crash record: loud, wild, dangerous, out of control, grotesque, unsettling . . . [and] impossible to pull your ears away from."

The first loud dissenting voice came from the Gay/Lesbian Alliance Against Defamation (GLAAD), decrying a strand of homophobia in *The Marshall Mathers LP* to them even stronger than its misogyny. A June 1 statement from the organisation declared: "[The] LP carries the warning 'Explicit Lyrics'. That's an understatement. Eminem's lyrics are soaked in violence and full of negative comments about many groups including lesbians and gay men . . . The hatred and hostility conveyed on this CD has a real effect on real people's lives as it encourages violence against gay men and lesbians. While hate crimes against gay people are on the rise, these epithets create even more bias and intolerance toward an entire community. The real danger comes from the artist's fan base of easily influenced adolescents, who emulate Eminem's dress, mannerisms, words and beliefs."

GLAAD's record in choosing targets for its wrath wasn't one to inspire confidence: its belief that the glossy bisexual killer thriller *Basic Instinct* (1992), which it picketed, was a threat to the well-being of gay and lesbian Americans was just one example of its propensity for confusing art and reality, which *The Marshall Mathers LP* so effectively examined. The phrase about "the artist's fan base of easily influenced adolescents", too, revealed them to be closer in their thinking to censor-happy, conservative anti-rock/rap groups like Tipper Gore's Parents Music Resource Centre (PMRC) than they may have wished.

The offending lyrics were anyway more humorously delivered than the venom Eminem reserved for women, if just as blatant. The video to 'The Real Slim Shady' in which, to the line *"there's no reason that a man and another man can't elope"*, Eminem squeezes between two bearded marrying males with a face screwed up in comical disgust, was his most visible statement. But the LP's closing track 'Criminal', in large part a good-humoured provocation which softens the bad taste of 'Kim', is more explicit. *"My words are like a dagger with a jagged edge,"* its first verse goes, *"that'll stab you in your head whether you're a fag or a lez . . ./ Pants or dress – hate fags? The answer's 'yes'."* It goes on to joke about murdered gay fashion designer Gianni Versace, while elsewhere Em's gay creation Ken

Kaniff orally services Detroit rivals Insane Clown Posse, in ways which are just funny.

Eminem was anyway wheeled out to deny he was homophobic to MTV's Kurt Loder, in the wake of GLAAD's condemnation. " 'Faggot' to me doesn't necessarily mean gay people," he said. " 'Faggot' to me just means taking away your manhood. You're a sissy. You're a coward. So, when I started saying 'faggot' on record, I started getting people going, 'You have something against gay people,' and I thought it was funny, because I don't."

In *NME* later that year, though, he was drawn into a fuller response. "[Faggot]'s the worst thing you can say to a man," he declared, "it's like callin' 'em a girl, whether he's gay or not. I don't give a shit about gay, if they wanna be then that's their fuckin' business . . . Just don't come around me with that shit, that's all." Why would that freak him out? he was asked. "Why would it freak me out? A man suckin' another man's dick?! I just said it! A man suckin' another man's dick." Then, too late, he eased back. "It's because hip-hop is all about manhood. It's about competition, about bein' macho. It just goes with the territory."

The fact that Paul Rosenberg had already called *NME*'s reporter, Sylvia Patterson, to one side to condemn her story in the previous week's paper detailing Cypress Hill's similarly injudicious comments illustrates how routine instinctive homophobia like that "dicksucking" tirade is in hip-hop. Or, as Patterson noted, in any pub.

With all his prejudices, raw nerves and blind spots, Eminem had still become inspirational like no one else in pop. *The Marshall Mathers LP* had put an uncensored, unhappy, angry, irritating individual at the centre of an American culture increasingly characterised by self-censorship, commercial second-guessing, and sanitised pictures of brotherly love between every race, sex and creed. Eminem brought the massive bulk of Americans too beaten down, hopeless or confused to be so perfect spitting back into the limelight, with a voice too clever and articulate to be ignored. His record stood at the top of the charts starting arguments, shoving and venting aggression. It was brutal behaviour, but the kind more Americans than their politicians and TV admit sometimes need to stay sane. The bruised feelings he caused were feelings, anyway. In my experience even his "victims", gay and female, don't fear his rage so much as recognise and relish such fury in themselves. There really is, it would seem, a little bit of Slim Shady in all of us.

Unfortunately for Eminem, there was now more than a little Slim Shady in him. *The Marshall Mathers LP* may have been able to separate art and reality. But, as the dramatic months after its release would prove, Eminem's relationship with his violent alter ego was no longer nearly so sure.

8

I AM WHATEVER YOU SAY I AM

JUNE 3, 2000. Saturday afternoon, outside a Detroit Record Shack. Unknown Insane Clown Posse employee Douglas Dail is getting a car stereo installed. The mundanity of the act and setting show we are back in the real world, far away from the feverish insults to Dail's bosses which litter the fantastic landscape of *The Marshall Mathers LP*. But here, driving by, comes the real Slim Shady anyway. According to the subsequent police report, the two exchange looks. Then Eminem steps out of his car, and says, not like a word-weaving artist, but a bar-room bully: "What did you say to me?" He is then alleged to have yanked out an unloaded, 9 mm semi-automatic pistol from his car, and screamed: "I'll shoot you! I'll kill you!", before driving off.

Hours later, and the possession of Marshall Mathers by his fictional creation seems to deepen. It is after midnight now, and he is with his wife Kim, outside the Hot Rocks club in Warren, not far from his old high school. It is reported he sees Kim "intimately kissing" former bouncer John Guerra and, assuming her unfaithfulness, assaults Guerra, some say pistol-whipping him, with the same unloaded gun. When nightclub bouncers see it fall to the ground, they call the police. Eminem, Kim and two others involved in the mêlée are arrested. Kim is charged at the scene with breach of the peace.

June 7, and Eminem turns himself in. He is photographed in the dock of Warren's 37th District Court, handcuffed, soberly dressed in black suit and dark blue shirt. He peers slit-eyed and suspicious at the judge. He is charged with assault with a dangerous weapon, and carrying a concealed weapon. He speaks only to say he understands the charges. Lawyers enter a plea of not guilty on his behalf, and $10,000 bail is posted. The maximum sentence is nine years. On the 8th, he returns to face charges for his altercation with Dail: possession of a concealed weapon (a felony), and brandishing a firearm in public (a misdemeanour). $1,000 bail is paid. *"I'm a CRI-MI-NAL!"* he'd taunted the naïve, on the album he'd released only two weeks before. And now, look, he really was.

In the April 2000 issue of *Hip-Hop Connection*, he'd wrongly claimed to be too clever for such a fall. "I can't get away with as much as I used to. I can on record, but not in public. Now if I hit someone I make them rich, so if somebody gets to me physically, or there's a confrontation, I have to bite my tongue. I have people who are there for me so that doesn't happen, and to do it for me."

The day he was charged with his nightclub brawl, true to form, Guerra sued for $25,000. Dail, perhaps wanting no more of their feud, refused to help police further, after his initial charges. Kim meanwhile, speaking to the *Detroit Free Press*, despaired at her husband's idiocy: "I don't think anybody in their right mind would cheat on a millionaire husband – especially with a nobody in a neighbourhood bar. The fact that he has just jumped to conclusions has gotten him and myself into a lot of trouble."

In hip-hop terms, of course, it was barely a parking ticket. Eminem had joined a depressing tradition including such disparate figures as amiable Dr. Dre, whose youthful indiscretions included viciously assaulting Dee Barnes, breaking a hip-hop producer's jaw, and a nightclub brawl; languid stoner Snoop Dogg, eventually judged a bystander in the shooting of reputed LA gang member Philip Woldemariam by his bodyguard; Public Enemy's loveable court jester, Flavor Flav, charged with the Angel Dust-aggravated, gun-wielding harassment of his girlfriend; Wu-Tang Clan's roguish Ol' Dirty Bastard, whose gun and drug-related crimes led to a notorious, failed spell on the run; even pop-rapper Puff Daddy who, accompanied by girlfriend Jennifer Lopez, was present at a nightclub where a gun was fired during a confrontation in 1999. And Tupac Shakur and Biggie Smalls' gangster fantasies were tragically realised, when both were shot dead in real drive-bys.

Ghetto and gang backgrounds apply to only some of those individuals. Instead, there seems to be something in the demands of hip-hop and its followers, for "keeping it real", ostentation and machismo, that makes so many of its stars pass through courtroom baptisms. Mild, music-loving Dre and bohemian, Shakespeare-reading Tupac are among those who have forced their personalities into tough guy masks. Eminem (like Tupac, a sneered at stripling as a boy) may have been playing that game, as he glared through his first court appearance. But it was the media outsiders to hip-hop he so hated, with their "Bad Boy Rapper" headlines ready-made to slip round his neck, who really gained as his actions seemed to strip the defence of artistic licence from his work.

In fairness, though, if you took away the unloaded gun, and Eminem's name, what he had done was no worse than the average Saturday night stupidity of other men and women. And the pressures which had built up on him before he took that pistol out, and let himself descend into rap cliché, made his personal boiling over no surprise.

First, there was the home he woke up in each morning. Bought when he had no idea how huge his fame would become, it was on a main road in Detroit, near his old stomping grounds. He had thought it would be a hedge against his success's eventual collapse, a sensible piece of security in his life. Instead, as the celebrity he grappled with on *The Marshall Mathers LP* consumed all such normal concerns, it made him feel like he was waking in a cage.

"The city won't let me put up a fence," he told the *Detroit Free Press*. "Everybody wants to treat me like a regular fucking person. But I'm not a regular fucking person. I've gotta have security guards sitting outside my house now because they won't let me put a fence up. I get motherfuckers coming to my house, knocking on the door. Either they want autographs or they want to fight. We've had people getting in our backyard and swimming in our pools. I don't like having security hold my hand to walk out to my fucking mailbox. There's something inside me that refuses to believe I can't walk down the street or be as normal as I want to be. Whenever something good happens, the bad always follows. That's the story of my life since the day I was born. I should have been out celebrating my record sales. Instead I'm sitting there in jail."

"I've always had a problem with people staring at me," he added to Britain's *Star* magazine. "And now they have a reason to stare, and I can't get mad at them. I'm not gonna tell you it's great to be recognised."

His relatives too, the people others looked to for comfort in times of trouble, made him sweat with distrust, draw further in upon himself. His mother was suing him, his grandmother was threatening to. He felt everyone with his blood, except his daughter, was a leech upon his soul. "I've got second and third cousins crawling out of the woodwork," he told *Muzik*. "I've got aunts and uncles crawling out of the slime, screaming they always knew I'd make it and they'd like some money and a car. It makes me sick to the bottom of my stomach, 'cos nobody in my family ever thought I would be anything."

Would he take back the last year, the *Detroit Free Press* asked him, when his anguish and dismay became apparent. "That's a real good question," he considered. "It's 50-50. Sometimes I feel like I'm living my life for everybody else. I wake up at seven in the morning, and the rest of the day is work. I can't sleep. I don't eat. It's just crazy. These past couple of years have really shot by for me. Shit is speeding now. Before I was famous, everything was moving in slow motion."

NME's Sylvia Patterson, interviewing Eminem the month before *The Marshall Mathers LP*'s release, drew out more of the racing, harried emotions pounding in his head in the weeks leading to his June 3 explosion. Perhaps it wasn't a coincidence that he was being faced, almost uniquely, by a female reporter. But in their short time together, he veered between the unsatisfiable hyperactivity of a child (swinging a hammer at Patterson, screaming in her face, sprinting to a window to holler at the street), the petulant hostility and sexual defensiveness of a teenager (threatening to "rape" her, staring sullenly, speaking flatly), and mature awareness of the state he was in (richer and more famous than he could ever have imagined, criticised and lusted after by strangers who wouldn't have bothered to spit at him 12 months before). After all the iron control he had poured into succeeding, this was a glimpse of his mind simmering to boiling point.

Eminem's barrier to complete meltdown, as his life swung away from his control, was stated several times in this period. "Right now, I feel like I'm on top of the world," he told *Newsweek*, discussing his reconciled relationship with Kim. "I did right for my daughter." "I figured I would secure the shit down at home," he told *The Source*, " 'cos realistically, truthfully, that's what I need. That's the main thing that keeps my head levelled, having that security at home. I would go crazy if I came home to a house by itself."

But the most disturbing holing of the walls Eminem claimed between art and reality came in just this private place, soon after his first court appearance, again through his own rash actions. On June 15, he started the massive, much-hyped Up In Smoke tour of the US, alongside Dre, Ice Cube and Snoop, playing 47 gigs in 10 weeks. The tour movie *Up In Smoke* (2000) emphasises blunted, schoolboy good times. But on that first concert night, safe among his boys, he couldn't resist kicking a blow-up doll of Kim around the stage. Back in record stores, his sales inexorably rose. In June, *The Marshall Mathers LP* hit five million. On July 2, 'The Real Slim Shady' became Britain's number one. And late on the night of July 7, at home with Eminem's beloved child, as she had been for almost all the last year while he publicised himself around the world, Kim saw video footage of her husband kicking her likeness for the pleasure of a roaring crowd. She slashed her wrists. Paramedics and police were called. She was treated at the scene, and taken to hospital. The next day, she went back home. Eminem was, a spokesman said, "obviously concerned."

"Kim doesn't like the fact [the song 'Kim'] went on the album," he had told *Newsweek*, "but I'm like – this music is a form of expression." "I tell her, 'Look, if you piss me off when I'm writing a song you might be in it,'" he had added to *Muzik*. "I sometimes regret mocking my fans and family on my records," he would all but repent to *The Face* that September, months after Kim's suicide attempt. "I just wanted to make regular people feel more in touch with me, like I was a real person."

Instead, the whole episode showed a childish failure of imagination, and demonstrated the awful selfishness Eminem's mantra of self-expression allowed. He is hardly the only artist to be this way. The British novelist Neil Gaiman has talked of writers gnawing off their own arm for raw material for a story, and standing at relatives' funerals thinking, terribly, "I can use this." But few artists have been so nakedly aggressive in strip-mining the feelings of their loved ones as Eminem. "I leave my anger in the studio," he's said of screaming through songs like 'Kim'. What, then, was his wife supposed to do with her anger when she heard it, and knew millions of strangers would, too? Turn it on herself, it transpired. *"I just said it – I ain't know if you'd do it or not,"* Eminem had shrugged, self-absorbed, on 'Who Knew'. But he must have known what emotions he was trampling on when he ignored his wife's pleas to scrap 'Kim'. In sculpting songs that tried to get "in touch" with his fans, he was smashing people in his own home. Exploding the harmful emotions mining his head, the shrapnel had lodged in those near him. "I gotta keep some sense of privacy about me," he had told *NME*, discussing intrusive journalists. "Some shit just isn't people's business." His wife had been denied that privilege. First he had transformed her life into a notorious song, then a literal punching bag. Outmatched physically, verbally, and in those who would listen to her, it's no wonder she slashed at her own wrists, doing what damage she could.

Eminem's response, in a guest spot on Xzibit's *Restless* LP the next year, 'Don't Approach Me', was to turn that into a song too. *"If I can hold onto my private life for five minutes longer,"* he rapped shamelessly, *"I might get my wife to let go with this knife / Just got in a feud in some parking lot with a dude over Kim / and she just slit both her wrists over this shit."* Not content with an arm, Eminem, it was clear, would devour a person's body without conscience, if the thought crossed his mind.

Still, in August, concrete retaliations for his music and deeds were launched, almost daily. On the 8th, Eminem cancelled his upcoming headline slot at Britain's prestigious Reading Festival, as he was denied permission to leave the country, with court cases pending. On the 9th, he was offered, and refused, a $2 million out of court settlement with his mother. He also learned that she would be releasing her own song about him, 'Why Are You Doing Me Like You Are?' "She needs to make some money," his grandmother Betty Kresin told a website, "because Eminem gives her nothing." His now-former bodyguard Byron Williams (clearly dispensed with before events in June) meanwhile published a book alleging serial on-the-road infidelities by his ex-boss.

On the 16th, little more than a month after his wife cut her wrists, Eminem filed for divorce. On the 21st, his mother filed a second lawsuit against him, claiming his comments about her first were defamatory. On the 22nd, Kim finally struck back at him in public, filing her own $10 million lawsuit – nicely matching the amount requested by his mother – for defamation caused to her by 'Kim'. On the 28th, the couple settled, for an undisclosed sum, and Kim was granted custody of their daughter. Back in the stores, the counter ticked over again. *The Marshall Mathers LP* had now sold six million.

As the lawsuits mounted, and the verbal battles his records had instigated at last began to bruise him too, Eminem's bitterness against his mother, in particular, grew.

"Ever since my success, shit hasn't been all good with me and her," he told *The Source*. "She wants to act like it is, and talk all this shit about, 'I love my son, and this is just a lesson that he's gotta learn. I love my son, but I'm suing him for $10 million.' In other words, 'I'm trying to take everything he worked for away from him but I love my son.' There's a lotta shit that I'm bitter for in my past that my mother has done to me that I never forgave her for to this day. And that's what sparked that whole thing. There's shit that I'm still bitter about that she won't admit to, to my face, and all I want is an apology and I can't get it. To tell you the truth, I could never look at her in the face again."

He told *Muzik* that, as was true even before the suit, he only spoke to her at all to keep ties to his half-brother Nathan, now 14. "When I call him I bite my tongue," he said, showing the paranoia that sets in with long hostility. "I believe she's listening on the other extension. I'm sure he's afraid of my mother and I'm sure she's doing the same things to him that she did to me."

The core of the verbal and legal carnage, the cut wrists and brawls that swirled round him in these months, might be hidden, in part, in the fine print of that *NME* interview. "If someone does diss me I will fuckin' demolish your self-esteem," he said. "I will fuckin' say everything I can in my fuckin' power to hurt you and make you wanna jump off a fuckin' bridge. I think I was given this ability to put words together like I do in order to do this. That's how I came up, in hip-hop circles, in battles, MCing – and through arguments with my mother, fights with my girl, period, that's just how I am. I'm a very spiteful person if you do me wrong." Did he run on vengeance? Patterson asked. Was that his main motivation? "Yeah," he said at once.

The balance in his idea of the sources of his art turns the key to it. It was the battles with the two women in his life, at least as much as with other MCs, that had been the perceived proving ground for his unique rage. It was these intimate furies, in cramped apartments and trailer homes, when it seemed impossible that anyone in the world would ever know of them, that were now being replayed on a ludicrous scale, in multi-million-selling songs and lawsuits. No wonder, perhaps, that so many of those songs had such misogyny purring through their veins.

But there was a further possible cost in the real world to his pouring such feelings onto tape. It applied to the one female he has never criticised: his daughter. The chasm between her and his wife in his head yawns in 'Kim''s opening: *"[to Hailie] Baby, you're so precious/ Daddy's so proud of you/* [to Kim] *"Sit down bitch/ You move again I'll beat the shit out of you!"* The potential damage to his baby, despite his love for her, of such hate for her mother, so violently expressed, never seems to have crossed his mind; even after his school sweetheart's wrists had been stitched.

The upside for some of those listening to such irrational lover's fury on record was, as with all his best work, one of identification, unavailable from more circumspect sources. "I guarantee you there's a lot of people

119

going through this kind of shit with their relationships," he told the *Detroit Free Press*. "With their girl, their man. I think a lot of people feel what I'm really saying."

But for himself, his mother, wife and child, the quickfire confessions and assaults on his albums were now causing only destruction. "That part is shitty," he admitted to *The Face*. "It's like I did this so that I could be a family to Kim and Hailie and raise my daughter the right way and not cut out on Hailie like my father did to me. And it's like all this success is working backwards." For the only recorded moment, he looked nakedly, fearfully bewildered, as if it was finally dawning on him what his confrontational success had cost. "My family is crumbling."

With home and marriage failing, his job seeming more like a trial, and the law closing in, his daughter was the only centre that still seemed to hold him. In interviews, her mention could draw out the vulnerability *The Marshall Mathers LP*, and his subsequent actions, had hidden. "I listen to everything my daughter listens to, and I watch everything that she watches," he told *Hip-Hop Connection*. "Hailie listens to both of my albums, and she likes them. Sometimes she'll say, 'Daddy put that one song on.' But she's a smart little girl and if she hears cuss words, she knows not to repeat them."

Eminem was, it seemed, the ideal, responsible parent for Eminem fans. Elsewhere, he gushed about her personality, and her vocabulary, with doe-eyed adoration utterly at odds with any other side of his combative public face. "She's gonna have everything when she grows up," he told *NME*. "She's gonna be able to go to college and be something I wasn't. If she never makes anything of herself, God forbid – I want her to do something, be a model, do music, be a doctor, anything – I'm gonna have that money there for her. It's about her now. We're here to reproduce. And I reproduced. So now my life is for her."

It was the one thing he and Kim could still agree on. So, on September 14, for Hailie's sake, they announced they would try to make their marriage work, again.

August had meanwhile brought a fitting artistic response from Eminem to his troubles. The video to the second single from *The Marshall Mathers LP*, 'The Way I Am', which swiftly gave him his by now expected spot at number one on MTV, worked as a brooding, coherent explanation of his state of mind. Though the song had originally been written as a response to Interscope's pressure to write a hit like 'My Name Is', the lyrics typically

Eminem, complete with hockey mask and unplugged chainsaw, during his infamous 2001 UK tour, at Docklands Arena, London, February 9. (LFI)

Eminem with his mentor, Dr Dre, in Las Vegas for the announcement of their Up In Smoke tour, May 11, 2000. (LFI)

Eminem stokes the crowd with Dre, at the Experience Music Project in Seattle, June 25, 2000. (LFI)

One of the boys. Eminem with Snoop Dogg, Dr Dre and Ice Cube, May 2000. (LFI)

Eminem embraces unlikely new friend Elton John at the 2001 Brit Awards in London, February 26, 2001. (LFI)

Role Model. Protestors outside the 2001 Grammy Awards in Los Angeles, objecting to homophobia in Eminem's lyrics. (REX)

Eminem, in a Warren courtroom charged with carrying a gun, stares out the judge. Privately, he was scared jail would end his life with Hailie - June 7, 2000. (REX)

Eminem with D12, boyhood friends and adult support group, June 2001. (BRAD MILLER/RETN

Eminem on stage with D12's obscene joker, Bizarre, at the UK Leeds Carling Festival, August 2001. (JOHN MATHER/RETNA)

Spiderman actress Kirsten Dunst dances for Eminem on the set of Saturday Night Live, May 2002. (LFI)

Eminem at the LA premiere of 8 Mile, the film that forced even mainstream America to take him seriously, November 2002. (REX)

made leaps into every tension now clenching his head: fans crowding him, media attention, Columbine hypocrisy, and lawsuits.

Fittingly the only *Marshall Mathers* track he pieced together with almost no help, its claustrophobic feel on the album was built from an ominous piano loop which Eminem made his rasped, harried rap cling to at all times, allowing no escape from his mood. The video intensified that atmosphere and, playing on MTV endlessly each day through the mean month of August, as Kim and Hailie separated from him, it seemed like a confession from a cornered man.

Shot as a series of shadowy and sunlit scenes intercut so swiftly the screen seemed to strobe, the visual beat was of an erratic heartbeat. Its star's three personas all seemed to be on hand. That was surely Slim Shady, standing on a skyscraper window ledge at night, gawked at by a curious public, roaring at them like King Kong. And it looked like Eminem, in a darkened room with Marilyn Manson behind him, fearlessly lancing Columbine falsities. But the character we were really shown on screen for the first time was Marshall Mathers. We saw him at a cafe with Kim (played by an actress) and Hailie, taking a seat in the sun to give their daughter a drink, an ordinary couple, not arguing or murdering. And we saw the presumption of a fan sitting down with them as if by right, and the others that swarmed in like locusts when Marshall signed an autograph. His eyes looked vulnerable and exposed. Later, as the scenes of indignity play out (*"But I can't take a SHIT in the bathroom/ Without someone standin' by it"*), those eyes look dead, not resisting what's being forced on him, but numbly taking it. Slim rages on, as he was starting to in real life: *"No patience is in me and if you offend me I'm liftin' you ten feet . . . Go call you a lawyer, file you a lawsuit/ I'll smile in the courtroom and buy you a wardrobe."* But Marshall, at least as he showed himself here, was not really that strong.

The most striking scenes were of him and Kim at home. For the first time in his art, as the acrimony over its brutalising of his wife climaxed, she was shown as the angry, embattled one, shouting and gesturing at fans as they crowded her baby, and at a passive Eminem in their apartment afterwards. For once, she was more than a pair of legs sticking out of a car, or the name of a notorious song, or a battered blow-up doll. It was a glimpse of why they had ever been together.

Eminem had only admitted once in print such understanding of his wife's problems with their changed lives. "Not to defend Kim," he had told the *Detroit Free Press* in June, "but I realise what has happened to me has probably been a strain on her, too. It's a crazy thing to deal with. You've really got to be in shape." In the month that she really left him, a video planned earlier now had the honesty to show Kim raging and packing her bags for that reason, and warmly kissing her husband as she left with Hailie, love at last mixed with hate in what Eminem showed of her to the world.

The final shots said even more. To the sound of a stopping heartbeat, Slim, who has leaped off that ledge, and snarled unrepentantly all the way down, suddenly realises what he's done. An image of Hailie flashes in his mind, and he screams and windmills his arms in fear and regret, then finds the ground softening to meet him. His wife, whose own suicidal mood seemed to be anticipated and perhaps explained in this video, art and life in these months too close to prise apart, may have understood. With an ambulance called before her suicide could be completed, and the hospital declaring her safe to leave the next day, neither of them, it seemed, really meant to leave their baby that way. The last shot of all, though, of the surviving Slim staring at us with unreadable menace, lets you take nothing for granted.

In September, *The Marshall Mathers LP*'s sales ticked over again, to seven million. No doubt that video helped, maybe the marital blood-letting did, too. But the record had also gained its own remorseless momentum. The controversies around it were no longer relevant to the various corporate arms which now attached themselves to any music with cash or credibility to convert to their own bland ends, with sponsorship and awards. As Eminem had shown with the "clean" versions of his albums, he did not object. The tortured bad grace with which white "alternative" rock stars like Pearl Jam's Eddie Vedder had collected corporate prizes in the Nineties had no relevance to him. Money, success and mutual backslapping had never been a crime in hip-hop, where all three were so hard to get.

So, in August Eminem collected the *Source* Hip-Hop Award for Lyricist of the Year and Music Video of the Year. In September, 'The Real Slim Shady''s video was nominated for two *Billboard* Music Video Awards, Maximum Vision Video and Best Rap/Hip-Hop Clip of the Year. In September, too, Eminem won the *MuchMusic* Video Award for People's Choice – Favourite International Artist. Somewhere in an Alaskan town hall, or a British video shop, or else some other blank corporate entity, even more ludicrously named and meaningless awards were being struck, to squeeze out a few more dollars from association with Eminem's intensely personal work. And a few more dollars would be slipped to him for letting them.

The MTV Video Music Awards, also in September, had no more credence, really, except that more people saw them. Eminem duly won three: Video of the Year and Best Male Video (for 'The Real Slim Shady'), and Best Rap Video ('Forgot About Dre'). He was also nominated for two more. Fortified by that many name-checks, he turned up to perform 'The Real Slim Shady' and 'The Way I Am'. But events outside the show were part of an opposite, in some ways complementary, groundswell, showing yet another way in which the months after *The Marshall Mathers LP*'s release had slipped from his control.

In the streets around the ceremony, protesters from GLAAD and the National Organisation of Women gathered, chanting and carrying banners. GLAAD also voiced their objections in a second anti-Eminem manifesto: "These are the words that kids hear in school hallways before they get beat up. For this kind of language to be put out there without any sense of responsibility on Eminem's part, or MTV's part, is simply not something that GLAAD can ignore . . . We are very disappointed that they continue to support him as heavily as they do."

Meanwhile, in Washington, DC, on September 14, the very day Eminem and Kim reconciled, Lynne Cheney, former Chair of the National Endowment for the Humanities, and wife of that year's ultimately successful Republican Vice-presidential candidate, Dick Cheney, was testifying to the Senate Committee on Commerce, Science and Transportation, about the entertainment industry. "They are producing violent, sexually explicit material and they are peddling it to our children," she declared. She singled out Eminem, for "propagating violence against women" and being a "violent misogynist", and imagining the "joys" of murdering women he met. She pulled out lines from *The Marshall Mathers LP*'s first track, 'Kill You', shorn of any context, to put before America's administrators: *". . . he's raping his own mother", ". . . painting the forest with blood", ". . . Bitch, I'm a kill you", ". . . I got the machete from O.J."* Columbine was also mentioned, and Marilyn Manson, the kindred spirit Eminem had made caper ghoulishly behind him, allies in adversity, in 'The Way I Am''s video, which played on MTV even as Cheney spoke.

October saw Canadian officials join the mounting outcry, as the Anger Management tour – pairing Eminem with Limp Bizkit to reach the rock

123

record-buyers Up In Smoke had missed – began in North America. "That's unacceptable to us in Ontario," the state's Attorney-General Jim Flaherty told newspapers, after a complaint by Toronto resident Valerie Smith, as a tour date in the city was booked for the 26th. Smith wanted Eminem's prosecution under Section 319 of Canada's Criminal Code, outlawing "communicating statements, other than private conversation, that wilfully promote hatred against an identifiable group". The legislation's focus on race and religion prevented a serious challenge.

A November 2 show at the University of Illinois was also protested against by a group of students outside the venue, whose unsuccessful petition trying to stop the event read: "We, the undersigned, believe that it is wrong for the university to promote and profit from a concert that will include hate speech, encourage violence and defame people."

The Marshall Mathers LP had predicted such attacks, of course, as if Eminem knew the critics that had goaded him into making it would eventually be superseded by sober law-makers, those who had come for Marilyn after Columbine, turning their ire on him. It did not take a genius to know he would attract such attention. The final way the real world attacked him for what he said he was in 2000 was merely one more skirmish in an unrelenting, 15-year war between American politicians and pop.

It was a conflict Eminem had been raised in. In his book *Night Beat*, critic Mikal Gilmore pieced together how rock in the Eighties, when in America its radical Sixties power was assumed to be spent, in fact faced its greatest assaults from conservative forces. Fuelled in part by a 1985 *Newsweek* attack by journalist Kandy Stroud on "pornographic rock" (Prince, Madonna, etc.), the Parents Music Resource Centre (PMRC) had been set up that year to push for the censorship of sex and violence in rock. It was co-founded by wealthy Washington wife Tipper Gore (whose husband Al would be 2000's Democratic Presidential candidate, leaving the radical American music fan in the year of *Marshall Mathers* with nowhere to run). The coincidence of the murderer-rapist the "Night Stalker", then terrorising Southern California, declaring on his capture that Australian heavy metal band AC/DC's 'Night Prowler' had inspired his crimes, the charging of British metallers Judas Priest with the "lethal use of subliminal messages" after a fan committed suicide in Nevada, and the general conservatism of America under Reagan, who judged rock to be about "violence and perversity", were enough to steamroller the record industry into "voluntary" labelling of offensive content (with the exception of gun-happy, conservative country music) soon after.

Eminem's whiteness and lyrical liking for sexist violence made him a combatant in that ongoing battle, a natural enemy of Gore and Cheney. And the American Establishment's loathing of hip-hop was still more fierce. Violence at the *Krush Groove Christmas Party* at Madison Square Garden in 1985 had begun media scare stories about the genre. In 1990, when a *Newsweek* cover story on "The Rap Attitude" called the music "repulsive", Florida lawyer Jack Thompson orchestrated the arrest of a record store owner for selling 2 Live Crew's "obscene" music, and of three members of the band for performing it, and pressure from conservative Congressmen caused CDs' compulsory labelling for "Explicit Content". What Thompson called "the opening shots of a cultural civil war" had been fired. Ice-T's dropping by Time-Warner, after he'd recorded 'Cop Killer' with his rock band Body Count, Virgin's dumping of The Geto Boys' début, and the severing of ties with Death Row by Eminem's label Interscope, once they'd squeezed its formula dry, were among the casualties of subsequent fire-fights.

L.L. Cool J had responded to the obvious racism in such crackdowns in 1986, to journalist David Toop. "You know how the press is. Things happen and they blow it all out of proportion 'cos it's black kids and it's rap and they don't understand neither." Eminem's turn in the trenches of this "cultural civil war", though, showed again what a freakish anomaly his colour, music and mentality made him. With all the troubles spinning round him, he would prove a figure no pressure group or politician could silence, and no record company could drop.

The lack of real heat in politicians' tirades at him, compared to the hounding of Ice-T and gangsta-rap, could be explained by his whiteness, on a number of levels. It not only increased his commercial clout, and the number of libel lawyers ready to protect him from censors. His blond, blue-eyed good looks also meant that, to adult whites watching his videos, he gave no worrying reminders of America's abandoned, intimidating black ghettos (even though that was partly where he came from). The implacably scowling Ice Cube, for instance, would always have a harder time. Eminem's wounded, young blond features also disarmed at least some of the women and gay men he lyrically lashed out at; as Sylvia Patterson told him, "you're so terribly good looking, you see."

Eminem himself accepted that the racial issues that made the best black rappers incendiary were not for him (a line in 'Criminal' goes, *"I drank more liquor to fuck you up quicker/ Than you'd wanna fuck me up if I said the word . . ."*, the unspoken "nigga" and its baggage something he couldn't touch). It was why he had prodded America instead on the raw nerve of its sexual attitudes, and by making his own fraught celebrity his theme. And so, in a way rare for movies and books, but natural for a rapper, he had put his own personality at war with his country's hypocrites, from the President down. Affronted Senators, students, protesters and pickets vanished into the funhouse reflections he'd prepared for them in *The Marshall Mathers LP*. Every line Lynne Cheney partially quoted to attack him had retorts waiting for her a word or two later. As he taunted on 'Criminal': *". . . every time I rhyme, these people think it's a crime/ To tell 'em what's on my mind/ But I don't gotta say a word, I just flip 'em the bird, and keep goin' . . . You can't stop me from toppin' these charts."*

The most popular six months of Eminem's life had ended with his marriage on rocky ground, three court cases pending, politicians denouncing him, and jail a looming possibility. But his greatest days of notoriety were still ahead. On October 28, he announced he would be touring Britain.

9

STAN

"PARENTS BEWARE! The world's most dangerous rapper is coming to Britain. Eminem will perform his controversial songs about murder, drugs and violence to women in February."

The Sun's shamelessly simplified warning, as Eminem dates for 2001 were scheduled in Manchester and London, was followed by a strengthening salvo of "shocked" tabloid broadsides, as his arrival neared: "THE TRUTH ABOUT THE REAL SLIM SHADY: The Astonishing Story Of The Bullied Trailer Trash Nerd"; "BULLY'S BRUTAL BEATING LEFT HIM FOR DEAD"; "RAPPER WAS SHY LONER"; "EMINEM LOVED DOLLIES"; "TOUR SHOCK FOR GAY HATE RAPPER"; "PUBLIC EMINEM".

"The show is the most outrageous ever," *The Sun*'s Dominic Mohan brazenly reported from the start of Eminem's European tour, in Hamburg on January 30. "I predict there will be a storm of controversy here . . . Take cover, Britain. Eminem's show should have a health warning."

But, rabid as the British tabloid press could be, no one's heart seemed to be in efforts to make him the nation's newest folk devil. Comparisons with the last rapper to achieve such notoriety in this country are instructive, and do no-one credit. Snoop Doggy Dogg had arrived in March 1994 to a *Daily Star* front page screaming, "KICK THIS EVIL BASTARD OUT!" Though the case of Philip Woldemariam's shooting was still awaiting trial (and Snoop would eventually be found innocent), and though the degree of violence and misogyny on his album *Doggystyle* which the tabloids (no strangers to sexism) condemned these days sounds mild, the media fury was unrelenting. No detail was sought about Snoop's life in the mainstream British press, as they did with Eminem, and nothing was asked about his music. Instead, the *Star*'s headline was accompanied by a mug-shot of Snoop looking brutal and unrepentant, redolent with echoes of the last black man to be so spotlighted on British front pages: Winston Silcott, who had been accused, and later acquitted, of the murder of PC Keith Blakelock. The stench of unapologetic racism then was powerful.

Eminem had certainly done nothing to soften impressions before his February arrival. On top of his own pending court cases and lyrical savagery, he had opened a new front of verbal warfare in November, after fellow white rapper Everlast, ex-House of Pain, sneered of him, while guesting on Dilated People's 'Ear Drums Pop', *"lift up your panties and show your skirt for the world to see."* Eminem immediately responded on 'I Remember', recorded as a B-side for D12's forthcoming début single 'I Shit On You': *"I just wish the cardiac would have murdered you"* (a typically tasteful reference to Everlast's near-fatal 1998 heart attack). With his usual city-flattening overreaction, he followed up with D12's 'Quitter' (eventually left off the group's *Devil's Night* LP). Here he told fans to *"hit"* Everlast *"with sticks, bricks, rocks, throw shit at him, trip him, spit on him, treat him like a ho, bitch slap him . . . Fuck you, fat boy, drop the mic, let's fight."* "I'm not gonna let someone else diss me on a record and not say something back," he redundantly explained. "It's in my blood; it's a competition thing."

But far more decisive in the public's reaction to him when he touched down in February was the December release of *The Marshall Mathers LP*'s third single, 'Stan'. Once that reached the radio, the tabloids' already weak outcry was muffled by a louder, less predictable noise: the sound of everyone in the country who still listened to pop talking, like they hadn't in years, in consternation, wonder and surprise.

"It's about an obsessive fan who keeps writing me and taking everything I say on the record literally," Eminem told the *LA Times*. "He's crazy for real and he thinks I'm crazy, but I try to help him at the end of the song. It kinda shows the real side of me." "I know I ain't got it all upstairs, but some people are sick," he added to *Muzik*. "There are people who write saying they're into hurting themselves. They're cult people, fucking devil worshippers, who say I'm right next to Satan in their thoughts. I've had skinheads and KKK members on my case, telling me they love my shit and how I'm one of them." Even as his manner in concert would show how much he loved most fans back, these "sick" ones at the margins weren't people he felt any tie to. "As a kid, much as I loved L.L. Cool J, Run-DMC and The Beastie Boys, I wouldn't have cried, hyperventilated, or had a fucking seizure if I met them," he told *Muzik.* "I . . . would have been real shy."

Stan, the single's progressively more unhinged stalker, had no such reservations. But the song, a 6½-minute, boundary-busting radio event like Dylan's 'Like A Rolling Stone' 34 years before, was a far more intricate, jagged piece of music than Eminem's summary even started to suggest.

'Stan''s masterstroke was its extensive sampling of 'Thank You' by Dido, one of the most daring, lateral record raids in hip-hop history. Dido Armstrong was then known, if at all, as a singer in her brother Rollo's British house act, Faithless. Although aggressive marketing by her label and the Eminem association would drive sales of *No Angel*, the début LP from which 'Thank You' was drawn, past one million in the US by the time of 'Stan''s single release, when Eminem started to build his track around her's in the studio, only he heard something right in it.

What Dido gave him, most of all, was a voice, mood and sound from a world far from his, the first part in what, with Eminem as superfan Stan and himself, would become a weaving, unpredictable, three-way dialogue. It starts with a crash of thunder, and Dido's 'Thank You' beaming in tinnily, then stronger, as if her voice is transmitting to a place that's hard to reach, a room submerging in lightning-streaked rain. *"My tea's gone cold, I'm wond'rin' why-y-y, I got out of bed at all,"* she sings. *"The rain clouds up my window, and I can't see at all."* The picture of an English bedsit on a gloomy Thursday is completed by the accent of her pensively accepting voice. Looking at the pictures of her lover on the wall, she feels happy, in the hemmed in way her country's cold and drizzle have trained her to be. But the voice and the beats are getting louder, as if someone's turned that radio up as far as it will go. And here, with no warning, comes Stan.

He sounds polite at first as he writes Eminem a letter, reasonable, informed, the kind of fan every artist wants. He likes the most obscure tracks, he's papered his room with his idol's pictures, feels he knows him in a way. He wishes he'd had a reply to his last letter, but he understands. Only a harsh, scratching sound, like a ragged typewriter, or rats in the roof, is disquieting. That, and the way the bass, guitars and beats loop claustrophobically, like they can't find their way out of Stan's head. When Dido comes back in, her kind voice doesn't sound as comforting as before.

Verse two, and Stan's sanity's taken a dip. *"I ain't mad, I just think it's FUCKED UP . . .",* he's writing now, still with no reply, so forced to pour more of himself onto the page. Stan says his father was a wife-beater and cheater, he cuts himself, his pregnant girlfriend can't understand, he's just like Eminem; only Eminem, who he met for seconds at a signing, is his friend. When Dido returns, her tea sounds cold as death. And in Stan's final letter, the sympathetic detail with which Eminem has entered this wounded fan's head spins into merciless farce: Stan's on the freeway, barking last words into a tape, his pregnant girlfriend screaming in the trunk, just like Kim, till he screeches and splashes into the river, unheard tape and all.

The swerve in mood has a logic you can only imagine after it's happened. And then, when you think surely there can be no more, here's Eminem himself, replying sensibly, conscientiously, "the real me", maybe, as he told the *LA Times*; but he's too late, as Stan is dragged from the water on TV. Psychodrama, stalker comedy, character study, shaggy dog tale, a sick, cruel joke: that was 'Stan', every time the radio played it.

The video, another automatic MTV number one in November, added even more nuances. It starts as a horror movie, with an actor as Stan and Dido as his heavily pregnant girl, arguing in an eerie house. Dyeing his hair blond, Stan peers at himself in the bathroom mirror, wearing a vest that makes him look like the poster image from *Henry: Portrait Of A Serial Killer*. But he sees only himself, turning into Eminem. The schizoid role-playing at 'Stan''s heart – Eminem impersonating his biggest fan pouring his heart out to Eminem – is now naked, as Stan retreats to his cellar, where he writes surrounded by torn images of his hero, eyes bright, remembering the times he caught real glimpses of the star. We see that Eminem, dead-eyed and self-protecting, as Stan grabs him to hug at a signing.

But it's a third Eminem, the one shown receiving Stan's letter in his trailer, who is really a new face for an artist so addicted to masks. This is again "the real me" he'd mentioned to the *LA Times*, but portrayed with a force the song could not match. More even than 'The Way I Am' 's video, the minute of film in which he acts out the final verse, studiously writing Stan back, wearing glasses to see the page, is a corrective to all the cruelties and fears he'd unapologetically mined elsewhere; evidence to suggest that that truly was play-acting. As he returns Stan to reality, recommending *"counselling"*, saying his songs are *"just clownin' "*, feeling *"sick"* when he sees Stan's crash on TV, these lines leap from the screen: *"I really think you and your girlfriend need each other. Or maybe you just need to treat her better."*

With Dido's strong, kind-eyed female presence in the video too, this advice to a fan who's taken in by 'Kim''s cruelties, on what would become Eminem's biggest hit, is his clearest, overlooked indication that, when at peace, he might not want to harm women, even with his words.

British reactions to 'Stan' were particularly acute because it was released as the least likely Christmas single in years. It was unmissable on the radio that December, hard, funny and fresh among a slew of novelty songs and bland boy bands. In the traditional race for Christmas number one, it looked briefly as if Eminem's astonishing stalker ballad would for once give the position some dignity. But his record company backed down, not trusting seasonal buyers' sense of adventure. 'Stan' was slipped out early in December, securing Eminem's second UK number one without serious opposition. Bob the Builder's 'Can You Fix It?', a grating children's song, toppled him in time for the turkey.

Still, it was 'Stan' and Eminem people were still talking about as 2001 dawned, and his UK tour neared. As was now routine around the world, his approaching entry was protested against as if he was a real convicted criminal. On January 30, Sheffield University Student's Union banned the playing, merchandising and promotion of Eminem on its campus, worrying that this would "intimidate" gay students, after three complaints. The stereotypical notion that its gay population were wilting flowers prone to cowering at people playing records was not challenged, and on February 3, the University's radio station, Sure, was fined £7,000 for playing Eminem. The Swedish manufacturers of the chainsaw he used in his act, Husqvarna, were also perturbed. "We make chainsaws for mature people," they declared, "who have genuine forestry work to do." The notoriously unhip and censorious Tory Shadow Home Secretary Ann Widdecombe then weighed in with her own condemnation, making both parties look foolish.

But the most striking aspect of the tour as it neared was that everyone had to write or say something. Because 'Stan' had been heard so widely, simple *Sun*-style vilification was no longer supportable. And the thematic baggage and dramatic life Eminem hauled behind him like contraband – the homophobia, the misogyny, the maternal strife, the bullied past, the beatings, the race – was so alive, it forced thought from literary critics and pop pundits, and people in the street. On ITV's *Tonight* news magazine, Trevor McDonald interviewed his mother. On Radio 4's more high-brow news programme of note, *Today*, his grandmother spoke. By the time Eminem and his entourage stepped onto a private plane in Paris on the 8th, after a gig in the city the night before, with their Manchester date now only hours away, a media thunderstorm not seen in Britain about a pop act since The Sex Pistols was boiling to a head.

Preview reports from across Europe gave clues on what to expect, and titillating gossip. In Hamburg, Eminem got the crowd to chant "Pop the pills!", before seeming to down two Es. A D12 member called them a gift from Marilyn Manson, also hauling a censor-baiting show towards Britain that month, and a guest of Eminem that night. In Paris, R&B artist Mya watched him parody boy band N'Sync's 'Tearing Up My Heart' as 'Tearing Up My Ass', before he and the French told each other, "I love you!"

But it was in Manchester that the jackals, the zealots and the curious gathered in earnest, news crews, protesters and young girls jostling for space outside the MEN Arena, on a crisp winter night. On his plane earlier in the day, Eminem had rested unawares, listening to the Xzibit album on which he guested. He walked down the plane's steps towards the Manchester ground like a T-shirted Pope, only to be sent back up by Paul Rosenberg, wanting to catch the moment just right for a possible video. When he cancelled his night's reservations at the Mal Maison Hotel, the day's first rumour flew. He was fearfully avoiding the city's nearby gay district, it was gleefully claimed. He had always planned to drive straight onto London, his label countered, barely caring. The fine points of this frenzy of attention no longer mattered.

Around 100 pickets gathered in the early evening, some in make-up, their literal-minded flyers showing why they could not challenge the man waiting inside. "EMINEM HAS GONE TOO FAR!" they warned. "Everyone knows Eminem's lyrics are oppressive to women, homophobic and they actually make fun of rape victims . . . Manchester is proud of its diversity, women, gay and straight. Why should we give this bigot a warm welcome?" But their own "rap" was no contest: "Eminem you are not funny, you oppress us to make money."

The teenagers and younger children, the majority girls, who filed past these protesters, not looking oppressed, had their own voices heard in a *Smash Hits* survey in the tour's wake. Were his lyrics offensive? "Nope, they're normal," said Sarah of South Wales. "Some, but I guess he's joking," said Katie of Wembley. "Only to people who have no life and actually take them seriously," said Jenna of Sutton. "He makes it clear he doesn't actually believe in what he raps about." As to dating the author of 'Kim': "Yes! He is the sexiest man on da planet!" "Most definitely, he's God!" Only Katie worried about getting "beaten up" for liking Westlife, too. Their unfussy good sense put most of the week's commentators to shame.

Inside, meanwhile, nervous expectation rose by the second. Outkast, the blistering Southern rappers due as support, failed to show, back in America due to family illness. British-Armenian rappers Mark B and Blade stepped into the breach, as the British garage act So Solid Crew, soon to be notorious themselves, would in London. But all that mattered was the moment, at 9.20 pm, when the lights at last went down. Now the crowd knew it was really happening, that nothing could stop Slim Shady striding to them.

All they could see at first was a 25-foot, broken-roofed shack, like the one on *The Marshall Mathers LP*. "This is the house I lived in when I was 13," Eminem would tell them later, and most thought it was a joke, a parody of his white trash image, a pretence he'd once lived in a hovel like a Thirties bluesman. To anyone who'd been to Detroit, the parody seemed only slight. He really had brought the broken home he hated with him to Europe, to dance and shout in its ruins. Video screens moved us inside, showing *Blair Witch*-shaky footage of two young burglars being attacked by a maniac in blue dungarees and horror movie hockey mask, wielding a whirring chainsaw. Then Eminem was standing on the stage, in that mask, with that chainsaw, and the crowd surged forward in ecstatic relief.

But what followed had little of the offence or illicit thrills the storm preceding it had promised. Instead, like in 'Stan''s video, the "real" Eminem stepped forward again. He swigged a bottle of "Bacardi", and declared he would "drink myself to death"; asked the crowd "if I'm amongst some drug addicts", to a positive roar, before taking two "Es"; appeared strapped to an electric chair; even touched on the Guerra court case, declaring, "Of course I pistol-whipped that motherfucker. Because I'm a . . . *Criminal!*" But all the while, he treated his near-child audience conscientiously, letting them swear and pretend they were addicts, ensuring they were in on the joke. He let them touch him, and brought one girl up on the stage. He didn't tell his fans he loved them, like he did in Paris. But it was there in the soft warmth of his voice. Apart from his daughter, it was hard to believe he loved anyone more. As he told *Q* when asked if he wanted to explain his lyrics to his fans, "They get it, they know what I mean. I don't need to explain it to adults and older people, or critics. If anything, I'd like to thank the fans for understanding where I'm coming from." For a man from a disrupted childhood who doted on his daughter, a mutual bond with these youngsters willing to join him in saying "fuck you" to the world was natural. When they shouted 'Stan''s words for him, new depths were tapped in its tale of fan love.

The problem with this increasing revelation of the sensitive, decent man Marshall Mathers felt himself to be, behind the Slim Shady mask others had taken so seriously, was that the emotional impact of this breathlessly awaited show was almost nil. D12 joined him near its start, for 20 minutes, letting him safely disappear in their number; there were set-changes (shack to castle), pantomime crowd participation, even an Eminem cartoon. Everything was safe, as if his art's jagged edge was being kept from minors. He railed against critics at the end. But once again, he seemed to have listened to them too much. He was so worried about fans falling for his "bad" example that he had sanitised himself. Those who didn't see him were lucky. They could still believe he was "the world's most dangerous rapper". But the Eminem seen live in Britain, as the excesses of 2000 slipped away, was someone more humane, and more ordinary.

His last three days in the country evaporated in gentle anticlimax. Police rushed to his dressing room after that first show, believing, like the concerned, naïve grown-ups they were, that the Es Eminem had necked were real. Once, maybe, they would have been. But Eminem, having slipped away already, explained the next day that the "pills" had been rolled-up chewing gum. The tabloids' disappointment was naked. Manchester Police Inspector Steve White seized video footage anyway. "I thought it prudent . . . to see if any offences had in fact occurred that might be in breach of the Misuse of Drugs Act," he declared, with Dickensian formality.

Eminem was already being driven to London, for two dates at the Docklands Arena. He dined at his exclusive hotel on egg mayo and chicken salad sandwiches, and buckets of Kentucky Fried Chicken, spending the first day shopping for Hailie, and the second in his room with his old D12 friends. Two years of limitless opportunity hadn't altered the people and things he liked. But two radio interviews showed the relaxed, confident, amused man he was beginning to become.

Asked by Kiss FM's Matt White about D12 solo careers, he spluttered:

"What do you mean? Like the group split up? Like this is a stepping stone for everyone's solo careers? We're a crew, we'll whip your ass! There's six of us in this fuckin' crew and we'll stomp you like there's 12 of us!" To Radio 1's Jo Whiley, he was sparkier still. If he had a time machine, when would he go back to? "I'd probably go back to the day I was born and kill my mother as soon as she had me." Would he let Hailie listen to his records? "Yeah, she listens to it, she walks around the house going, 'Fuck, fuck, fuck!' She's my little secretary at home too. She answers the phone, 'Shady Records!'" Would he get into movies? "I've been so busy with doing what I'm doing and I'm so drunk all the time that I can't possibly . . ."

By the time he flew back to America, in the early hours of Sunday, February 11, the storm he had aroused had broken, in the dawning realisation that he had given no evidence of evil, or genius. He must have known he could not have the same impact again, and seemed glad of it. His farewell words summed up his time in the tabloid fire. Looking at the papers on his arrival he'd wondered why he bothered. "Why do you guys all hate me so much?" But the fans' screams had changed his mind. "I totally didn't expect that reaction. Respect. I love y'all." He'd come as Johnny Rotten. He left polite like Johnny Mathis.

The closing months of 2000 had meanwhile seen him collect another batch of random, meaningless awards from various US show business corporations. In November, the *Rolling Stone* and MTV: 100 Greatest Pop Songs list placed 'My Name Is' at 67. The same month, Eminem was named *Spin* magazine Artist of the Year, and picked up two awards each from MTV Europe and *Billboard*, as well as the "My VH1" prize for Most Entertaining Public Feud (Eminem vs. Everyone). *The Slim Shady LP*'s sales clicked over to four million, doubled in its successor's slipstream. And, in December, *Billboard*'s Year-End charts declared Eminem Top Artist – Male, and *The Marshall Mathers LP* the year's second-biggest US seller, now up to 7.9 million.

These vacuous bashes, cobbled-together lists and crushing sales statistics placed Eminem in the same global pop arena as Britney, Christina, N'Sync and all the other production-line pop stars he loathed so bitterly. An Internet rumour that he had died in a crash – like James Dean, or like Dylan nearly did at a similar exalted, exhausting stage – was so pervasive that, on December 17, he had had to deny it himself. The story seemed to confirm his sudden worldwide ubiquity.

But it was the biggest music awards of all, the Grammys, which pushed the public's awareness of him up still another notch at the start of 2001. *"You think I give a damn about a Grammy?"* he had sneered on 'The Real Slim Shady', *"half you critics can't even stomach me, let alone stand me."* The video's nightmare vision of Eminem attending the awards, squeezed next to a simpering Britney, had been hilarious, but hardly ingratiating. Yet when the awards' shortlist was announced on January 3, *The Marshall Mathers LP* was on it, for Album of the Year, part of an unusually risky list for the Recording Academy's annual prize-giving – Radiohead's *Kid A* and Beck's *Midnite Vultures* were also there, alongside Paul Simon and Steely Dan. Eminem had three more rap nominations, too. Perhaps 'The Real Slim Shady''s brinkmanship had embarrassed the Academy, perhaps *Marshall Mathers*' sheer weight of sales had forced their hand. Grammy President Michael Greene certainly sounded equivocal. "This is probably the most repugnant record of the year," he said, flinching, "but in a lot of ways it's also one of the most remarkable records of the year." The nominations might still not have mattered very much more than the countless others Eminem had already absent-mindedly collected – though the Academy talked the Grammys up as their industry's Oscars, their commercial impact was far less. It was 'Stan' which again helped him haul in yet more fans, when it was announced he would perform it at the Awards: as a duet, with the famously gay Elton John.

Though John's own creative vitality seemed long spent by 2001, he had a pop scholar's interest in fresher talent, and had not been slow in supporting Eminem – "ELTON TELLS EMINEM: I'M RIGHT BEHIND YOU", as *The Sun* tastefully put it in August 2000. "It feels like the nuclear bomb has just hit," he said of *Marshall Mathers*. "This is really hardcore stuff – funny, clever. It's poetry and also musically interesting."

John's willingness to share a stage with an accused homophobe, though, brought instant fury on both their heads. In America, Eminem's old critics swiftly regrouped. Of his nominations, GLAAD spokesman Scott Seomin declared, "What this says is a little scary. It's about murdering, stabbing, slitting throats, and putting women in the trunks of cars. It's about violence." As to the duet, "GLAAD is appalled that John would share a stage with Eminem, whose words and actions promote hate and violence against gays and lesbians." Senator Lynne Cheney, wife of the current US Vice-President, turned her latest attack on John. "Elton John has been good in the past about speaking out on issues of equality for gay people, on issues of being against violent language against gay people," she noted. "I am quite amazed and dismayed that he would choose to perform with Eminem." Peter Tatchell, of British gay rights protest group Outrage, was more succinct, and vicious: "It's a curious alliance – a bit like a Jewish performer doing a duet with an avowed Nazi." Only Ed Robertson, of fellow nominees Barenaked Ladies, could see the positive side: "Wow, Sir Elton! Eminem is going to call him a fucking fuck, kick him, and walk off the stage – it's going to be great!"

The ability of a gay pop star to enjoy *The Marshall Mathers LP*, and his willingness to then support its maker, seemed to be the real hook under the skin of Eminem's detractors this time, more than anything he had done himself. It revealed the enlivening, unpredictable nature of his words and possible reactions to their potency, the point of his work at its best, but one which was anathema to the pious, literal-minded pressure groups he so easily inflamed.

John's reaction was unrepentantly open-minded. "I don't know why everyone is getting so crazy about this – it's just pop music," he reasoned. "As a gay artist, I'm asked by a lot of people, 'but what about the content of Eminem's music?' It appeals to my English, black sense of humour. When I put the album on for the first time, I was in hysterics. If I thought for one minute that he was hateful, I wouldn't do it." John's disgust at real homophobic violence would be confirmed the next year, with *Songs From The West Coast*'s strong protest song about a gay student's murder, 'Wyoming'. But his reported promise to "have a word" with his new partner about toning down his musical message sounded unlikely. Eminem for his part declared he hadn't even known John was gay when their duet was suggested. But his reaction to finding out showed a tentative maturing of his suspicion of gay men. He told *Q*, of John's support: "I think it's hilarious and I think it's fucking great, because it shows that Elton John gets it. He understands where the fuck I'm coming from. My music is about what goes on in the world, I don't say one thing on my record that doesn't happen."

Hundreds of gay and female protesters demonstrated outside the Grammys, anyway, when they were finally awarded at LA's Staples Center, on February 21. Inside, Eminem won his three rap nominations. Dre was heard to mutter afterwards that the controversy had denied them the real prize of Best Album: "I think we was robbed." When Elton and Eminem walked on for their party piece, its more musically minded critics had their own fears confirmed. The waddling, hair-transplanted Briton, dressed for the occasion in a pink–polka-dotted yellow suit, looked ludicrous next to the new pop king; and his grandiose boom was no substitute for Dido on 'Stan' (his designated, gender-bending role). Plans to release the episode as a single in aid of musicians' charity Musicares were wisely shelved. But it spoke well for the sense of absurd, fearless theatre in both parties that it happened at all. On TV and newspapers around the world the image of a determined looking Eminem holding the raised fist of a clenched-jawed John, each looking as if they'd achieved something, sent a message quite apart from the music.

"I would say, 'Why?' to both of them?" GLAAD's Scott Seomin said when it was over. To which Eminem's press conference that night sent a clear reply: "If I didn't make a statement tonight, I don't know what else to do. I came to make an impact, I came to make a statement, and I guess I came to piss some people off." He felt, he added, that Elton's on-stage presence was the only way to answer the criticisms of the likes of GLAAD. "I didn't know anything about his personal life. I didn't really care." Before they performed, John added this: "I've met Eminem and I can say absolutely that he is not homophobic." Eminem had somehow managed to retract his homophobic reputation even as he enraged those it offended even more. He enjoyed his characteristic trick so much that he and John repeated their duet at the Brit Awards, in London on February 26. Returning to Britain mere weeks after his tour, Eminem was given his Best International Artist award by his unlikely new friend.

The early months of 2001 saw the more threatening, legal aspects of the fallout which had followed *The Marshall Mathers LP* start to settle, too. On February 14, in between his UK tour and the Grammys, Eminem appeared at Macomb County Court, Michigan, and agreed to a plea bargain from prosecutors over his alleged pistol-whipping of John Guerra. Wearing a dark suit and spectacles, he accepted the dropping of the felony charge of assault with a dangerous weapon, in return for pleading guilty to the potentially five-year felony offence of carrying a concealed weapon without a permit. "Mathers' attorneys will request a sentence of straight probation, and Marshall is looking forward to putting the matter behind him," said Interscope spokesman Dennis Dennehy. Probation was what even County assistant prosecutor David Portuesi expected from the judge when sentence was passed in April. "Mathers has no record and there was no serious injury," prosecutor Carl Malinga added.

Only Guerra's lawyer, John J. Gaber, was unhappy, claiming his client had not been consulted on the prosecutors' deal. "Eminem walked into a court with two or three lawyers," he sneered, "maybe the prosecutors are impressed with that. Through manoeuvring, they just have possession of a concealed weapon without a licence. That's a violation of the law without a victim . . . and the prosecutors are going along with this? And you tell me why."

A fresh, queasy aspect of American celebrity was certainly suggested by the squad of high-priced, middle-aged, neatly bearded lawyers pictures showed putting their sheepish client's case, on his return to court on April 10. Interscope's corporate funds were surrounding their most prized asset, a force field to prevent the law making his misdemeanours bring him low. The difference if Eminem had faced his charges three years earlier, coming to court alone from a trailer park, could only be guessed.

April's sentencing went smoothly, anyway. Judge Antonio Viviano imposed only two years probation. The terms included refraining from excessive alcohol or drug use, undergoing counselling, avoiding "assaultive behaviour", and a ban from owning or possessing weapons. Eminem also needed the judge's permission to leave the country. Viviano cautioned him that any violation of his probation, or criminal trouble, could lead to the full five years jail-time, for carrying a concealed weapon. Eminem was also fined $2,500, plus $500 in court costs, $60 to the Michigan crime victims' support fund, and $30 a month in supervision fees during probation. "I don't think it's a slap on the wrist," Viviano said.

His mother had been in court, seeing her son for the final time to date. "I'm sure he was worried," she told *NME*. "He wants to portray himself as a tough guy, and he's not." His look of inward concentration, hand rubbing his chin, as he was photographed standing to receive sentence, supported her claim. When it was over, he was, as he had been at the Grammys, unusually sober with reporters. "I'm glad the judge and the courts treated me fair and as a human being," he said. "I just want to get it behind me, and get back to spending time with my little girl and making music." Afterwards, "he didn't celebrate," his lawyer Walter Pisczatowski told *NME*. "We talked and then he went out to lunch with his family. It was just a small get-together."

On June 28, Eminem would admit charges of carrying and brandishing a concealed weapon, during his other altercation a year earlier, with Douglas Dail. He was sentenced to a year's probation, and $2,300 in fines and costs. With barely a whisper, the consequences of his Slim Shady eruption, which had loomed over him for so long, had vanished from his life.

On March 1, something still more central finished. Kim filed for divorce a second time, citing "a breakdown of the marriage relationship . . . and [because] there remains no reasonable likelihood that the marriage can be preserved." By the 20th, it had already been agreed that she and Eminem would share legal and physical custody of Hailie, and that Eminem would keep their $450,000 home, and write her a $475,000 cheque for a new one. "It was easily arrived at," Eminem's lawyer on this occasion, Harvey Hauer told the *Detroit News*, "because each person was concerned with the family and concerned with the well-being of their daughter." It was "not contentious" at all. The divorce was finalised without fuss that October. "It's always been Marshall's desire that whatever happened, happened in the best interest of the child," Hauer said. The heat and bruising fury that had hurt the couple for so long, and fuelled Eminem's most extreme art, had burnt out. The one-time wild teenage lovers were now civilly distant adults, for the sake of their daughter. Eminem's most gruelling love had stopped in its tracks. 'Kim''s argument was over.

On May 1, Mathers-Briggs agreed to settle her court case, too, the $10 million in damages she'd asked for plummeting to $25,000. But the complications that followed showed this legal war was still causing strain and hurt, with Eminem's mother now the one suffering, and no healing in sight. She fired her lawyer, saying she had been "confused and pressured" into the settlement, which she then appealed. Betty Kresin depicted the wounded bewilderment her daughter appeared to be experiencing to a reporter: "Debbie dropped the lawsuit because she wanted to try reconciling with her son. But she's told me she wants to bring it back, and then she doesn't, and I don't know what's going on." Judge Mark Switalski enforced the original settlement on June 6 anyway, on the basis of Mathers-Briggs' verbal agreement, recorded on a voice-mail to Gibson, and Gibson's letter on her behalf to the court. Subsequent "remorse", he said, changed nothing. After costs, Mathers-Briggs was left with a derisory $1,600. "Marshall thinks that's hilarious," she sighed to *NME*.

Suddenly, all Eminem's troubles since *Marshall Mathers* were gone. Now, all he had to do was follow it.

10

THE DIRTY DOZEN

East Detroit was where the next salvo came from. That was where Eminem's schoolboy compadres D12 still lived, anonymously, in the sort of chipped clapboard houses their star rapper had abandoned. That was where *Spin* magazine was forced to seek them out, listening to the group's five black members' sanguine stories of police harassment, carjackings and shootings, in April 2001. The occasion was the release of D12's début LP, *Devil's Night*, on June 19. Eminem's name was written boldly on its back, as its "Executive Producer", a patronage-denoting title previously used by Dre on him, and he played his full part inside. But, barely a year after *The Marshall Mathers LP*'s full-frontal assault, *Devil's Night*, it was quickly clear, was covering fire.

D12's six members, six years after its inception, were now all veterans of the Detroit hip-hop scene which had burgeoned around them: Rufus Johnson, aka Bizarre, 25, had released an EP, *Attack Of The Weirdos*, and shared time with Eminem in The Outsidaz; Denaun Porter, aka Kon Artis, 25, had followed his production work on *Infinite* by producing other underground Detroit rappers, and recorded an unreleased EP as Da Brigade with Von Carlisle, aka Kuniva, 25; Deshaun Holton, aka Proof, 27, had made an unreleased EP with the group 5 Ela; Ondre Moore, aka Swift, ex-Rabeez With Baredda, was the replacement for Bugz, shot two years before. And then there was Marshall Mathers, aka Eminem, aka Slim Shady, aka the eight-million-selling man, the 28-year-old senior player. But that *Spin* piece showed events since their inception had not unbalanced D12 in the ways you would expect.

"The thing about D12 is there ain't no leader," Bizarre told the magazine, even if "Em did sell eight million copies, so his opinion does matter."

"We'll still whip his ass [if he's in the wrong]," said Kuniva. "We don't think about it like, 'Oh, this guy, he sold eight million records, we can't speak to him," Bizarre added. "We think about him as our boy, who we always known all our life. He never changed, really."

"The crew's got to stay together," Eminem concluded. "There's gonna be fights. But we're always gonna be friends, because that's what we were before any of this shit. That's the most important thing. Just to fuckin' remember that we're friends."

"We agreed that the first one who made it would come back and get the others," he simply added to another reporter, suggesting a romantic bond more like the till-death blood brothers of The Wild Bunch than the immoral Dirty Dozen; the honourable Western outlaw self-image they'd started with in 1995 was clearly still strong in their hearts.

The photos in *Spin*, of D12 with the Lafayette Coney Island hot dog diner to themselves, impishly clowning with staff, confirmed the comfort of his posse for Eminem. Relaxed and laughing, for the only time I know of in public (apart from one early photo of him dancing and hugging with D12 and Kim, everyone innocently happy), he is lost in pleasure at the others' antics. For once, as the fat and slyly funny Bizarre perches a British bobby's helmet on his head, and Kon Artis takes charge in the kitchen, no one is watching Eminem. In the pictures, he looks like just another scrawny, amiable white guy, pleased to be allowed in the gang. "There's no fucking master plan, no pressure, no commercial intent with D12," he explained to *Q*. "It's just something I do with my friends and it's fun. It's not a career thing at all. I don't have to be in the fucking limelight all the time, which is good."

Devil's Night was further evidence of Eminem's diluted, unpressured presence in D12. When it came out, so soon after the group had done little but get in his way at his lame British shows, I reviewed it dismissively, calling them Eminem's Wings. Like Paul McCartney's wilfully democratic post-Beatles band of musos, their presence excused him from any sudden shortfall in talent after *Marshall Mathers*' heights. He could even have a flop record with them, and not get the blame.

Listened to more carefully, though, D12 and *Devil's Night* had more substance. Eminem had started his own imprint, Shady Records, to get his friends released through Interscope, and, also producing eight tracks (to Dre's four, and Kon Artis' two), it showed him using his success to seize a new level of control. Rapping alongside the Detroit crew he'd grown up with, some of his more freakish attributes were suddenly given context. And when he did take the mic himself, he had the old implacable presence. At its best, *Devil's Night* took the previous year's notorious ammunition, and resumed his war with the world.

It was a Detroit record through and through. Intense, isolated sessions in Dre's studio did not feel right this time. Instead D12, and Eminem's key collaborators – Jeff Bass, Mike Elizondo, even Dre – decamped to the 54 Sound studio in Ferndale, a small white suburban community to the west of Warren, with almost identical battered frame bungalows, and the inevitable southern border, 8 Mile. There, cheap motels, a cemetery and the State Fair surrounded a bare bus terminal which would shoot you straight back into downtown Detroit's ghetto heart. In this place, the slickness and self-absorption of Eminem's last two LPs fell away, and the references to the city – as Detroit, or Amityville – piled high. Even native son Iggy Pop got a mention.

Eminem's increased involvement in production, and new Dre directions, also made *Devil's Night*'s sound at once more basically, funkily hip-hop, and more inclusively American. Simply, it was more like rock music. The influence of Eminem's method of composition – building ideas by bouncing them off Jeff Bass's guitar and piano riffs – must have been significant, as his own rock knowledge was slight. But the single 'Purple Pills' was typical of this barrier-breaking mood anyway, its scratching and booty-moving bounce ending in a redolent harmonica solo by Ray Gale. Dre-produced track 'Fight Music' meanwhile was built from an ominous Elizondo bass line, clearly echoing Led Zeppelin's 'Kashmir'. Rasping hard rock guitars were all over the record, as were welcome female R&B voices, for the songs about sex and filth, and, on the Eminem-produced 'Blow My Buzz', a West Coast-pleasing snatch of P-Funk.

This base-covering was nothing new: hip-hop's initial crossover into mainstream acceptance in the Eighties had come from Run-DMC's use of Aerosmith's dinosaur rock, and the example of Cypress Hill's grunge-rap ten years later, and hip-hop's subsequent domination of the American charts, had shifted rock towards rap's beats, in the form of the massively popular Nu-Metal. But while Eminem and Dre were not above considering such commercial factors, the blurring of demographic lines in *Devil's Night* went deeper.

As it was made by five young black men from the ghetto, and a white best friend who was partly raised among them, and who had the ear of more black and white listeners than the rest put together, such crossed borders were perhaps inevitable. But tracks like 'Fight Music' and 'Devil's Night' showed the changes that could cause. The former, Eminem barked, was *"just some shit for some kids to trash their rooms to/ just refuse whenever they're asked to do shit/ a drastic movement of people acting stupid."* On the latter, he tauntingly imagined *"a whole generation of kids blowing their brains out to this Kurt Cobain music/ . . . as soon as they heard it went out and murdered and maimed to it."* Though the reference to Cobain was ironic – and disrespectful – these songs moved surprisingly near Nirvana's old constituency of disaffected young whites. Eminem's commentary on Columbine – hardly a hip-hop staple – was also resumed, his amused sympathy with the reviled white killers even more explicit: *"making fun of your trenchcoat/ that's how students get fucked up . . ."* His Cobain-like solidarity with alienated teens was then confirmed in a personal context at the climax of 'Fight Music', even as sonically it veered towards a white nu-metal anthem: *"I came to save these new generations of babies/ from parents who failed to raise 'em 'cos they're lazy."* In the same song, meanwhile, other D12 members imagined crashing through a club with casual reference to black icons: *"any nigga looking too hard/ We Rodney Kinging 'em."* "Nigga" was now a sayable word on an Eminem album; though not, of course, by Eminem.

The sampled, confrontational opening of Curtis Mayfield's 1970 '(Don't Worry) If There's A Hell Down Below We're All Gonna Go' – *"Niggers! Crackers! Whiteys! Jews!"* – on 'That's How . . .' showed D12's playful awareness of their racial confounding. The fact remained that, on what had been intended as an underground, uncommercial hip-hop album, Eminem's own contributions moved it closer to white concerns than anything he'd done before. The deliberately brattish rebellion of 'Fight Music' – making kids *"trash"* rooms and not do anything they're told – was a 13-year-old white suburban idea of punk attitude, the sort of self-indulgent sulkiness which had eventually made grunge risible. Black hip-hop fans with more pressing concerns in South Central LA or downtown Detroit must have found it quite hard to give a fuck. But D12 were merely shoving at the door into the mass market gangsta-rap had long catered to; with a white rapper on board, that door could be snapped off its hinges.

Most of *Devil's Night* was ideal anyway for sniggering teens of all colours, in a less contentious way. It was a foul-mouthed stoner album *par excellence*, the least "meaningful" record its makers could manage. Fair warning was given of what was coming in the opening "Public Service Announcement", helpfully listing D12's favourite offensive terms – "lesbian", "faggot", "fudgepacker", "clit-licker". "It's not that they don't have no creativity," the announcer (aka Kuniva) chided. "That ain't the case. We just like saying shit like that just to fuck with you . . . bitch."

"It was to be disgusting," Proof said of their aims to *Spin*. "To piss people off, raise eyebrows," Eminem concurred. "Our politics are a little more incorrect than Eminem's," Proof added, with frightening accuracy.

This was the obscene badinage Eminem and his one-time roommates had amused themselves with in private, put on record; the mind that had carelessly toyed with *"raping his own mother"* egged on by five equally untrammelled friends. 'Shit On You', the single released before the album, showed how far below the belt D12 had deliberately set their sights, as did LP opener 'Shit Can Happen', both single-mindedly scatological in a way Eminem on his own showed no interest in.

Nor was he always the strongest swearer. Bizarre's claim in *Spin* that he had "the foulest style" proved true, causing even Slim to feign dismay – *"Bizarre, you're on Capital!"* With a voice sometimes slow, deep and flat like a stone killer, then on the verge of childish tears at chastisement of his peccadilloes, Bizarre was a memorable sex monster in the style of the Wu-Tang Clan's Ol' Dirty Bastard. Whether fucking his dog, enticing under-age girls and putting his mother on the game, or wanking into anti-freeze till his penis was burning, fucking groupies with genital warts and eating his girlfriend's miscarriage, he was an object lesson in deflecting disgust with creativity, and in showing up Eminem's suddenly pedestrian "potty" mouth. It was still left to Eminem, of course, to defend such art in *Spin*: "Remember how fun it was to cuss when you were in the first grade? Just to be like, *'Fuck.' 'Shit.'* But still, it's just words." Kuniva put the case best in *Loaded*: "Look, freedom of speech is the shit. If I just did a whole song about fuckin' dogs in they ass and it sells a million records, why are you mad at me? It just means there's a million motherfuckers that wanna hear that. Where's the problem?"

D12 certainly gave full value when it came to swearing, and sex ('Nasty Mind', 'American Psycho', 'Pimp Like Me'), drugs ('Purple Pills', 'Blow My Buzz', 'These Drugs'), and punch-ups ('That's How', 'Fight Music', 'Instigator'). As a successor to *License To Ill*, 2 Live Crew, or Cheech & Chong, they had done a decent job. As a successor to *The Marshall Mathers LP* though, my original disappointment remains. *Devil's Night* confirmed the faults first exposed when D12 took the stage in Manchester that year. In their comforting company, one voice among six, the creative tension Eminem had felt battling the world with his words mostly melted. His desire to dispel the monstrous myths about him to that young crowd now filled what was largely a comedy album. It was as if, in reaction to *Marshall Mathers*' shattering success, he was slowly returning his artistically vital Slim Shady side to the shadows. Now he preferred us to see him with the mask off, swearing and spliffed up with his mates. But the results on *Devil's Night* were so often sluggish, meandering, repetitive, and short on the synaptic leaps he had previously made with ease that you couldn't help wishing he'd drop his friends, put the mask back on, and sell us the evil, angry myth again. Fortunately, there were corners of the album where Slim and his compulsive demons still breathed.

Eminem's autobiographical instincts, for instance, were still unflinching. He sketched an update on his troubles since he'd last been heard from over several tracks, seeming to like skating on thin legal ice. 'Pistol Pistol' and 'Words Are Weapons' responded aggressively to his disarming by the courts, while 'Purple Pills' returned to another litigation scene: *"Cool, calm, just like my Mom / With a couple of valium inside her palm."* But the most fascinating development was in his attitude to Kim. D12 had added some unsavoury memories of their relationship to 'That's How . . .' – *"Choking your wife all in front of your peeps ('Bitch!') / She tossed a brick through the window of your jeep / They're back together by the end of the week."* But on 'Girls', written after their personal battles were over, Eminem saw Kim more clearly, as someone who, like D12, was on his side, not the world's: *"Now I've got five dogs that'd die for me like I'd die for them / I'd fight for them, swing or shoot, like I'd fight for Kim / All of them been with me through this fucked up life that I'm in."* It was a lone, late admission but, after 'Kim', an unexpected and touching one.

Devil's Night also included one track the equal of anything Eminem had done before, on which every member of D12 played their part. The album's climactic effort, 'Revelation' was a jolting reminder of why he had seemed so dangerous and essential, six short months before. Produced by Dre, it confirmed the Doctor's own increasing rockist inclinations, as it began and ended with wailing guitar riffs from Mike Elizondo, and was built on an ominously unresolved, rising guitar line. Pink Floyd's anti-education 'Another Brick In The Wall' was also quoted, but 'Revelation' was a far more sophisticated work. Eminem sang its chorus in a sulky, petulant voice, a teenager throwing a tantrum. But his words built into an excoriation not only of education, but of the pious hopes of liberal America, and ended in territory he'd never broached before, somewhere between existential hedonism, and imminent rapture: *"I don't wanna go to school/ I don't need no education/ I don't wanna be like you/ I don't wanna save the nation/ I just wanna live my life/ Every day a celebration/ One day I'm gonna leave this world/ I'm waitin' for the Revelation."* Whether he was playing another role, in suddenly voicing this apocalyptic spiritual vision – which must swim in the heads of many alienated, Midwestern teens – or really had such religious dreams himself could only be guessed. But he had never before "acted" attitudes which were not partly his.

Within this, 'Revelation' played out a more ordinary apocalypse, of teenagers refusing education, railing against parents, and falling by the wayside, sometimes by their own gun-wielding hand. With each D12 member taking a verse, the similarity of black and white adolescent experience was emphasised. Bizarre led off with his usual six-feet-deep deadpan humour, concluding his tale of inter-family crack-dealing and AIDS by declaring, *"There's three things that keep me from being a Nazi/ I'm black, I'm gay and my Dad's Liberace."* For the rest, though, the stories of threatening a female teacher and mother who try to corral a boy's wild-ness, student, parent and teacher bullies creating trench-coated outcasts, truant escape, peer pressure to drug-deal, drunk, lazy, violent and sexually abusive parents are jaggedly individual but uniform pictures of teenage devastation.

Though the jet-black jokes keep coming (*"Daddy no!"* and *"I'm gonna kill myself!"* were screamed with satiric exaggeration, like the female begging on 'Kim'), Kuniva's verse in particular touched hurt as deep as anything Eminem had managed. Ignored or punched by his Dad *"like a grown fucking man"*, he flees, feels sexually useless, flicks through porn and pines for a gun, to fix things, crying he's *"about to lose my mind."*

The lack of personal responsibility in these adolescent voices, left float-ing in a world blamed on useless, oppressive adults, is a telling American tale in itself. It was how Eminem had always excused raging at his mother, an immature, arrested development that 'Revelation' suggested was shared by all his friends. His teenage-fit parody on its chorus at least indicated he knew how childish this was. And, for once, safe in the company of his old gang as they too cried and confessed, Eminem used his own verse for adult reflection on his teenage self. *"My mother was unable to raise me,"* of course.

But then, Marshall too was *"full of crazy rage, an angry teenager/. . . ooh, I was stupid, no one could tell me nothing."* Most movingly, this was where he remembered how gangsta-rap derailed his ordinary life, sounding lost in its spell again: *"hip-hop overwhelmed me, to the point where it had me in a whole 'nother realm/. . . it felt like we was on welfare but wealthy."* This second supernatural vision of transcendence was broken by a typically snotty "fuck you" to the Lincoln school he left for rap: *"a dropout that quit. Stupid as shit, rich as fuck, and proud of it."*

The track as a whole offered no solutions, accepted no blame, nursed no social wounds; if anything, it inflamed them. "All I see is violence," a voice said somewhere in the mix, and rage was offered in return. Rip up your schoolbooks, shoot your father and slap your mother, it seemed literally to advise. But, moving between parody, commentary and confession with practised ease, what Eminem had really done, near the end of an inessential, stopgap release, was once again show more of what squirmed in America's underbelly in one five minute song than most artists managed in a career. 'Revelation' proved he still mattered. *Devil's Night* meant it had to.

The album was received adequately. Reviewers treated it with less respect than an Eminem record – "not exactly pushing the envelope", said *NME*; "feels a bit perfunctory", said *Rolling Stone* – and sales followed suit. In the UK, it entered the charts at number two, with sales of 54,000, the most for a rap band's début. In the US, it reached number one, and sold a million. The drop in interest whenever D12 played without Eminem showed the real reason for the sales. Considering its faults, it did him no harm.

Censors and politicians certainly trailed him through 2001 as if his threat was undiminished. On June 6, the US government's Federal Communications Commission levied a $17,000 fine on KKMG, a Top 40 station in Pueblo, Colorado – a Republican, Bible Belt community – for playing the edited version of 'The Real Slim Shady', after a listener complaint a year earlier. Even in bleeped form, it was deemed "patently offensive as measured by contemporary community standards", with "unmistakable offensive sexual references . . . that appear intended to pander and shock." The draconian decision "sent a tremor throughout the radio industry", according to *Billboard*, and radio corporation Clear Channel Communications warned its stations that "the industry is deemed to be on notice of the song's indecency, and subsequent fines for broadcasting the song may be higher." An immediate outcry from musicians, radio programmers and First Amendment activists, and a keynote address on indecency by Def Jam co-founder Russell Simmons at the following week's inaugural Hip-Hop Summit, forced the FCC to back down and rescind its fine in January 2002. It was a rare victory in two decades of censors' attacks on pop. "Freedom of speech is the shit," as Kuniva had wisely observed. But few other than Eminem at that moment could have drawn such absurd, unsustainable fire in the first place.

On June 22, three days after *Devil's Night*'s release, MTV then banned its single 'Purple Pills' for its unmissable drug references. As with the "clean" versions of his solo albums, Eminem raised no murmur of protest, and D12 re-recorded the song as 'Purple Hills'. He might believe in free speech, and think his band was "underground" but faced with people not buying his records, he always went with the flow.

July 5 saw a more serious attack, as Australian Prime Minister John Howard condemned an upcoming Sydney concert, saying Eminem's lyrics were "sickening, demean women and encourage violence". Ticket sales slumped as the possibility rose of his visa being denied. Christian Democratic Party MP the Rev. Fred Nile meanwhile called for the concert to be 'R'-rated, banning it to under-18s, in the fiercest terms: "Eminem's rap songs are obscene and provocative as they incite violence and rebellion against parental and police authority. The audience will also be encouraged to chant in unison socially unacceptable, obscene words such as FUCK, over and over again! . . . Something has to be done, as Australia already has the highest level of teenage suicides and increasing teenage school and gang violence, which is incited by Eminem's violent, murderous message of death and depression." In America, they could have used that on the posters. Of more consequence to Eminem was that, according to the Christian Democrats, they had the support of his mother. Raising her voice for the first time since her court humiliation, she was quoted as saying: "My son's foul-mouthed material should not be heard by children. I would say ban these shows for people under 18." On August 1, the Scottish Catholic Charismatic Renewal Group also handed a petition to Glasgow Council, calling for a ban on Eminem playing there that month.

As in Canada, and as in Britain previously, all this uproar amounted to nothing in the end. For all the traditional authoritarian language used by his official enemies, what Eminem was proving on this year of touring was that it was he, with his multinational backing, money, fame and free speech rights, who had the power in modern democracies. Ministers, church or Prime, could rant, but they were no threat to him now.

Dre, speaking to *NME*, did not even bother to hide the attacks' positive effects: "It's exciting to me as long as it doesn't go any farther than this. I don't want to go to a position where our stuff is being watched so closely that we're going to have to watch what we're saying in the studio. Any time you've got genius and you're presenting it to the masses, you're going to be looked at in a certain way. That's the reason N.W.A. was getting so much flack, because we had every kid in the ghetto's ear and they were ready to wear what we wore and said what we said, y'know? And that's the reason for all the turmoil with Eminem."

When Eminem reached Sydney in August, for a reputed (Australian) $1 million fee, his single show had failed to sell out, and his chainsaw's teeth had been pulled, the furore doing at least that much harm. Still, he told the audience, "I'm lovin' this shit . . . I might buy a fuckin' house out here! Bet your fuckin' Prime Minister wouldn't like that though." Kim was called a "cheating bitch", he pretended to have brought his "pistol" with him. But everything else – the setlist, the props, the "pill-popping" – was the same pantomime routine he'd trailed round the world for over a year. And, as in Britain, the response, once the storm around it broke, was disappointment. *NME*'s reporter noted that "it is near-impossible to take him even remotely seriously . . . he's little more than a hip-hop Robbie Williams."

When he returned to Britain at the end of the month, for his biggest ever gig there, a slot headlining the Reading Festival that court cases had delayed by a year, the response was muted, and the set was still unchanged. *NME* again: "Performing with D12 for the first half hour, with a ten-minute cartoon intermission and huge inflatable props, it seems like the most famous pop star in the world has difficulty walking his walk unaided." A "secret" warm-up gig at London's medium-sized Astoria theatre had failed to sell out, to smirks from a British music press which had previously stoked Eminem's notoriety. But that fire could not be relit. In September, after almost 100 near-identical shows supporting *The Marshall Mathers LP*, a US version of Reading signalled the tour's end. The idea of it had made him a national nightmare around the world. The reality had revealed too much of the nice American boy he could so often be. And, because it wasn't a very good show, it had made him not only more famous, but less of a star. The "shack" 's demolition was long overdue.

11

THE WAITING ROOM

With the very last juice squeezed from *The Marshall Mathers LP*, everything else that happened to Eminem in 2001 took on a sensation of drift. It was as if he had entered a sort of limbo between albums, with his celebrity sustaining enough atmospheric force to attract unrelated fragments of gossip, rumours of sex and violence. Cut loose from his teenage Detroit sweetheart, he was said to be dating other stars: first, 19-year-old R&B queen Beyonce Knowles of Destiny's Child; then, Irish pop singer Samantha Mumba, 18, glimpsed with him in posh LA hotels; even the fading diva Mariah Carey was placed at his house. None of it seemed quite real.

Violence, meanwhile, now happened in his name, without him lifting a finger. In August, rival Detroit rapper Esham alleged he had been attacked by D12 and dozens of their hangers-on while on tour in New Jersey, and blamed the absent Eminem, although the accusation went nowhere. Eminem told MTV Asia that, when he rejected two groupies who followed him to his hotel after a gig and left them in a room, they fell to fighting on the floor over whose fault it was, and continued their wrestling in the parking lot. "Little did they realise I didn't like either of them," he smirked with lordly disdain.

In Britain, his influence was still more distant. In March, a 14-year-old Devon boy sent home from school for stabbing a girl with a pen kicked in his house's door and stairs and scrawled on walls, after his mother criticised Eminem, whose "disturbing" lyrics were attacked by his lawyer. In August, a 24-year-old Kent man brutally thumped his girlfriend over the head with a dumbbell and shoe, and stabbed her foot with a screwdriver, after she turned off an Eminem CD because she didn't want her four-year-old hearing his lyrics. In January, a coroner in Teignmouth had criticised those lyrics at the inquest into the suicide of 17-year-old David

Hurcombe, who had printed out the words to 'Rock Bottom' before jumping in front of a train. In March, another inquest heard Hampshire 13-year-old Kayleigh Davies had become obsessed with Eminem before hanging herself. In July, an Oldham primary school headmaster discovered at least five of his pupils had cut their arms with pencil sharpeners, which they reportedly blamed on seeing "a fan" slash his wrists in 'Stan''s video (which contains no such sequence). "It has all been instigated by this idiot Eminem," the headmaster decided. PC Graham Jones was called in to explain to pupils "that what their idols do is not gospel. It is quite worrying that parents are allowing children to watch things like this. It could lead to serious injury, even death." The fact that those "things" did not exist to be watched in the first place showed the ill-informed, headline-led nature of the fuss. Eminem had done all he could to tell his fans not to follow his music's example. This rash of sad deaths, stupid, thuggish violence and juvenile experiments in Britain merely showed that the lost and unpleasant young souls in his songs existed outside America. His name's attachment to them showed it now had a life beyond his control.

In the absence of a new record, others also began to make records about him. In September, Tori Amos released *Strange Little Girls*, a selection of songs written by men but reinterpreted with female characters at their cores. Among covers ranging from Tom Waits' 'Time' to Slayer's 'Raining Blood', Eminem's ''97 Bonnie & Clyde' was the track critics zeroed in on. Leaving the lyrics as they were, Amos sang them starkly, in the previously erased voice of the wife lying in the trunk. By its existence, it dragged Eminem's misogyny into terrain he could not have anticipated. A woman had finally returned his hate to him, in his own words.

"I've always found it fascinating how men say things and women hear them," Amos told the *LA Times*. "In 'Bonnie & Clyde', that was Eminem – or one of the many people living inside him – and he killed his wife. What intrigued me in the way he told the story was this rhythmic kind of justification. You have to have empathy for him. I did when I heard it. But she has to have a voice." To MTV, she spoke almost mystically of her relationship to the battered Kim of the song. "'Bonnie & Clyde' is a song that depicts domestic violence very accurately, right on the money. But there was one person who definitely wasn't dancing to this thing, and that's the woman in the trunk. And she spoke to me. She grabbed me by the hand and said, 'You need to hear this how I heard it.'"

Like my female friend with experience of misogyny and male violence

Amos, a rape victim, wasn't threatened or surprised by the song, and wanted its angry, unchecked words to be heard. "Music is always a reflection of the hearts and minds of the culture," she told MTV. "If you're singing songs that are about cutting women up, usually these guys are tapping into an unconscious male rage that is real – they're just able to harness it. So to shut them up isn't the answer. They're a gauge; they're showing you what's really happening in the psyche of a lot of people."

It was as mature, insightful and fair a response as Eminem could have wished for; better than the man who on 'Shit On You' accurately rapped *"over-reaction is my only reaction"* managed to female and gay attacks on himself. Where she split from him was in his defence of his work's careless extremity, repeated so often by now that he hardly seemed to hear the phrases as he mouthed them: that *"I didn't know if you'd do it or not"*, that these were just words, that speech was free. "I would hear a lot of people say, 'They're only words, what is everyone going on about?'" Amos countered, to MTV. "I believe in freedom of speech, but you cannot separate yourself from your creation. Words are like guns. Whether you choose the graciousness of Tom Waits or the brutality of 'Bonnie & Clyde', they're equally powerful."

In the North-east of England, meanwhile, The Pet Shop Boys were recording a similarly cogent response to Eminem's homophobia. "Eminem's defence of the homophobic lyrics on his albums has always been that he's not speaking as himself, he's speaking as a character, and he's representing homophobia in America," their singer-lyricist Neil Tennant noted. "I thought it would be quite interesting to take that method and just to present rap in this homosexual context. I mean, there obviously are gay rap stars."

'The Night I Fell In Love', one of the strongest songs on The Pet Shop Boys' March 2002 album *Release*, was therefore a narrative of a teenage boy's night of lust and love with a barely disguised Eminem. To a softly swelling, romantic melody, he's introduced to this nameless rap star backstage, and taken to his video camera-equipped room for a *"private performance"*, ending with the rapper joking at breakfast the next morning *"about Dre and his homies and folks"*. Tennant had obviously thought about his subject enough to penetrate past Eminem's image to his private character, as the boy notes, *"I was surprised he spoke so politely"*, and *"he couldn't have been a nicer bloke"*; the boy's seduction is gently consensual.

In some ways, 'The Night I Fell In Love' is an answer song to 'Stan',

Tennant clearly inspired by it to write another angle on fan love, with Stan's advances responded to more positively. Tennant's rapper even quotes 'Stan''s lyrics, as if nervous he's about to vanish into the song: *"Hey, man! Your name isn't Stan, is it? We should be together!"* So Eminem's greatest work had yet another layer added to it. Tennant's cleverest critique, though, was simply to sing the fan's memoir in his own, fey, Northern English voice, bringing the rapper's street Americanisms thudding down to earth. The breakfast they shared was surely an English fry-up, and Tennant saved his best deflating line for last, when the lovers part quickly: *"but I thought that was cool/ 'cos I was already late for school."*

"I was thinking of the boy as the schoolboy in *Queer As Folk*, someone like that, going to see a concert at Manchester Arena or somewhere like that, and he ends up backstage because he's cute, and he gets off with the rap star," Tennant explained. "I think if rap's going to be provocative that you can be provocative back about it. I like Eminem's records. I think he's brilliant." "I've got his doll on the mantelpiece," fellow Boy Chris Lowe added, helpfully.

When the schoolboy *"asked/ why have I heard so much about him being charged with homophobia and stuff/ he just shrugged"*. But Tennant, as a critical gay fan of Eminem, had constructed a far more accurate, effective undermining of his homophobic leanings than any of the outraged pressure groups who had tried to shut him up, and just fuelled his fire. 'The Night I Fell In Love' begged for a single release, to take the argument into the charts where it belonged. Eminem offered no public response to either Tennant or Amos (a spokesperson said he was "aware" of the latter's effort, but "hadn't heard it").

Nor did he comment on the equally cheeky "Eminem Look-Alike 8-Page Pull-Out Special" in the April 2001 issue of gay porn magazine *Euroboy*. In dungarees (initially) and hockey mask, 18-year-old Matthew licked his chainsaw, and gently inserted it where even the toughest rapper might hesitate. Editor Sean Spence told *NME*: "The common consensus here is that Eminem is an asshole and gay men shouldn't waste money on his records. But personally I like his music and think he's attractive. We're making a political statement and having a bit of a laugh. Matthew really wants to carry on as Eminem, stripping at hen parties and gay clubs." Matthew himself added: "Even my mum thinks I look like Eminem. I love his music, his lyrics – in fact, I love everything about him. People say he's homophobic, but I'd still like to give him one!"

The army Eminem had imagined in 'The Real Slim Shady' 's video had come true, doing his work for him all over the world, while he vanished from view. But recruiting had taken place without his permission. So these Slims not only trashed their rooms and screamed, "Fuck you!", but stabbed their girlfriends, slashed their arms, hanged themselves, resurrected his wife, made him come out as gay, and saucily stripped for gay men and straight women. The value of letting him speak could not have been clearer. The unpredictability of responses to his songs of provocation, satire and rage, and the ability of the groups he targeted to enjoy and turn his words, and good looks, to their own ends, had been demonstrated all over the world.

The real Eminem, meanwhile, continued to live his life as best he could. It was his fractious relationship with his family, still, which damaged and dominated it, the hurts of childhood ruling his heart even now, after so much success.

In August 2001, on the eve of his Reading appearance, the *News Of The World* published an extensive "letter" from his long-lost father, Marshall Mathers II. The accompanying picture showed a 50-year-old, bespectacled, grey-mulleted man, gaunt in the face and heavy in the belly, in a jumper that was too big for him. The letter – actually an interview with the tabloid's reporter – explained that this Marshall had been told of his now-famous namesake by his son Michael, 23 (one of two children by his second wife, along with Sarah, 21 – "They're the half-brother and sister you never had," he said, enticingly). There followed a plea of innocence for every sin Eminem had laid at his door. *He* hadn't been drinking and doing drugs when his baby was born; *he* hadn't been fucking Debbie's best friend while his wife was giving birth; it wasn't *him* who walked out (reading Debbie say that made him "choke with tears of rage"). When Debbie left with his darling boy, he had searched everywhere for them. "On the word of God" he knew nothing about the letters Eminem said he sent to him, and had got back, "returned to sender". A photo of him going into an Alcoholics Anonymous meeting was just "lies" – "I was going into a DONUT shop." He had a new girlfriend now, Teresa Harbin, 40. "You'd like her. Me?" he continued, as if his son had just respectfully cut in. "I'm a construction worker . . . I'd get on a plane right now, this second, and go anywhere in the world if you'd meet with me. Please get in touch." The apologia seemed credible in parts. But its tone of wounded innocence, and its disingenuous claim that, "I'm not after any handout", made in a tabloid notorious for paying its informants handsomely, didn't sound like a loving, pining parent.

Eminem's response came in 2002, in *The Source*: "Fuck him!" He remembered with perfect clarity his father ringing his father's aunt's house, while he played there as a little boy, and never speaking to him. He recalled it in a tone of still childish dismay, as if that part of his life was still frozen. He had already seen his father, such a painful absence for so long, blundering back into view with his pleas on TV, trying to reach his rich, famous son. "For 24, 25 years of my life, he never wanted anything to do with me," Eminem coldly noted. "And him saying he couldn't get in touch with me, it's bullshit. It was cool to see him to know, hey, this is what I'm gonna look like when I get old, but that's it. All I can say about him is, fuck him."

But it was Eminem's relationship with his mother, so much more active, angry and intimate over so many years, which remained the worst sore in his life. It just got more poisonously bitter as each month went on, none of the good things that happened to him making him relent. In this time their bond, once one of love, took on the shape of genuine tragedy, perhaps the greatest he was a part of. Although, blinded by hate, he was of course unable to see it that way.

Debbie Mathers-Briggs' first action after the effective failure of her lawsuit had been to follow up her single about her son by writing a book with the provisional title, *My Life With Eminem*. It was not the sensible course of someone seeking reconciliation, and when *NME* spoke to her before Reading she revealed his inevitable reaction: "He's pissed about it. He's like, 'You and my dad are trying to cash in on me, now you're writing an effing book, go ahead and try and ruin my career.'" There was hypocrisy here on his side, of course – that career had partly been based on exploiting his fiery rows with his mother and Kim, so sulking that Mathers-Briggs, having failed to silence him, should comment back was not fair. But then fairness and restraint didn't seem on the agenda of anyone in the family by this time, and the book, bound to anger, was just another chip in a furious game which hurt its players with each new turn.

Mathers-Briggs' comments to *NME* about her son's alleged continuing drink and drug intake ("He needs to go into rehab") showed her uncompromising mood. She indicated, too, that money was a factor in her writing the book, allied with resentment ("He's never done anything for me in his life, and I was behind him every step of the way"). Eminem's attitude was revealed in what she said was their last conversation. When she called, he had told her he had a woman with him (Mariah Carey, went the rumour), but if she wanted to move back to Michigan, he would help. The next morning, she said, he called back, to spit: "I lied, I had company. The only thing I would put you in is a damn pine box." The undeclared motive in his mother's sometimes confused, impulsive or stupid moves in their feud, which would become clearer as the months went by, was perhaps one of self-preservation, as Eminem moved to cut her out of his family and life with all the vicious concentration of those final words.

The first step had been taken before that August interview with *NME*, and explained her frustration in it. Eminem had finally moved from his exposed old house in the heart of Detroit to a large new property in a gated, secure community, a place more practical for a man of his suddenly vast fame and wealth. He had immediately moved in, not his mother (naturally), but her 25-year-old half-sister, Betti Schmitt, and her husband and children. For Mother's Day, Eminem had given Schmitt a new car, with "not even a card" for Mathers-Briggs. He wasn't thinking straight, she complained, he couldn't "move them in and replace your own blood, which is me and his little brother Nathan." But such an act could be about nothing but replacing blood – choosing who would now be his family, and who would not. Still seething about all the times he'd been cast out of his mother's home, there was something more naked than symbolism about the way he now locked her out of his mansion.

Mathers-Briggs and her mother were united in thinking Schmitt was a "gold-digger", which they both also thought about the suddenly divorce-rich Kim (Eminem, the lone multi-millionaire in a poor family, must himself have been racked with suspicion about each relative's motive in talking to him, almost as much as he was with new "friends"). But the strain of events was now also tearing Betty Kresin from her daughter, even as that daughter lost her son. That ill-starred lawsuit was again the damning act. "I turned my back on my daughter," Kresin told the *Sydney Sun-Herald*. "I said, 'If you don't drop that lawsuit I'm going to come to your house, run you over and go to prison myself. How can you do that to your own son?'" Of the book, she told *NME*: "She sued her son, and I'll probably sue her." As to Eminem, Kresin too was feeling the chill. In February, she admitted to Trevor McDonald on ITV: "Our relationship is not a good one. It has changed. It was good up until Christmas 1999." She would not elaborate on what had caused her exile.

But it was in *The Source* the next year that the now unshakeable, central nature of Eminem's hate for his mother became apparent. It was here that he told the story of her wishing he had died instead of his uncle, with undimmed resentment. "I want her to apologise," he said, in a flat tone suggesting things had gone too far for that. "But that ain't enough because I know she ain't gonna change. She'll go right back to doing what she was doing. She's not right, not now." As to what she was doing, he wouldn't say: "I don't want to get sued again." But the degree of distaste he now felt for her was shown in his decision not to let her granddaughter, now six, set eyes on her. "I don't feel like Hailie would ever grow up to resent me for that," he said, echoing his refusal to see how demonising her mother Kim, his other female *bête noir*, might harm their child. "I feel like when Hailie is old enough to know better and wants to find out about her grandmother, she can. But right now her mind is too young to be around that. I don't trust my mother around my daughter. My mother wrote her letters, before she could even read. Real sick letters that she wanted me to read to Hailie or somethin'? I don't know. I throw them in the trash."

In his childhood, his own letters to his father had never been read by their target; his own grandmother had sometimes been kept from him. Now, like a petty child suddenly turned into an upside-down family's head, he was using his unexpected powers to repeat these offences, to get back at the grown-ups who'd hurt him. The imbalance of his millionaire adult status right now, and the weakness of his mother in the face of it, wasn't something he could see, it seemed. But his mother's actions in the closing months of 2001 showed the damage she was starting to sustain.

According to a report on Sony's Musiclub site in January 2002, when he would no longer take her calls, she had moved to an apartment near his Detroit mansion, to try to get close again. Betty Kresin's comments on what happened next showed she too was still outside the mansion's warmth: "My daughter was involved in a car crash when she first moved there. She nearly killed herself when she was driving Nate to school. She was taken to hospital in an ambulance, but Eminem wouldn't change his behaviour or visit her. She even tore her book up in the hope her son and her would get back together. She did make some mistakes, but she just wants her son back. She's hurting, she's so sad. And she's so thin, she looks like she's just about to die. She misses her son so much. She's living in a condominium as close as she could get to his house, but he's as hard-hearted as ever." Whatever wrongs his mother had done him,

Eminem's apparent inability to see her as a fellow, hurting human being, with flaws and motivations of her own, showed how much he was still a child when it came to his family. The irrepressible, disproportionate vendettas which made his records so much fun when applied to Britney Spears also tasted sour when turned on a mother withering from them. This was still the stony place in his heart, untouched by his achievements, the ground where he was worst and weakest.

In every other respect, though, the Eminem glimpsed in this time out of the spotlight seemed to have matured appreciably. However much he rapped about the probation conditions which had narrowly kept him out of jail not taming his wildness, he had in large part obeyed them. He knew very well how close his day of Slim Shady madness the previous year had come to ruining him. Keeping clear of drink, drugs, guns and "assaultive behaviour", at least in public, and maintaining a new fitness regime, he was in better shape physically and mentally. He was also more understanding of the price of his fame, as he told Q, when considering the familiar complaint that he couldn't play basketball where he used to any more, as the people he had played with now just stared, and asked for autographs. "Gotta build a fucking basketball court in the backyard," he laughed. "That just might be the way ahead – all the shit you want to do and miss doing, you just go and do it in your own backyard. Then you shut up and respect it."

As Jennifer Yezvack told me when she took my order at Gilbert's Lodge when I first went to Detroit, Eminem anyway continued with the places, people and acts that were natural to him, in spite of his fame. He had not become an alienated celebrity, severed from his roots, lost and mad. Instead, in short, chaos-trailing bursts, he still hung out with the friends who had loved him when he had nothing, and went to the movies, or the clubs. "He goes to all the right places where the hip-hop fans go to," Detroit promoter Michael Saunders confirmed to *NME*. "It's not like he's from Detroit but you never see him. He's here all the time. You would not believe he's on MTV by some of the venues he goes to."

Though the spectre of Elvis' Memphis Mafia of live-in home-town disciples (who had eventually asphyxiated his sense of the outside world) loomed when you looked at Eminem's Detroit Dirty Dozen, the latter crew seemed vastly healthier. Only Eminem's immutable diet really recalled the King. "Everyone wanna eat *filet mignon*," Swift laughed to *Spin*. "He still hollerin' about Taco Bell." The material temptations of his status, out of reach so long, simply meant nothing to him. "A lot of motherfuckers are living way better than me," he told *Spin* indifferently. "Their houses make mine look like shit."

His peaceful, reflective state when away from his parents was summed up in *Q*: "I've made plenty of mistakes in the past, I'm only a human being, but I learned from my mistakes, and I'm definitely old enough to know right from wrong. I've got some regrets, but that shit is all besides the point as long as I know I'm raising my daughter right, and she doesn't have to live in a 'hood any more, and go through the things that I went through."

While Eminem got his head together and was briefly almost forgotten, the pop world he would have to come back to was of course moving swiftly without him. In hip-hop, only Eminem's ties to him had kept Dre's production style (changing and improving though it was) really current. The likes of Timbaland and The Neptunes had developed techniques based on skittering, micro-sliced beats which made Dre sound slow. It was a single by Timbaland's main accomplice (and Eminem fan and one-time collaborator) Missy Elliott, the skeletally funky 'Get UR Freak On', not D12, which had defined the form in 2001. That year, Timbaland also unveiled his own million-selling white rap protégé, Bubba Sparxxx. His *Dark Days, Bright Nights* LP and hit 'Ugly' had no similarity to Eminem (except for the unusualness of a white rap point of view). Nor was he quite good enough to challenge for his predecessor's crown. But in interviews, he thanked Eminem for breaking the curse of Vanilla Ice, as Eminem had thanked 3rd Bass: "He gave credibility back to the institution of white people being involved in hip-hop." The arrival of a second black rap entrepreneur with a money-making white boy in tow, so opposite to the arrangement which had previously held in American music, was perhaps still more significant.

The Southern funk of rap veterans and Eminem tour alumni OutKast and their massive hit 'Miss Jackson', and the sonically astonishing re-imagining of New York's ghettos as electronic iron tombs to be transcended in Cannibal Ox's *The Cold Vein*, indicated underground currents. Jay-Z, who by year's end had registered his third straight US number one LP, *The Blueprint*, and 12 million sales, remained Eminem's biggest commercial rap rival. White rock fans meanwhile, though still in thrall to the brainlessly macho nu-metal, were also favouring Slipknot, whose deliberately obscene style, and assumption of enough intelligence in their depressed, rebellious teen fans to understand its subtleties better than their elders, was precisely in Eminem's vein. The success of acts like Nickelback and POD in early 2002, with their songs of white broken homes, wife-beating and teenage suicide, also showed Eminem's heartland constituency was not changing in his time away.

The only seismic change in America as the follow-up to *The Marshall Mathers LP* gestated, in fact, had nothing directly to do with music. The terrorist obliteration of the World Trade Center on September 11, 2001 briefly made the solipsism of most modern American art seem foolish. The hysterical self-absorption of Eminem, as much as the narcotised materialism of many of his rap contemporaries, was brought into sharp relief by the sight of their fellow Americans windmilling to their deaths from high windows, or being squashed to paper thinness in rubble. The dark cloud of dust, stone and glass which rolled through New York City, coating it black, made even Cannibal Ox's hellish vision of the city, or Eminem's bullet-riddled Amityville, look tamely pleasant.

In the atrocity's immediate aftermath, there was much talk of an end to senseless violence and "negative" feelings in movies and music, that America's seemingly unquenchable taste for such art had been gorged by the real thing to the point of vomiting. That soon passed, of course. Six months later, the music and movie charts looked the same as ever. But for Eminem, who on *Marshall Mathers* had sometimes seemed ready to wrestle his country till one was bundled to the floor, the attacks had to be dealt with. Would the man who had dared compare Columbine unflatteringly to the forgotten carnage in Detroit's ghettos be so bold, or feel the same, about New York's 3,000 dead? He had called himself a "political rapper". In a nation being kept in a state of insular panic well into 2002, hyped up for a phantom war by regular TV news stories showing gas-masked preparation for apocalypse, how far would he be able to take up that mantle? Appetite for the total freedom of speech he had advocated for so long had suddenly tumbled in America. Would he rise to the challenge, risk the martyrdom of a Lenny Bruce or Muhammad Ali, become truly great? Or fold? Or simply, and typically for his generation, find he still cared more about exploring his own fucked-up head, and the fucked-up family which orbited it?

The only instant reaction by any pop figures, oddly, anyway came not from him, but the other five members of D12. Stranded in London when planes to America were grounded after the World Trade Center was hit, they collaborated with Damon Albarn's pop-rap band Gorillaz and ex-Special Terry Hall, on a track called '911', which was released to download on the Internet within a month. "We had organised the collaboration beforehand," Albarn explained, "and the terrorist attacks added a different context, to say the least, to what we did together." Over sinuous Middle Eastern instrumentation and an ominous bass, D12's disparate personalities worked to good effect, summoning the moment's anger, helplessness and confusion. The traditional rap response of verbally gunning down all enemies, even before their names were known – *"whoever did this, we gonna getch'all"* – dominated. But Kuniva also sounded lost and frightened, imagining himself in ash-blinded New York: *"so much smoke you can't tell the difference between night and day / next time you hear a verse from me, you might be caged"*. Most affectingly, the track caught the spacey drift of five young men from Detroit stranded far from home, losing themselves in chaotic dreams of showering glass, perhaps putting themselves in those Tower-toppling planes: *"I ain't never going home, 'cos I'm too far gone / . . . as I sit in my seat and remain calm, I close my eyes."*

"You don't have to tell me the world is fucked up" was the nearest thing to a political statement from the rappers. Hall's muezzin wail and Albarn's chant of *"we are one"* in the chorus were attempts at balance from the Britons in the studio, at a time of heated jingoist rhetoric. The only hole in the track was where Eminem, still missing, should have spoken.

He did make two, relatively unremarked appearances without D12 in 2001. But neither really indicated new directions. First, there was that guest spot on Xzibit's *Restless*, in which he tastelessly complained about Kim's suicide attempt (*"she just slit her wrists over this shit"*). His part on 'Renegade', on Jay-Z's massive-selling *The Blueprint* was little more revolutionary. But this meeting between the world's most popular black and white rappers did reveal both were aware of their complementary roles in racially schismed America. Jay-Z, sometimes criticised for his money-loving raps, described how he was still *"influenced by the ghetto"*, and *"bring 'em a lot closer to where they pop toasters / . . . I'll bring you through the ghetto without riding around"*, perfectly capturing the voyeuristic relationship white suburban kids felt to the black rappers they worshipped. When Eminem spoke, he didn't have to mention he had come from that world to meet Jay-Z in the studio. He simply admitted he also had an influence, then launched into one of his most surprising and challenging lists of what that might be: *"maybe it's hatred I spew, maybe it's food for the spirit / maybe it's beautiful music I made for you just to cherish."* And yet still *"I'm viewed in America as a motherfucking drug addict"*, sparking another assault on his mother's generation, and Bill Clinton's: *"Like you didn't experiment?/ That's when you start to stare at what's in the mirror/ and see yourself as a kid again and you get embarrassed/ stupid as parents/ you stupid do-gooders/ too bad you couldn't do good at marriage."*

It was as incisive a dismissal of the hypocrisy of baby-boomer authoritarians, the faded, smug rock'n'rollers his contemporaries were displacing, as could be managed in so short a space: he stripped them back to their own hormonal, experimental, raging adolescences, when their faces were as twisted, silly and slapdash as his; then he left them mired in their messy attempts at maturity. It was a Biblical switch, staring out from their mirrors to ask if they were without sin. His religious description of his own work (*"food for the spirit . . . beautiful music"*) then led to a second verse which imagined him as *"Jesus Christ . . . Satan, a scatterbrained atheist"*, battling whole Christian sects. The fresh quirks in this short performance were added to by a chorus in which he screeched *"I'm a re-ne-ga-yaade!"* in a rising howl borrowed from rock's former Anti-Christ, Johnny Rotten. It seemed he was now consciously exploring his lineage beyond rap. Producing the track alone for Jay-Z, its synthesised choirs, sombre strings and organ were also quietly effective.

The year's last sliver of Eminem output was a video compilation of the cartoons that had interrupted his gigs, *The Slim Shady Show*, released in November in the UK, just in time for Christmas. Originally made for MTV at the station's request, but fresh to most British fans, they were the worst thing he had put his name to. Relating the adventures of inept Marshall Mathers, evil Slim Shady and their friends (including Ken Kaniff), its animation was cheap even by MTV standards, and the pall of laughlessness that descended whenever they were screened at British shows was now stretched over 60 minutes. Hired scripter Matt Cirulnick gamely trotted out the usual targets, from Christina Aguilera to Kim (whose silicon breasts Slim rips off, having paid for them pre-divorce, the only interesting gossip, or slander, on view). But with Eminem and Paul Rosenberg as Executive Producers (for their own Shady World Productions), and Eminem as lead "Voice Talent", the buck for the farrago stopped at Slim's door. "If I read the script, and I'm not feeling it, I'm not gonna do it," he told a "Making of" documentary, revealing how much he could misjudge a foreign medium. Still, it was his first vocal acting job, helpfully played out in a recording studio. He liked slipping "into character", he explained of his technique. "You see the line, and just run with it."

Other news around him had thinned to a drizzle. In September, 'Stan' was nominated for five MTV Music Video Awards. In December, with staggering cheek, De Angelo Bailey, the bully who had concussed the child Marshall Mathers by shoving him in a snowbank, resurfaced to sue Eminem for $1 million, claiming 'Brain Damage' had harmed his reputation, and hampered his ambitions in the music industry, apparently being pursued from his current position as a Detroit dustman. His lawyer said Bailey "completely denied" the song's allegations, despite merrily elaborating on them to *Rolling Stone* in 1999. Following in the footsteps of Eminem's mum, he also released a CD, threatening to break down the gates of his one-time victim's new home and kill him, which didn't really help his case. "He got my address wrong," Eminem sighed to *The Face*, in mock-despair at his now-impotent tormentor's carelessness. "He's making himself a public figure, which is where my mother fucked up. But," he added, with the mature perspective he was now gaining in non-family matters, "if you have nothing else and you haven't made nothing with your life, then what the fuck? If Eminem says my name on a record, why not get money? I'd do it."

By year's end, though, such minor distractions ceased to matter. The stasis that had settled around his artistic life after *The Marshall Mathers LP* at last began to shake. A follow-up album was nearing completion. What's more, a film with strong autobiographical elements, first called *Detroit*, and finally *8 Mile*, was due to wrap in December, with its own soundtrack album being written by Eminem and Dre. The next testing stage in Eminem's career was suddenly thundering down the track. 2002 would secure his crown, or dash it.

8 Mile was the main reason there had been any gap at all in his previous headlong rush. It had begun as a casual idea for a hip-hop equivalent of *Saturday Night Fever* or *Purple Rain*, during a conversation between Jimmy Iovine and Brian Grazer (producer of *The Nutty Professor* and *A Beautiful Mind*). Two other rappers were considered, before Grazer saw Eminem's range of expression at the 2000 MTV Music Video Awards. Eminem had meanwhile been interested in an acting role beyond those hapless cartoons for some time, and there had been rumours of films before, no doubt floated by hopeful producers (*Lazarus*, in which he would have played an evil dead rapper returning to life, was typical). "Eminem had a lot of scripts. He didn't want to do a jokey movie," Bizarre confirmed to the *Launch* website. When Eminem agreed to meet Grazer, he was at first offputtingly aloof, not looking at him or saying much for 15 minutes, distrustful, perhaps, of Hollywood temptations. But when he did start to speak about his life, Grazer found him "articulate" and "passionate" about the subject, and "humble", and "damaged", he told *Premiere*. Eminem, a man who had never finished a book, forced his way into the script by Scott Silvers (*The Mod Squad*), and the deal was done. "It was a good enough script for me to put my music on hold for, like, four, five months," he confirmed to *Premiere*, with a suggestion of the sacrifice that was to him in this central time in his musical life.

Curtis Hanson, of *LA Confidential* and *Wonder Boys*, agreed to direct, having decided his untried star's potential was worth the risk, and immediately *8 Mile*'s credentials climbed. The script, as it developed, seemed to adapt aspects of Eminem's life with all the freedom a movie might take with some literary source, but the resultant fiction still let him draw on strongly personal memories: he would play Jimmy Smith, Jnr, a Detroit factory worker living in a trailer park with his mother (Kim Basinger), who has a fractious relationship with his girlfriend (Brittany Murphy), and hip-hop dreams he starts to realise, during one week in 1995. But neither Hanson nor Eminem wanted the rapper to simply play himself, and pushed hard together for something more. There was a generous six-week rehearsal period, during which the 57-year-old Hanson, a Hollywood veteran, became the first man since Dre to mentor Eminem in a new art. For a second, briefer time, he had a father figure to test himself against. "He was good to work with because he was real," he told *Premiere*. "Curtis didn't sugar-coat anything. If something sucked, he would say that it sucked. At first I would take it to heart – like, 'Damn, how could he say that to me?' And then I would take it in."

Removing his blond bleach and disguising his tattoos, Eminem also worked to smother the inflections and rhythms he had developed on record. Effectively, he was killing Eminem and Slim Shady when on set, and replacing them with still another persona, this time with an actor's sense of craft. Hanson's instructions before filming had included handing Eminem a stack of films containing great breakthrough performances from young actors like James Dean, Jon Voight, Dustin Hoffman and Robert De Niro. Hanson said his star had shown a special interest in Dean, astonished at his iconic fame after just three films. But, Eminem confessed to *Premiere*, he had, not for the first time, ducked his homework: "I was so into this movie, I didn't wanna see what other people had done. I didn't wanna copy anybody or anything. I felt like as long as I felt real in a scene, that's all I needed."

8 Mile's filming through late 2001 returned Eminem to his childhood heartland, places he had barely left even now. The Continental Mobile Home Village on the 8 Mile border of Warren, almost identical and adjacent to the trailer park where Eminem had grown up, was the major set, its residents cordoned off by Warren police, or compensated by Universal Pictures, as a neighbour they had never noticed came back with power and wealth at his command. Their homes and bodies were now extras in a Hollywood movie about a place which, until Eminem, America had ignored. It was something about which Warren, like the principal of Eminem's school there when I talked to him, could feel only confused and uneasy. The production put millions into the local economy. But, like so many Eminem had used in his art, they worried they would somehow be sullied. There were a few pickets. When a building in Highland Park, in downtown Detroit, was burned down (with injuries to four crew-members), as part of a scene in which it's torched, after a rape behind its walls, there were complaints that the area was being given a bad name. "The fucking white trash capital of the world?" Eminem asked *The Face*, exasperated. "I'm white trash, so what the fuck? You can't tell me. I grew up in it."

As Hanson's cameras explored the empty lots and industrial husks of Detroit almost as much as Warren's trailers and trash, true to the city's theme of division which the road he took his title from expressed, sensible residents should have been calmed. Hanson, a long-time friend of Robert Towne, writer of the legendary cinematic excavation of LA *Chinatown*, was fascinated with urban America too, as proven by his own *LA Confidential*. By bringing such an insightful director back to his home, as much as by making his records, Eminem was putting the broken city he loved back in America's thoughts. Once it had been known for Henry Ford's residence there. Then, for the slow closure of Ford's factories. Now, the refusal of the country's most infamous pop star to leave it behind seemed like one of Detroit's few signs of hope.

Taryn Manning, who played Jimmy Smith's bitter ex-girlfriend (and had also appeared in Britney Spears' rather different vehicle, *Crossroads*), watched Eminem as he worked in Warren. She sensed he was under great pressure. "He just knows he has the power to create something that could have a lot of longevity," she said. "He can feel it inside. He's focused. He's intense. He's also really goofy." Part of the strain came from Eminem having to co-create the movie's soundtrack with Dre, a task far from complete as he started to act. "Any downtime, he was writing," Manning said. "You could see him formulating stuff in his head." The composition of a second album for 2002, even as he finished his first major film, showed the drive behind *Marshall Mathers* had not withered. But it was Eminem's first release of the year, *Marshall Mathers*' belated, official follow-up, for which the world was really waiting, still.

Interscope let intimations of its content trickle out in the early months of 2002, preparing the atmosphere for their artist's return, delicately building expectations. The title, it was confirmed in February, would be *The Eminem Show*. *Nothing Mathers* had been considered. Eminem had produced it himself, with the help of Dre and the Bass Brothers. It would be, Marky Bass told a fan website, more "serious", the same thing insiders had said of *Marshall Mathers*. "It's better," Bass continued. "He's matured since the last one, and he's been through so much since then, good and bad. He kept going and wrote a fantastic album. He's a tough kid – it's brilliant."

"I do feel he has matured as a lyricist," Dre chipped in, to MTV, "but I don't know if saying he's moving in a different direction is accurate. His stuff is really crazy to me because just when you think, 'Okay, he has run out of stuff to say, he can get no crazier than this,' something comes out of his face that gives you chills. Makes the hair crawl on your skin. So I think the shock value of Eminem is definitely going to still be there." With this new stimulus, rumours flew around Eminem's name again, but this time with a force near to fact, as Interscope leaked and manipulated news, till the day when the waiting would be over. There would be a Seventies rock direction. Eminem would appear as bin Laden in a song. Kim would be back again. "Ohhh, Kimmy, Kimmy," Bass teased. "You'll hear all about her on this one. Is she at the bottom of the lake, or is she in Bel Air? You'll find out . . ."

In March, Eminem himself broke his silence, to *The Source*, but said nothing about the album, except the idea behind it. "The concept is my life becoming a show," he told them. "All my personal shit people are able to know about. Nothing I do is behind closed doors, so it's kinda like *The Truman Show*, Springer Show. The album is more personal than I've ever gotten." The same magazine contained an advert for the record: red curtains, a spotlight, an empty stage, and the words, "Coming This Spring", the show now so real you could almost touch it.

The release date was pushed back. First it was April. Then May. Finally, June 3 was set as the day *The Eminem Show* would start. The few copies in existence were being kept under the tightest security. Almost no one at his own label had heard it, a few weeks before the world would. But nothing Interscope did could control what happened next.

The Marshall Mathers LP had briefly made its maker the most notorious and brilliant man in pop. But the two years since had cooled everything. In his show and other actions, he had worked to dismantle his monstrous image, and succeeded. He was now a veteran artist in hip-hop, a genre more dismissive of the past than any other. He was a pop star in an era when attention spans flickered at light speed, and the durability of a Sixties star on the streak of genius he had so far ridden seemed impossible. He had imprinted British culture with fear and fascination not seen since the Sex Pistols, for a couple of months. Since that heady instant, he had worried no one. To still be the force *The Marshall Mathers LP* had made him would need not only an astonishing record, but for him to buck the nature of his times.

And so, the show began.

12

EMINEM

The first reaction was disappointment. When 'Without Me', Eminem's first solo single since 'Stan' came on the radio, he sounded like a man implausibly low on material. After the suicide attempts, divorces, brawls, lawsuits, terrorist outrages and wars of his time away, it was a song consumed with himself. Built around a lyrical reference to Malcolm McLaren's hip-hop proselytising early Eighties single 'Buffalo Gals', and 'Purple Pills'' sax riff, it had the childishly bright, bouncy addictiveness of his previous, album-introducing worldwide pop hits, 'My Name Is' and 'The Real Slim Shady'. It just seemed to lack anything new to say. *"Guess who's back? Back again?"* a voice taunted before the first verse began. Interscope had ensured everyone knew that answer. The question that needed asking in return was: why?

"I just settled all my lawsuits. Fuck you, Debbie!" seemed to throw down a gauntlet, and a queue of other enemies were slapped: Limp Bizkit, Moby, Canibus, the FCC and, most memorably, Lynne Cheney, who was tactfully warned that the famously delicate heart condition of her Vice-President husband Dick was *"complicating"*. But as Eminem repeatedly rapped *"we need a little controversy, 'cos it feels so empty without me"*, it seemed a perfunctory, insufficient reason to return. Even his bragging of the *"revolution"* he could start with his lyrics *"infesting"* teenagers' ears, *"nesting"* in suburban parents' homes, said nothing new. Only two references to Elvis Presley, who his life paralleled in so many ways, suggested a fresh, fascinating awareness of this fact. Elvis' first appearance was as an embarrassment, still on the unfashionable stereos of parents, who Eminem's teen fans drown with their own hero's hollers. But Eminem himself was more wise to the chain he linked: *"Though I'm not the first king of controversy/ I am the worst thing since Elvis Presley, to do Black Music so selfishly/ and use it to get myself wealthy."* Superficially embracing the black rap view standardised by Chuck D of Elvis the culture-thieving *"flat-out*

racist", and dumping himself in the same bracket, Eminem's understanding of the eruptive, miscegenating, parent-appalling force of himself and his ancestor a half-century before was clear.

Another American hero sucked into 'Without Me' was Batman, as Eminem imitated the TV show's theme, and presented himself as a superhero come to save the pop world from his own devastating absence. His life-long fascination with comic-books then spread to the accompanying video. Shot largely as if it was a comic, complete with speech balloons, it co-starred his half-brother Nathan, who sneaks a Parental Advisory-stickered Eminem CD home, while Rap Boy (Eminem as Robin) and Rapman (Dre) bounce their heads to the beat. TV was also sampled and satirised once more, with Nathan as young Eminem and Eminem as a blonde, big-haired Debbie clone on a Springer-like show, then, with the nearest thing to real controversy, a cut to live "ENN" footage of Osama bin Laden (Eminem again, in joke-shop beard and Stars-and-Stripes-patched turban). Found and threatened in his cave by D12, they all make up and dance to 'Without Me'.

No one was really offended, but Eminem explained anyway: "With the Osama thing, I was trying to make light of a bad situation. If we don't address the issue, that's not a healthy thing. Although this will not take away the pain of what happened, I'm trying to lighten the mood a little and help us get past it."

Whatever its merits, 'Without Me' predictably went straight in at number one in the UK on its May 20 release, and number two in the US. But Interscope's carefully escalating build-up to *The Eminem Show* had already been thrown into sudden disarray. By May 11, nearly a month before the album's official release, one of the few, jealously guarded copies in existence had found its way onto the Internet, where it was down-loaded, bootlegged, and for sale on New York street corners for five dollars within minutes.

Interscope tried to be sanguine about what was an industry-wide problem (Oasis' *Heathen Chemistry* had been downloaded three months early). Eminem was understandably less open-minded. "I think that shit is fucking bullshit," he announced. "Whoever put my shit on the Internet, I want to meet that motherfucker and beat the shit out of him, because I picture this scrawny little dickhead going, 'I got Eminem's new CD! I got Eminem's new CD! I'm going to put it on the Internet!' Anybody who tries to make excuses for that shit is a fucking bitch. I'm sorry; when I worked nine to five, I expected to get a fucking pay cheque every week. It's the same with music; if I'm putting my fucking heart and time into music, I expect to get rewarded for that. I work hard, and anybody can just throw a computer up and download my shit for free."

The underground, illicit spread of the album forced Interscope's hand anyway. On May 27, billboards sprang up around London, advertising: "THE EMINEM SHOW. OUT NOW. BECAUSE THE WORLD COULD NOT WAIT." The posters showed the record's sleeve: a spotlit mic-stand on a wooden stage, with velvet, gilt-tasselled curtains parted, in this typical theatrical scene, just wide enough to reveal a besuited, sharp-shoed Eminem, sitting with his head in clasped hands, lost in thought, waiting to go on.

When the fans who flooded record stores that day took *The Eminem Show* home, a week early, they found the theme of its title – of Eminem's whole life as an exposed, *Truman Show*-style performance, just as he'd said in April – spread through every part of its package. When they flicked through the CD booklet, it was illustrated with closed-circuit TV pictures positioned in every part of his gated, exclusive new Detroit residence – in the mailbox when he reached in for letters, by the swimming pool as he and Hailie played, in his walk-in wardrobe as he picked from a wall of shoes and row of jackets; as he put out the trash in his yard, and scribbled raps in his clean white kitchen, CD headphones and spectacles on; even as he recorded *The Eminem Show* with Dre. 3:23AM.04-09-02 WORKINPROGRESS>VIEW354>STUDIOSCREENWITHDR. DRE ran computer type alongside, letting you know the very second of his life you were spying on. A skulking, hooded paparazzo was shown too, pointing his long lens at the house, suggesting by whom the rapper felt stripped. But in showing us his new home, Eminem was of course doing more to help us picture the mundane details of his life than any *Hello!* shoot or celeb-snapping helicopter dive. The booklet's final images then twisted the satire inside-out: in open-necked office shirt and loosened tie, Eminem looked up from the business pages to coldly inspect us. In the darkened room (BACKSTAGE), a bank of TV screens let him watch each showbiz snapper. The very last page showed the MAINCONTROL-ROOM of the TV station running *The Eminem Show*. But Eminem was running it. Like all his best lyrics, he had spun his feelings of celebrity intrusion and insanity around, until self-pity was shredded, and he con-trolled what we thought.

When you put the album itself on, nervously, after such long expectation, that almost arrogant grip did not loosen. 'Without Me''s disappointment was forgotten. Eminem had refined and focused all he'd done
before, and matched every hope. *The Eminem Show*, intended as the close
to a loose sort of trilogy, did not try to retrieve the raw shock of its previous instalments. He had become more dangerous in a harder, more lasting
way: by getting better.

So sure was he of what he'd done that his thoughts on what you were
listening to were hard to find. After previous media blitzes, and in a year
which would also include a soundtrack album and major film, only four
carefully spaced print interviews were permitted. They gave only the
barest of insights.

To *The Face*, he considered the production style, which built on
changes begun with *Devil's Night*. "I just took the record on as my own
project," he said. "I know how to produce now. I've soaked up everything. When I first got with Dre I was like a sponge, asking him questions.
What is this called? What's this button do? And now I know how I want
my shit to sound. I was trying to capture a Seventies rock vibe for most of
it. We treated this record like it was a rock record, as far as how it's produced. It's, like, loud. There's a lot of guitars in it. There's a lot of hip-hop
shit, too. I tried to get the best of both worlds. But I listened to a lot of
Seventies rock growing up, when I was real little," he added, something
which – perhaps in denying his "little flower child", Hendrix-adoring
mother – he'd never admitted before. "When I go back and listen to them
songs, you know, like Led Zeppelin or Aerosmith or Jimi Hendrix . . .
Seventies rock had this incredible feel to it."

To *White Teeth* author Zadie Smith in *Vibe*, too, it was sonic shifts he
wished to discuss. "I learned how to ride a beat better, that's what I
wanted to focus on," he told her. "It's not easy. Sometimes I'll spend
hours on a single rhyme, or days. Even if I have my ideas stacked, if I'm
flooded with ideas, I'm always trying to figure out how to make it better,
make it smoother." To *Rolling Stone*, he added, "I'm paranoid as fuck
about anything of mine sounding like a track I just did or anything out
there. I practically live in the studio, apart from spending time with
Hailie."

But he also looked back for *Rolling Stone* on some of the swirling
turmoil in which *The Eminem Show* had been composed. "I have songs on
the album that I wrote when I went through that shit last year, with a

possible jail sentence hangin' over my head and all the emotions going through the divorce. I went through a lot of shit last year that I resolved at the same time, all in the same year. And yeah, that's when the album was wrote. I was in that shit, and I didn't know what was going to happen to me – I thought I was goin' to jail. But the scariest thought was, 'How am I going to tell this to Hailie?' What am I going to say – 'Daddy's going away and he's been bad, and you have to come visit him in jail'? I never told her anything, because if there was a slim chance that I could get off, then I didn't want to put her through that emotionally – being scared. She hates when I go away, any time. The first song I wrote for the album, 'Sing For The Moment', is that frustration and all that shit. There I was, in the fucking precinct getting booked, and the police were asking me for autographs while they were fucking booking me, and I'm doing it, I'm giving them the autographs. But I'm like, 'My life is in fucking shambles right now, and you look at me like I am not a fucking person. I am a walking spectacle.' I signed it. 'They're the police, and I'm sure that if Marshall is a good guy, word will get around, so okay, fuck it, lemme do it.'"

To Smith, he added, "I had a wake-up call with my almost going to jail, like, *slow down*. That was me letting my anger get the best of me, which I've done many times. No more." But to *The Face*, he ruefully admitted how such confrontation still fed his art. "It's funny, it's like I need drama in my life to inspire me a lot, instead of just trying to reach for something. Last year was like a really rough year for me. You know, divorce and trying to raise my little girl. Obstacles are thrown at me – you've just got to fall or you don't fall. And I can't fall."

He also talked to Smith about the catastrophe that had happened in his absence, the terrorist assault of September 11: "That was, like, a dark day. It's a subject I couldn't really bring myself to make fun about – then I'd just have no fucking morals or scruples at all."

Whether that contradicted his comments on 'Without Me' 's video or not, *The Eminem Show* did anything but ignore how America had changed. Instead, Eminem passed the radical test this presented, in a way few previous musicians had managed. Without the groundswell of support among politicised fans which cushioned Dylan in the Sixties; at a time, in contrast, when the streets of Warren he drove through to his studio in Royal Oak were draped with Stars and Stripes, and dissent had vanished from America's TVs, he attacked its government and wars directly. There was no easily identifiable anthem on the record, no self-conscious stance.

Eminem's politics just poured naturally out, with all the other shit in his head.

The first few seconds of the album were deceptively peaceful, a theatre curtain being winched open over a classical prelude, then the clearing of a throat. Then came the first word: *"America!"* It was how *The Godfather* had opened too, the subject of both, no matter what bloody distractions occurred along the way, made plain from the start. The song was called 'White America', and Eminem spat his nation's name in the Rotten snarl he'd perfected on 'Renegade', pronouncing it like a Black Panther: *"Amerikkkaaa!"* To a heavy rock beat, his next words, dripping with irony, were: *"We love you! How many people are proud to be citizens of this beautiful country of ours / . . . The women and men who have broken their necks for the freedom of speech the United States government has sworn to uphold . . ."* Darkly, he murmured: *". . . Or so we're told."*

He then asked everyone to listen to the lyrics (something he'd never done before), and used them to discuss the politics of his own situation, how his white skin had probably doubled his sales, and how he and Dre had traded fans across the colour line. As he told *The Source*, "I'm not saying anything different than any rapper has said. I reached into them homes of Middle America because white kids looked up to me, because they looked like me." It was this suburban fan-base that made Congress and protest groups pore over his lyrics like no one else's, that made censors want to silence him, and made him feel watched and throttled and paranoid every time he picked up a pen: *"Surely hip-hop was never a problem in Harlem, only in Boston, after it bothered the fathers of daughters starting to blossom."* It was the same class and race distinction he'd drawn between Columbine and Detroit before, with the added fear of miscegenation which powerful American music had always fingered; except that white boy Eminem was the contagion now.

At first glance, attacking his country's Congress just because it attacked him seemed like a self-aggrandising way of thinking. But in the final verse, Eminem showed how seriously he took this battle, and his outrageous position as the channel for a generation's unfocused rage, *"the poster-child, the motherfuckin' spokesman now, for White America."* It made him have visions of patriotic sacrilege no one without his commercial clout would ever have been permitted to record, especially not post-Twin Towers: *"Sent to lead the march right up to the steps of Congress and piss on the lawn of the White House and to burn the* [something here so sensitive it's erased from the printed lyrics, and muffled on record: the Presidential Seal? The Bill of Rights?] *and replace it with a Parental Advisory sticker/ To spit liquor in the face of this democracy of hypocrisy/. . . Fuck you with the freest of speech this divided states of embarrassment will allow me to have, Fuck You!"* And then, with the taunting get-out clause with which he'd closed *The Marshall Mathers LP*'s provoking misogynistic opener, 'Kill You': *"Ha-ha-ha. I'm just kiddin'. America, you know I love you."*

It was the 1963 March on Washington or the Million Man March, deliberately devolved into working-class desecration, spitting and pissing on corrupted symbols of power, an expression of utter contempt for a Government whose post-Afghanistan approval ratings were monumental. And another track was still more specifically radical.

'Square Dance', set to a parody of the titular white trash beat, hauled off on another enemy made between albums, Canibus (the first black rapper he'd publicly dissed), for much of its length. It said a lot for his sense of democracy that President George W. Bush was treated with equal, if more serious scorn. Eminem had returned, he revealed, *"with a plan to ambush this Bush administration, mush the Senate's face in and push this generation/ of kids to stand and fight for the right to say something you might not like."* He was thinking of the same incoherent army of kids he'd imagined in 'The Real Slim Shady', his clumsy, unhappy comrades working in supermarkets and burger bars. But he knew September 11 and Bush had raised the stakes for them all, and that incoherence would no longer serve. In one verse aimed directly at those kids, from the position of an older friend (he admitted to 28 now; maybe it was even true), he laid out a modern Desolation Row, of teenage boys getting their call-up papers at band practice, and others choking from Anthrax-stained napkins, as assassins crashed screaming trainloads of people, and Uncle Sam used the excuse to draft a generation. *"You're just a baby . . . they gon' take you 'fore they take me,"* he sadly said, in words reminiscent of Bruce Springsteen's touching advice to Reagan kids not to join up, on his mid-Eighties tours. *"When I say Hussein, you say Shady,"* he added, before picturing himself hanged, expunged like that other Bush bogeyman.

The rest of the record returned to his own life, digging over all its details one more time, trying to make sense of the year's travails. The mêlée in the parking lot with John Guerra was replayed as a movie scene in 'The Kiss', in which Eminem sees his girl kissing another man, and leaps out of his car, unloaded gun in hand, before his friends can stop him; in 'Soldier', he bragged about what he'd done. But on the D12-assisted 'When The Music Stops', he cursed the pressures that made rappers try to live up to their music's tough images; while on 'Say Goodbye To Hollywood' and 'Sing For The Moment', he reflected on success with sorrow which had not been there the last time he bullishly discussed it, on *The Marshall Mathers LP*.

'Say Goodbye To Hollywood' begins with the sound of sirens, and handcuffs closing on Eminem's wrists. To a contemplative tune, he then adds more details to the Hot Rocks fracas: his gun falling to the floor unseen by him, a friend picking it up before bouncers pile in; and his rueful disappointment when Kim doesn't stand by him. But its biggest revelation was the state of his head as he contemplated jail. How, even as Kim slashed her wrists, he too pondered a second painkiller overdose as he skidded to rock bottom again, his brain pounding from the moment's pressures, only the example of his absent father staying his hand: *"thank God, I got a little girl/ and I'm a responsible father, so not a lot of good, I'd be to my daughter, layin' in the bottom of the mud."* The "Hollywood" he wanted to flee to survive was two-fold: the futile melodrama of his life, distorting to fit his public image; and fame itself, which for the first time seemed a true curse. The music that had freed him from poverty-stricken despair was now a cage. He'd never have rapped, he declared, if he'd known: *"I sold my soul to the Devil, I'll never get it back."* He and his daughter were now freaks: *"It's fuckin' crazy, 'cos all I wanted was to give Hailie the life I never had, but instead I forced us to live alienated."* A harmonica solo outroed his millionaire's blues.

'Sing For The Moment', though written almost as soon as the cuffs were off, was a more considered, moving response to his predicament. It was also the album's most complete adoption of Seventies rock, building its chorus on the surging guitar riff of Aerosmith's 'Dream On', with crashing rock drums.

In it, he replayed the moment when he signed CDs for cops even as he was fingerprinted. But he was more interested here in the implications of his fans' reactions to rappers' records and acts. For the first time, he admitted raps could do harm: *"I guess words are a mothafucka they can be great/ or . . . they can teach hate."* Though still dismissive that his lyrics could make someone cock a gun, he bemoaned the mixing of gangster postures with showbiz, the glamorisation of violence that came when ghetto rappers were unexpectedly made stars.

But finally, he rejoiced in rap's effect on fans, in the transcendent tones last heard in 'Revelation'. Voice softening as it always did when considering youths as he had been, he imagined fans with nothing, crying in their rooms and wanting to die, hanging on to the rap records that kept them hoping. And Eminem revealed that his hopes for salvation now lay with those fans, just as much as it had rested with his idols when he had nothing. The only afterlife he hoped for was through them remembering his lyrics, the receptacle of his *"spirit"* . He might curse Satan he'd ever rapped some days. Others, he thanked the Lord.

Money and damnation were also visited even-handedly on his mother, on what became the second single, 'Cleanin' Out My Closet'. Woodblock beats gave it a gentle sound, and its chorus – *"I'm sorry, Mama, I never meant to make you cry"* – suggested he'd heard of Mathers-Briggs' lonely despair on her return to Detroit months before to make up with a son who wouldn't see her, and repented. But against that, the song's verses were a vicious rejection of any blood-bond she still hoped they shared. Recalling life with her, he repeated now more carefully worded accusations (how she popped *"prescription pills"*, and convinced him he was *"sick"*), with the added offences of her CD and court-case. In the last verse, he lured her in, in a voice that whispered and insinuated in the ear, as if he wanted her to huddle to the radio to hear his remote-control, poison message: *"guess what, yer gettin' older now and it's cold when you're lonely, an' Nathan's growin' up so quick, he's gonna know that you're phony/ And Hailie's gettin' so big now, you should see her, she's beautiful/ But"* – voice starting to growl louder, now she's listening – *"you'll never see her, she won't even be at your funeral! Ha-ha!"* The *coup de grâce* revisited the terrible moment when he was 20, and she'd wished he'd died, and his uncle had lived. *"I am dead,"* he snarled, with controlled savagery, like he was cutting a throat. *"Dead to you as can be."* It was strange stuff to reach number five in the UK chart.

"Yeah, it's a harsh record," he admitted to *The Face*. "But I feel like my mother has done some harsh things to me. You just try your whole life to get away from that person and make a life for yourself and not have to deal with it any more. And it's so hard to break away. And they keep coming back to haunt you, trying to weasel their way into your life somehow. That's my closure song, I guess. It's like I'm washing my hands of it. I'm cleaning out my closet. I'm done."

His attitude to other women hadn't exactly improved either, on the standard-issue rap misogyny of 'Drips' (Em is hoodwinked into catching

AIDS from a *"dirty ho"*), and the more personal 'Superman', in which he refuses to commit to any of the star-fucking, gold-digging one-night stands that now apparently constitute his sex life. There was something queasily realistic about the slapping and neck-snapping he's an inch away from giving all of them (even though, as in real life, *"I don't wanna hit no women"*, and the songs' stacked circumstances give him cause). But both tracks seemed born from simple hurt and distrust, in the aftermath of his divorce from Kim.

In *Rolling Stone*, he had recalled how that scarred him. "Divorce is the hardest thing I went through," he'd said, "not that I'm bitter or anything like that. I'm a better person because I went through it, but it was hard at first. I've known this chick all my life, she's the first true girlfriend that I ever had. You grow up with this person and then they want to leave you. And at first you don't know what to do. You know, I put the blame on everything. I put the blame on myself, I put the blame on my career. But as I got through it, I stepped back and looked at the whole picture. I realised it wasn't my fault and there's nothing I could have done. It was inevitable. It's cool, me and Kim are on speaking terms, we can communicate, no hard feelings, fuck it. Didn't work, you know, after 11 years." Then he added, more fiercely: "I would rather have a baby through my penis than get married again. I can't take what I went through last year. I don't ever want to experience that again." The degrading of women in songs like 'Superman' now came straight from this; he didn't dare lay himself open to really love another woman, and be let down again. How many times had he been in love, *The Face* asked him. "Once," he said. "And that's enough for me. And when Hailie was born."

'Hailie's Song', coming straight after 'Superman' on the album, made the contradiction between his distaste for women and love for his daughter obvious. It was the sort of shamelessly soppy ballad Paul McCartney used to write about Linda, and Eminem used to write about Kim on *Infinite*. It was also his first, okay attempt at singing. It was about the pressure he had felt when Hailie was away living with Kim, and the relief of having her back. The only thing that made it unsuitable for a bedtime lullaby for his child was one last verse of bile at her mother (*"what did I stick my penis up in?"* he wondered, amidst more borderline actionable comments, which couldn't hide how he'd once felt, and his drained relief those times were done). It finished with a repeat of his ''97 Bonnie & Clyde' promise to never leave Hailie, and a kiss.

"I made it just for her," he told *Rolling Stone*. "I'm singing on it, for Christ's sake, or trying to. I wasn't going to use it, but I played it for a few people, and a few of them cried, actually. So I said, 'Fuck it.'"

In its original form, it was built around a sample of George Harrison's Beatles song 'While My Guitar Gently Weeps' – an unlikely connection with old rock royalty which almost came off. "From what I understand, he heard it before he passed and liked it," Eminem surprisingly revealed. "He was going to allow it. But his wife has control of his music now and she said no, so I had to re-sing it all."

The Eminem Show's finale anyway made far more telling use of his daughter, and pulled together every one of the record's strands. 'My Dad's Gone Crazy' was one of only three Dre productions (the other 17 tracks were all by Eminem), and the lone one on an often dark, hard album to recall the cheekiness of their first days together. An unlikely duet with little Hailie, it begins with the sounds of a radio announcer discussing fatherhood, coke being snorted, and the creak of a door as Hailie enters to see what Daddy's doing. He's *"gone cray-zee!"* she declares. Dad cheerily admits it, daughter's soon making chainsaw sounds, and Eminem lays waste to the world once again: declaring he and Dre are gay (*"I've been lying my ass off all this time!"*), insulting gays, imitating his Mum, announcing he's a genius, and beyond salvation. As typically seesaw Dre beats are built on by thunderous drum-rolls, bells and brass he even, despite what he said to Zadie Smith, uses September 11 as a metaphor for his own writing skill, unable to resist making even that the subject of his satire. In a climactic rush, comes this: *"More pain inside of my brain than the eyes of a little girl / inside of a plane aimed at the World Trade, standin' on Ronnie's grave, screamin' at the sky, till clouds gather, it's Clyde Mathers and Bonnie Jade . . ."* In those moments, he dashes every doubt that *The Marshall Mathers LP* could be topped. "You're funny, Daddy," Hailie loyally concludes.

Every minor cast-member of the previous two albums – Paul Rosenberg (weary), Steve Berman (shot) – had also already appeared, except for Ken Kaniff. He took the mic after the curtain on the Eminem Show winched closed. Voice echoing, as if on the wooden Lincoln stage where Marshall Mathers had first performed, he was swiftly drowned out by bird-song, nothing else, really, left to hear. The LP trilogy, and the slice of Eminem's life it had mined, was done.

Of course, it was number one everywhere. In the US, the first day's sales slammed it there. Reviews, mostly by writers who had listened once in Interscope's offices days before its rushed release, really failed to grasp what they'd heard, but went along with the unstoppable flow: "the greatest 'Show' on earth," said *NME*; "finally, in his own scattered way, in his own mind, at least, Eminem is fighting for something a little bigger than himself," *Rolling Stone* saw. But what was most noticeable, as the dust of expectation settled, was how quickly it became possible to forget *The Eminem Show* had been released at all.

In the UK especially, where only interviews with *The Face* and Radio 1 were granted, and 'Without Me' as the lone single for months, the record was left to sell itself, slipping into people's homes without a noise in the wider culture. The shock-waves of 'Stan' and the 2001 tour were no longer detectable. It was hard to tell, for all the CDs being bought, if Eminem did still matter as he had, only twelve months before.

Certainly, he wasn't waving pistols or making headlines. Instead, the solid authority of his new album seemed based on a sudden maturity in his life, as he neared 30. Discussing the probation conditions which kept him mostly drink- and drug-free with *The Face*, he seemed glad of their discipline. "I almost wonder, do I see a reason to even start back again after I've been clean for so long? I'm able to do things that a couple of years ago I couldn't do without freaking out. You know, trying to take care of a little girl and trying to do the Daddy things, and trying to make the music." He was almost announcing, without fanfare, the death of Slim Shady, the demon who had made the previously soft, sober Marshall dive into drugs in the first place, back when that derangement did him good.

Zadie Smith, watching him rehearse for a show, found him tired, but utterly professional. Describing a typical day to *Rolling Stone*, it revolved around making Hailie cereal, watching *Power Puff Girls* with her, taking her to and from school, or the studio, where he spent all his other time. He had succeeded at something as important to him as rapping, without anyone noticing, or caring, probably. He had not become his father, abandoning a family. He had saved himself, instead, and become a stable adult, for Hailie's sake. No more records would be sold on tabloid scandal.

There were still some scraps of new gossip, to be sieved from what reports there were. "Kim is pregnant," as he told *Rolling Stone*. "I have no idea who the father is. I just know she's due any day. So Hailie is going to have a baby sister. It's going to be tough the day she asks me why her baby sister can't come over. I've tried to keep her sheltered from those issues. Of course, she's going to find out shit as she goes through life. But I really don't want her to learn all the fucked up shit on my shift." *The Face* observed the new family unit he'd formed around himself, with not only Hailie but D12, and his half-brother Nathan, now permanently taken from their mother. With his dyed blond hair and pasty complexion, Nathan looked like Eminem's smaller shadow. What was living with Marshall like, *The Face* asked, catching him on his own. "Better than living with my Mom." Did he like the album? "It's good. I just wish we didn't have to let other people hear it." Such private attitudes were no longer possible, of course, in Eminem's world.

In the US, at least, another Anger Management tour helped sustain the rapper's profile. An earlier live comeback, as part of a festival in Washington, DC on May 25, had been marred when surging fans lost their footing, leading to four hospitalisations as he begged them to "back the fuck up". But the first of his full shows, in Buffalo, New York on July 18, supported this time by Xzibit, Ludacris and Papa Roach, and watched by *NME*, was a more promisingly dramatic affair than 2001's chainsaw-wielding flops. Footage of his politician foes – Lynne Cheney and the rest – preceded him. The set this time replaced a mock-up of his old home with a 50-foot Ferris wheel and fairground ride mouth, the broad American carnival of *The Eminem Show*'s concerns brought to life. 'White America' was played to police sirens and glitter showers, with a more radical cartoon in the background than last time, showing Eminem's army of fans being abused and assaulted till they shot their schoolmates, while Eminem wiped the blood from his face, to reveal dollar signs. A cartoon Hailie to duet with on 'My Dad's Gone Crazy', and the shotgun shooting of a Moby dummy (the techno star seemingly now the new Insane Clown Posse, on the basis of criticising Eminem in interviews) were other highlights. Eminem's continued lack of live charisma, and tireless wondering if his young fans "popped pills", showed some things never changed. But by the time the tour finished, in Detroit on September 8, with a five-hour party (staged for a DVD), it seemed a success.

A fresh set was struck for Eminem's traditional appearance at the MTV Video Music Awards, in New York on August 29. He performed 'White America' from the podium of a mock Senate, behind the seal of the "United States of Emerica", and was pelted with paper planes by fake Congressmen. His nakedly political stance was becoming hard to miss. But real boos came only when he undercut it by calling Moby a "girl". True controversy and cultural electrifying seemed suddenly elusive.

13

THE TOP

But the quiet was deceptive. Almost as soon as *The Eminem Show*'s discernible impact dissipated, he had a second major work ready for release. *8 Mile* had finished filming in Detroit back in January, but took till November to reach the public. It had always seemed the larger test of just how big a figure Eminem could become in his country's life, what limits there really were to his talent. When I spoke to its director Curtis Hanson in London, in the week of its US release, he recalled how delicate the process of even starting to make the film had been.

"It might have been the incentive of others to make a movie with Eminem in it," he told me of his initial misgivings, "but to me that was a big question mark – whether he could deliver a performance of sufficient emotional truth to anchor the kind of movie I wanted to make. I knew his work. I knew it was dense and serious and provocative. I also knew there was controversy around him. People said to me, 'Do you really wanna get involved with this guy?' My feeling was that I'd been involved before with actors of . . . reputation [Russell Crowe made his name in *LA Confidential*, and Rob Lowe and Robert Downey, Jnr. had been cast by Hanson when at disgraced lows], and I'd always tried to put that to one side, and see how they dealt with me, one on one. So I said to myself, 'I don't care about Eminem. I care about Marshall Mathers, the actor with whom I'm going to work.'"

When the pair met, after producer Brian Grazer had convinced first rapper then director to consider the project, both men were on tenterhooks, wondering how the other would be. "It was like we were on an extended blind date," Hanson remembered. "We were feeling each other out, getting a hit on each other, and deciding if we wanted to take a leap of faith."

As part of this courtship, Hanson asked Eminem to escort him around the landmarks of his life. Over the course of a long day, they toured the places of pain and pleasure that had made Marshall Mathers into Eminem. The fact that he was returning to the sites of boyhood humiliations as a grown man, wondering whether to be a movie star, didn't seem to phase him. His life had been that unreal for some time. "We went around the various places where he used to live," Hanson said, "where he went to school, where he met Proof and the guys from D12, where his girlfriend lived, and where they used to perform. None of it made him uncomfortable. He was looking back on it the way we all look back on different things. If there was something he didn't like, he was more laughing about it. In fact, I remember him showing me the place where he got beat up badly. He could laugh about that now. Or he was saying to Proof, 'Remember that, where we did dah dah dah . . . remember where we met on that street?' The reminiscing was more coloured by nostalgia, than the emotions he had back then."

Yet Grazer had famously said of his first meeting with Eminem that he felt "damage". Did Hanson feel those scars were still there – or that his star had hauled himself over them, long ago? "Oh, sure," he said emphatically. "I feel he's very strong now. Very focused."

As the tour continued, Hanson was offered another insight. "As we went around these neighbourhoods, there was always this feeling of good will towards him – from kids on the street, and people who poured out of their houses when they knew he was there. It was very different to how the Detroit media treat him. When we were shooting, they would have these stories: "Eminem Movie Causes Traffic Jam!" "Eminem Movie Burns Down House!" Whereas with the people, there was this feeling of pride, and familiarity. He was one of them. He was in his world."

And that world slipped under Hanson's skin. "The degree to which I wanted it to work out with him kept growing, because not only was I getting to know him, I was also spending more and more time in Detroit." The broken grandeur of the place, its roofless factories and mud alleys and scorched houses and silent streets, had slowly hypnotised him, as they did me. Eminem had brought another convert to his abandoned American home.

"It's a city of ghosts," Hanson enthused to me. "Everywhere you look you see reminders of its industrial past, and it's almost like there was another civilisation there, like Aztecs or Mayans, that vanished without a trace, a civilisation that's not connected to the young people living there today. And yet while you have this apparent visual grimness, you also have the populace, the citizens, who have this astonishing energy and spirit, and that's resulted in Detroit's incredible musical history. I wanted to try and capture that reality, and how Detroit and Eminem are inseparable."

He had been keen-eyed enough to notice something else about his possible subject, too. "What's unique here is that at first glance you think you have a story of race. But instead you have a story of class. The character Eminem ended playing, Jimmy Smith, is white, and all but one of his friends are black. But they're all from the same class. And that's the truth about Eminem as well. He grew up around 8 Mile, that's why his voice is authentic. As Future [the film's Proof-like character, played by Mekhi Phifer] says, 'Once they hear you, it won't matter what colour you are.' And that's something new in America."

Eminem and Hanson got along, too. So the deal was done, and work began on the script. Scott Silvers (of indie critical success *johns* and mainstream bomb *The Mod Squad*) had already drafted the sort of updated but standard tale of showbiz struggle Grazer had requested (his "hip-hop *Saturday Night Fever*"). Now Silvers and Eminem sat and talked about the rapper's life, deciding which details to incorporate into his character. "There were some things that were taken out of my real-life story," Eminem explained to MTV Asia. "I've had a lot of stuff happen in my life that not everybody knows about. I can't tell everything in my music. Then there are a lot of instances that are made up. Because you know, I'm not playing me in the movie. Just somebody like me." But those script sessions left the line badly blurred. In its final form, it showed Jimmy living with his unstable, unemployed, often drunk mother and little blonde sister in a Warren trailer park, having been kicked out by his manipulative girl-friend, as he struggles to succeed as a lone white boy in rap battles, supported by his small posse of mostly black friends. Like his records, the story let him draw on his own early days one more time, and add a further layer to what was becoming the most baroque, unreliable, extreme and endless American autobiography. His mother for one didn't fall for it as fiction. "She was bitching about Kim Basinger playing my mother, and calling the movie people," he sighed to *The Face*. "They were like, 'Yo, your mother keeps threatening to sue us.' I'm like, 'Does she know I'm not playing me? I'm a kid named Jimmy?'"

Hanson, meanwhile, added his own touches. He didn't care if it was Eminem's story, so long as it was Detroit's. The production company's

Detroit comes to Hollywood. A pensive Eminem arrives at LA's Westwood Village cinema for *8 Mile*'s premiere, as his stardom's peak approaches. (REUTERS/CORBIS)

Eminem wins Best Video of the Year for 'Without Me' at the MTV Video Music Awards at Radio City Music Hall, New York, on August 29, 2002. (REUTERS/CORBIS)

King of Pop? Eminem re-enacts Michael Jackson's notorious baby throwing incident – with a doll – at a Glasgow hotel window in 2003. His satire of Jackson in the following year's 'Just Lose It' video enraged Jackson, and Stevie Wonder. (CAMERA PRESS/WATTIE CHEUNG)

Eminem accepts his Best Rap Album Grammy for *The Eminem Show* in New York, February 23, 2003. His great comeback would see him up for Best Album in 2011, for *Recovery*. (REUTERS/CORBIS)

The Shady Gang. Eminem, 50 Cent and Dr Dre at the Shady National Convention in New York, October 28, 2004. (JOY E SCHELLER/LFI)

Eminem at the 2006 BET Awards in LA. He remembered little of such events, in a period when his pill addiction secretly took hold. (MARIO ANZUONI/REUTERS/CORBIS)

Enemy of the people. Eminem as Osama Bin Laden in the 'Without Me' video.

Eminem plays mum Debbie in the 'Without Me' video.

Eminem and Jay-Z perform at the launch of the *DJ Hero* game at the Wiltern Theatre, LA, on June 1, 2009. (JARED MILGRIM/CORBIS)

After four troubled years away, an unusually animated Eminem accepts the award for best hip hop video from Jennifer Lopez at the 2009 MTV Video Music Awards in New York. (GARY HERSHORN/REUTERS/CORBIS)

Ass like that. Sacha Baron Cohen, in character as Austrian fashion guru Bruno, lands on Eminem at the 2009 MTV Movie Awards in LA in a prearranged stunt. (MARIO ANZUONI/REUTERS/CORBIS)

In aptly old school garb, Eminem presents Run DMC at the Rock and Roll Hall of Fame 2009 induction ceremony in Cleveland. (AARON JOSEFCZYK/REUTERS/CORBIS)

Eminem and Lil Wayne perform at the 2010 Grammy Awards in LA.
During his depression, a jealous Eminem had fantasised about attacking
the younger star in a rap. (MIKE BLAKE/REUTERS/CORBIS)

Eminem and Rihanna perform *Relapse*'s big hit 'Love The Way You
Lie' at the 2010 MTV Video Music Awards at the Nokia Theatre, LA.
(PICTUREGROUP/EMPICS ENTERTAINMENT/PRESS ASSOCIATION)

Eminem, back fit and firing, at the Epicenter Music Festival, September 25, 2010.
(TIM MOSENFELDER/CORBIS)

plan to shoot in some more standard American city, with Jimmy as a hotel bellhop, was vetoed in favour of a job in an auto plant, and filming in Detroit's run-down heart. Scenes expressive of the city – like the symbolic razing of one of its plague of abandoned buildings – were inserted. And one more aspect needed to be changed. "We moved it back to 1995," Hanson said. "The idea of a white guy trying to express himself in that medium and being questioned doesn't really resonate in the same way today. We had to set it in a world before Eminem."

Next, a high quality cast was assembled, including Basinger, Mekhi Phifer (*Clockers*), and Brittany Murphy (*Clueless*), as Jimmy's new girl-friend Alex. They had six weeks of rehearsals, during which Hanson had to turn Eminem into an actor. "I didn't watch his videos before we met," he told me, "they didn't matter to me, neither did knowing he had another persona, Slim Shady. When you adopt a persona, it's artificial, you hide behind it. What I wanted was the opposite. I needed him to appear to be naked, and be still, and do nothing, so you would feel you were seeing his essence. I was brutally frank. I told him how long and difficult the process was going to be. And I wanted to be frank, because I wanted him to know, I didn't want him to enter into it lightly. And as frank as I was, he still didn't get it."

"I wanted to dabble in movies, I wanted to see if I could do it. I didn't realise it was gonna be this big a deal," Eminem would ruefully admit to MTV Asia after it was all over. "Then Curtis Hanson got involved, and Kim Basinger, and it got massive, it got out of control. All of a sudden it was like, 'Whoa. I gotta take this seriously.' I thought when I read the script that it was gonna be impossible for me to remember all those lines. But the truth is, we did a lot of rehearsing, eight hours a day for two months up until we started shooting. It was gruelling. I couldn't help but become this character. It took me back to that time, to that place. It stripped me of all ego, to before I was Eminem, before I was anybody."

With rehearsals done, *8 Mile* began shooting deep in the Detroit winter of 2001. For his cameraman, Hanson chose Rodrigo Prieto, best known for his work on the draining Mexico City melodrama *Amores Perros*; Hanson told him to make Detroit look "like a weed emerging from the sidewalk". Trying to mimic visually the free-styling of its rappers, *8 Mile* was filmed with mostly hand-held cameras, improvising and following the actors. Locations were chosen, too, for their correspondence to hip-hop's habit of recycling the past, easy in Detroit, where the money to knock down and start again never comes, and everything is gutted or patched. For the central rap battle scenes in The Shelter, the actual club where young Eminem was booed and abused was ignored, in favour of the shattered glory of the Michigan Theater, which production designer Philip Messina found "one of the most bizarre things I'd ever seen in my life. It was literally gutted from the roof down, with a quarter of its proscenium and tattered curtains intact, and the rest is a three-level parking garage." Understanding the religious nature of Eminem's devotion to hip-hop, expressed in so many of his songs, Hanson put a cross on his Shelter's exterior, making it "a church of hip-hop, where people go for a sense of community and hope". The interior was then styled more like a boxing venue, the site of *8 Mile*'s *Rocky*-style rap battles.

There were few rough moments during its shoot. The biggest strain was in its inexperienced star's head. Not just trying to act, but charged with writing the rap battles, and spending spare moments in his trailer writing soundtrack songs in the character of Jimmy, or in a mobile studio completing the soundtrack and *The Eminem Show*, he had stretched himself to the limit. Hanson's warnings had not been enough. Being a movie star was draining him.

"It was unnatural to him," Hanson said. "There's great courage necessary to lay oneself open as one has to [in order] to give the kind of performance I wanted. There was also courage involved because he wanted to be good. He wasn't entering into this lightly. He felt he had a lot at stake. He has sufficient ego and pride that he wanted his performance as well as the movie to appear truthful. And it took over his life. It was also challenging for him because it's very different than his normal process. He is somebody who does what he does in a very solitary way. Much the way we show in the movie, when we show Jimmy writing – those papers are Marshall's work-sheets – that little tiny writing, densely packed all over the page. It's a very private and interior process, and in making a movie not only did he have me to deal with constantly, but also the other actors, and the mechanics of movie-making. It was very invasive in his life. He found it wearing."

"I work a lot of hours in the studio, but it's on my own time and it's something I'm in control of," Eminem agreed to MTV Asia. "It hurts being on somebody else's schedule and somebody else's time. It was gruesome. It was like acting boot camp. It was tough, five in the morning till seven, eight at night. Then literally have enough time to go to sleep, and come right back." To Zadie Smith he confided, "acting was hard, not second nature, like rapping. I might do another, but not one where I'm in every scene and the whole thing's riding on me." As Hanson remembered, "After we were into it a few weeks, he said to me, 'You weren't kidding . . .' And the last day of shooting, I asked him, 'How do you feel?' And he said, 'Never again.' And he meant it. It was hard. But rewarding, for both of us."

Once the film had wrapped, word swiftly started to build that it had all been worthwhile. The first, rough cut was seen by critics at the Toronto Film Festival on September 8.

It starts in a toilet. Eminem as Jimmy is shadow-boxing, holding his hand like there's a mic in it, preparing for rap battle. His eyes look dead, and he's so nervous he starts to throw up. Urged on stage by fellow members of the Three One Third crew – 313 is the Detroit city phone code, 810 signals the suburbs, skin colour read in digits, like the number of Miles high you live – he looks out through dim, smoky air at a hostile black crowd. A taller black rapper, his opponent (played by Proof), gets in his face, and uses his 45 seconds of their battle to say people laugh at him "'cos you're white". At Jimmy's turn, he just clutches the mic to his throat like it's choking him, eyes scared, brain blank, saying nothing. Boos rise around him, and he leaves the stage. It was all the humiliations Eminem had suffered at the real Shelter and other clubs in one scene, the years of failure his fans had never seen revived in his first major film.

Elsewhere, *8 Mile* ranged round its star's private Ground Zero with investigating eyes. The cathedral-like car park of the Michigan Theater, the burnt buildings left to rot in the middle of streets, the indoor gun range outside his mother's trailer park and domestic nightmare behind her door, the bus rides up 8 Mile to his auto plant job; it was the subliminal background of his records given flesh, Hanson's fight to film there justified. In one powerful scene, where Three One Third roam through an abandoned, once prosperous family house, in the unsafe hollows of which a little girl has been raped, then burn it to the ground, as their militant member DJ Iz spits, "Does the city tear it down? No, too busy building casinos," the dramatic addressing of a Detroit issue for a global audience showed what a thorn Eminem now was to his home town, and how important. As Jimmy and his crew capered in the flames, the scene, Hanson's idea, recalled the thousands of such dangerous eyesores burned down by angry citizens during "Devil's Night" (Detroit's Halloween, as in the D12 song) in 1995, the riot inferno of 1967, the prosperity building and its city had once enjoyed, and the happy family home Jimmy and Eminem were denied.

Everyone watched, too, for more clues to Eminem's own past, the new details he had confided to Silvers. Basinger's glamorous but unstable, unreliable Mom showed more tired if incompetent love for her son than Debbie had in Eminem's memory, though her drunken rages and leeching from slob boyfriends seemed familiar. Her grand offer to hand Jimmy her car for his birthday so he can get to a job he can't afford to lose the next morning, only for the rustbucket to die when he turns the key, seems a symptomatic exasperation, stored from life, as does Jimmy's fight with the boyfriend she sides with, because she needs his money while his little sister cowers in a corner. But the melding of fiction and biography made it all guesswork, the forthrightness of his voice on record impossible here.

The most revealing scenes were of creativity: scribbling on his pad on the bus, or trading rhymes with Future in a sunny street, pleasure brightening his face. Eminem's whole performance, which carried the film, was built on such simple truthfulness; his high, light speaking voice, unfamiliar smile, and blue eyes capable of soft dreaminess as well as deadness, and his slight, white frame compared to almost everyone around him, made him vulnerable and sympathetic, where the public voice he had built since the times the film recalled could be strident and divisive. In a discreet sex scene with Murphy, the relieved need of his sighed out breath and drooping head as he came was unusually tender and erotic. And in the battle scenes, a lightness of touch quite different from his own raps remained, even in the pitch of desperate intensity of his final, winning confrontation. "Come on, Elvis," taunts his gigantic black opponent, fanning a pack of race cards. Jimmy's Eminem-scripted reply simply lacerates his own white trash flaws better than his enemy ever can, a return to the crushed esteem of *The Slim Shady LP* that success had seemed to bury. The choked silence of Jimmy's start has been spat out, to clog his speechless enemy's throat. But, true to the limited triumph of working-class rappers who don't become Eminem, he follows his victory by going back to his factory shift. The last shot shows a harried, private smile as he wanders away.

The Toronto screening exceeded everyone's hopes. The crowd, including Festival attendees Michael Douglas, Sharon Stone and Dustin Hoffman (though not Eminem, gigging in Detroit) roared Jimmy on in the battle scenes, and Hanson left the cinema feeling exhilarated. He told reporters: "The reception took my breath away." Early reviews were good, too. Eminem then stoked local flames with a surprise, MTV-sponsored live show after an *8 Mile* preview at Michigan State University, on October 11. Students queued for eight hours, just in case their state's most famous school drop-out showed.

Eminem then added one element of substance to the building hype, by releasing *8 Mile*'s soundtrack on October 29. The talents he'd assembled for it showed his unquestioned hip-hop status now, the distance he'd dragged himself from the desperate unknown the movie recalled: Jay-Z, Nas and Gangstarr were among the stars who contributed mostly strong, battle-style raps. Eminem also produced tracks by rough, Shady Records-signed Detroit rapper Obie Trice, and early copies included a second CD spotlighting Shady talent. Eminem's silent, sudden transition from Dre's protégé to Detroit's new Berry Gordy, picking up the city's raw music talent, left in the gutter since Motown fled for LA in 1972, was confirmed when he described his A&R policy to *Launch*. "Every artist I've signed so far is from Detroit – and that's kinda how I'm gonna keep it in the family. So, no matter what Detroit says about me, how much dirt they wanna spread and gossip, I'm doing something for the city. So suck my dick." Ironically, the one exception to his rule, New York rapper 50 Cent, also on the soundtrack, would soon prove to be Eminem's most successful discovery.

The soundtrack's real thrill, though, was its three new Eminem songs, plus his appearance on two more, a further track on the second CD, and seven producer's credits (including taking charge of his only commercial rap rival, Jay-Z). It was more than half a fresh Eminem album, four months after the last, and just before a major film. It also marked, incredibly, an instant musical and lyrical break from *The Eminem Show*. Eminem, having possibly reached the limit of his own life as raw material, had levered open a new part of his brain, to inhabit Jimmy Smith.

It had been Hanson's idea to show Jimmy constructing a rap during *8 Mile*, littering the movie with fragments of its words and beats, and climaxing with the finished work over the credits. Eminem wrote the track, 'Lose Yourself', during filming. *8 Mile*'s fictional rapper, in effect, had created its musical centrepiece as the movie was made, a reality-bending first Eminem was built for. "We talked a lot about what rap's opportunities meant to the character, and what the song needed to express," Hanson recalled. "And it was a struggle for him. Because his music, up to that point, all came from within, in whatever form he felt right, and it was all extremely personal and self-referential. Here, he was doing something that was also an assignment, and it needed to apply to his emotional life as reflected in his character Jimmy."

Released as a single on December 2, 'Lose Yourself' was Eminem's first US number one, and one of his most powerful records. Effortlessly commercial, it was based around a stabbing bass riff suggesting the unreleased, repetitive tension of Jimmy's life (rock by now integral to his sound) and triumphal Eighties synths, echoing the themes of the *Rocky* films *8 Mile* resembled. Within this hit frame, 'Lose Yourself's crafted nature seemed to sharpen and discipline its writer's wits, forcing him into Jimmy's head. It was in this song and its *8 Mile* companions, more than his performance in the film itself, that Eminem truly reached back into his depressed, almost hopeless past as Marshall Mathers with an actor's skill. His lyrics re-created his sweaty palms and stalling brain and choking mouth as he failed in the real Shelter, the cold shock of reality reasserting itself as defeat destroyed his dreams again. 'Lose Yourself' slipped into Jimmy's home life too, the subtle separation from Marshall more evident in this apologetic line: *"Mom, I love you, but this trailer's got to go."* How fictional that apology was, and how much a soft corrective to 'Cleanin' Out My Closet', could only be guessed, in the grey zone of this new writing style. But more innovative still was the verse when Eminem suddenly broke character, jumping into a cautionary vision of his own success's underside, and possible future collapse: *"he's cold product, they've moved onto the next shmoe who blows/ the soap opera's told."* Reminiscence and premonition, fiction, autobiography and obituary, 'Lose Yourself' showed that, even with *"the soap opera told"*, inspiration still flooded Eminem's veins.

Of the other new songs, '8 Mile' was almost as striking. Including another startling series of metaphors for the cramped depression Jimmy/ Marshall suffered before success saved them – asking *"am I just another crab in the bucket?"*, wanting to jump right out of his skin – what lingered from '8 Mile' was its sound: the wail of a train horn, followed by the click-clack rhythm of old railway tracks, which Eminem imagined trudging down, till his home was left behind. He had begun wanting to be Ice-T. By 2002, Elvis, Aerosmith, and the symbols and sounds of Depression bluesmen and hobos were welcome in his world, too.

The *8 Mile* soundtrack went straight to number one in the US, selling 703,000 and sucking *The Eminem Show* back into the Top 10. The next week, the final part of Eminem's extraordinary year of achievement fell into place. On November 7, he attended *8 Mile*'s US première, held, of course, at the Phoenix Theater, the only first-run cinema left in Detroit. Family members he was speaking to and friends were all with him. Ever the responsible father, he put his hands over Hailie's eyes during his sex scene. By the end of that weekend, the film had made $54.5 million at the US box office. Stepping into a mainstream medium, to be judged by Americans to whom he had until now been just a filthy rumour, reviews too were effusive. *Entertainment Weekly*'s critic was not the only one to dub him "a hip-hop James Dean", while many also grasped the new lessons on US class and race Hanson and his star were trying to teach. Some also noted the disappointing conservatism of the plot compared to Eminem's own unbound records, as in *LA Times* critic Kenneth Turan's insightful review: "*8 Mile* is very much an old-fashioned somebody-up-there-likes-me kind of story, replete with traditional plot devices that . . . are decades old. This . . . facilitates the mainstreaming of rap, enabling civilian audiences to feel the safety and security of familiarity that's simply not on the cards when listening to Eminem's earlier, more nasty and threatening work . . . [But] his hostility, savagery and disgust as well as his undeniable musical gifts come from too deep a place to be completely blanded out the way Elvis' talents notoriously were . . . Eminem is an actor with a rare gift for rage, and movie careers, even big ones, have been built on less."

It was true that the film came most alive in Eminem's self-scripted battles, and in that sense was a standard pop showcase. But in also crafting Hollywood's first portrait of working-class Detroit, and the dreams that can thrive there, director and actor could be well satisfied. Eminem was sure of the positive message he wanted to give: "No matter where you come from, you can break out of that cycle. You can make something of yourself." America's most politically radical pop star still believed in its Dream, and wanted others to. Even false hope was better than the despair he'd known in his darkest Detroit days.

In the general surprise at *8 Mile*'s success, there was even talk of an Eminem Oscar. He downplayed his prospects to MTV Asia. "It could or it couldn't. Steely Dan beat me out one year for a Grammy so, you know . . . Whatever comes I'll take, but I'm not looking for that. I just wanted to make an authentic movie about the place where I grew up."

But as his movie's triumph became apparent, the shocked exhaustion at shoot's end which had made him dread ever making another seemed to fall away. "Now that I've had a taste of the movie business, I want some more," he decided. "I want to do something completely different. I would love to play a comedy character or something. People wouldn't expect that of me." His family were, as always, free with their advice. Said grandmother Kresin: "I was one of the first in line to see *8 Mile*. Now I would love to see him finish what he started, by making a sequel, showing how he cut his first CD." With the spectre of Elvis the movie star now looming (an early, relatively good Presley film, *Loving You* (1957) had been very much in the raw, semi-biopic style of *8 Mile*, which hadn't stopped the sewage that followed), Eminem's cautious advisers seemed to feel the same way.

There was one more strangely resonant piece of bad news for the rapper, as *8 Mile*'s takings roared in. It was revealed that on November 7 Kresin's one-time home in Warren, Eminem and his mother's bolthole on so many occasions through their lives, had been sold by Debbie's brother, Todd Nelson (who had previously fronted a cheap video about his nephew, *Eminem – Behind The Mask*, in which he had claimed to be his rapping mentor). "This is a very emotional thing for me, because this house has been in our family for over 50 years," Nelson told the *Detroit Free Press*. He couldn't be accused of exploiting his relative on this occasion. Short of money, he sold up for $45,000, in an area with an average house price of $90,000. The buyers, St. Clair Shores lawyer Sebastian Lucida and real estate developer Roland Fraschetti, then coolly put their new property up for auction, with a minimum bid of $120,000. By the start of December, the house Eminem had built a replica of to reveal his "white trash" background as he toured the world, situated close to the 8 Mile colour line he'd made notorious, the place where he'd crayoned pictures for his vanished father, and the nearest thing he'd had in his unhappy, unsettled life to visible roots, had a bid for $12 million considered. Nelson observed that Eminem was upset. It was just one more garish sign that he really could never go home again now.

Instead, he found himself standing at another crossroads. His influence was at its zenith, his powers seemingly at their peak, everything he touched in every medium a dazzling success. He was the biggest and best pop star in the world. His home life was the happiest it had ever been. And yet, the details of that real life became rarer and duller, as his fame continued to grow. The touchstones of all his work, as Eminem, Slim, or

Jimmy – the beatings, depression, poverty, arrests, savage maternal and marital scraps – were buried in the past. They had been strip-mined and alchemised and turned into fiction. But they might stay the hot core of a cooling life. "That's my worst fear," he confirmed to *Rolling Stone*, "that I'll wake up tomorrow and won't be able to write. That if there's not drama and negativity in my life, all my songs will be wack and boring." As he had in 'Lose Yourself', he could imagine the day it all ended. "I've felt since my first day of rapping that my time is ticking. That's how I've based my whole career – that this might never happen again. Fans are so fickle and so quick to turn on you. Suddenly, you're not cool no more, even if at first you're the greatest thing since sliced cunt."

The collaborations of Hollywood could yet soften him into spineless-ness, too, Elvis all over again. And yet, the inexhaustible resource and radicalism of his work in 2002 suggested a happier comparison. Openly battling his nation's rulers in a time of scared consensus, picking at the sores of sex, gender, race, class and violence, spilling astonishing words as easily as breathing, he was like the great, late poet Allen Ginsberg. Both men are big enough to write about America every time they write about themselves, and themselves when they write about America. Neither subject has an end.

There was one more thing that may save Eminem from falling. The hurts of his past didn't only survive in his songs. His struggling, despairing years as Marshall were also a warning of where he might return, and the doubters and bullies he'd meet there. "Vengeance is my motivation," he's said. And that work is never done.

"It's kinda like that thing where you struggle all your life to get it," he told *The Source*, "but it's just as hard to maintain as it is to get there. I have to keep working if I'm gonna keep being able to laugh at them people who said I wouldn't be shit. I do feel like, 'Look what I've accomplished, ha-ha.' At the same time, there's the feeling that: 'How do I know that I got the last laugh?'"

14

THE CLOSET

The next year saw no new Eminem album, and no conclusive answer to how his music would survive contentment. Instead, he slipped behind the scenes, signing and producing some of 2003's biggest stars, as if rehearsing for his oft-mooted retirement from rapping. By the year's end, the dramas of his past would stake their claim on him anyway. His whiteness, which he had worked so hard to downplay, would once more cast poisonous doubt on everything he did.

Such thoughts were far from his mind that March, as the Oscars neared. Wild rumours of a Best Actor nomination for his *8 Mile* performance had sensibly come to nothing. One of the favourites to win that award did, though, have a sliver of Shady in his soul. Daniel Day-Lewis' ferociously intense turn as the demonic Victorian villain Bill the Butcher in Martin Scorsese's *Gangs Of New York* had been inspired by an unusual piece of Method preparation. He blasted out Eminem's 'The Way I Am' in his trailer each morning, using its snarling, trapped rage as fuel for Bill's lupine savagery.

Eminem's 'Lose Yourself' was meanwhile nominated for Best Song, against competition from the likes of Paul Simon and U2. Strangely, though, he chose the most prestigious awards ceremony of his life to break his habit of attending them all. Rumours circulated that he had refused to tone down his performance of 'Lose Yourself' for the organisers – unlikely, in such a career-minded man. At any rate, when his song was announced as the winner by Barbra Streisand – with a gasp signalling either shock, or an approving welcome into her conservative, Old Holly-wood world – keyboardist and co-writer Luis Resto stepped up to accept the award. "It means a lot to him, believe me," Resto claimed backstage. "I just don't think he expected it."

The success of 'Lose Yourself' and Eminem's rumoured boycott of the awards on a petty point were anyway insignificant in the night's wider context. Headlines were grabbed by documentarist Michael Moore, who used accepting his Oscar for *Bowling For Columbine* to deliver a raging protest against the just-launched invasion of Iraq by the US and Britain. Forcing anti-war sentiment onto American networks otherwise bellicosely uniform in their patriotism, provoking boos, cheers and frozenly inscrutable smiles from the assembled stars, daring even to attack the President – who he called "fictitious" – in time of war, it was an incandescent moment. Eminem's disinterest in even attending such a forum at such a time did him no favours. Instead, he saw his music used for the war. The brooding aggression of 'Lose Yourself' themed BBC radio's coverage of the conflict's first night, as if George Bush and Saddam Hussein were competing rap champions. And Eminem was one of the most requested artists on British and US forces' radio, joining The Clash's 'Rock The Casbah', another record to have its oppositional intent turned inside out.

The unauthorised internet release in December of five songs he was working on for his next album – dubbed the *Straight From The Lab* EP – showed Eminem's true attitude to his government. 'We As Americans' – titled like an alternative State of the Union address – included these lines: *"Fuck money, I don't rap for dead Presidents/ I'd rather see the President dead"*. His press office immediately distanced him from the "lost or stolen" songs. But, in the prevailing mood of jittery paranoia, the shadow of the Secret Service fell on him anyway, as they considered how potent his implied desire to assassinate Bush might be. The agency was "concerned about communications that can be interpreted in a manner perhaps not intended by the artist", spokesman John Gill intoned. On December 8, however, this threat was removed. It was a rare moment of common sense. But the Shady file in the alcove of state where earlier radicals like John Lennon had been monitored surely thickened another inch.

Eminem's official releases in 2003, though, were desultory and absent-minded. In the UK, 'Sing For The Moment' was *The Eminem Show*'s third single. Eminem's disengagement was shown by the video. Where the clips from his first two major albums had been marvels of inventive wit, now dull tour footage sufficed. The clip for final American single 'Superman' just enhanced its misogyny, as Eminem cavorted with a silicon-pumped porn star. This was an extra on *8 Mile*'s DVD, a greater priority by now than the LP he had honed so lovingly.

During this new period of apparent drift, Eminem's presence was, as always, still felt in the world. In Istanbul in November, Hayrethin Demir hawked T-shirts of the rapper with the cry, "Eminem, my Eminem!" It was the name of a passing 19-year-old's mother. In the knife-fight that resulted, the teenager was killed. On the internet, sites of "slash" fiction (erotic fantasies about the fictional or famous) proliferated, as women and gay men imagined Eminem, Kim and others in a series of obscenely unlikely positions. On the BBC, meanwhile, Nobel-winning Irish poet Seamus Heaney was asked if anyone now stirred interest in language in the way Dylan and Lennon used to. "There is a guy Eminem," he said at once. "He has created a sense of what is possible. He has sent a voltage around a generation. He has done this not just through his subversive attitude but also his verbal energy."

Eminem's greatest impact in 2003, though, was not as a writer, but as a businessman. This was the year he parlayed Shady Records into an empire. And the champion who carved out that kingdom for him was called 50 Cent.

Born in 1976 and raised by his drug dealer mother in the Jamaica district of Queens, New York, 50 Cent's early life under his given name Curtis Jackson was so appalling, and yet unexceptional, it made Marshall Mathers's sufferings seem mild. Marshall's mother wished he was dead. Curtis' mother just died. He was eight.

"She got killed," he explained to *Bang*. "Somebody put something in her drink and then turned on the gas to cut off her circulation, but her life-style was kinda like that. Of all the things that have happened to me, some of it is hard to explain even to myself."

Abandoned by a father who was rarely around anyway and raised by his grandmother, Curtis gravitated to his mother's old crooked acquaintances, the only people he saw with money and power. He became a crack dealer, soaking up violence and jail-time. Any softness in his nature was shut down, any emotional wounds cauterised.

Did he have a conscience? *Vibe* recently asked. "A little bit," he replied, "but it goes away. Anger is my most comfortable emotion. If you hurt my feelings, instead of hurting, I get angry. When you come from my neighbourhood, you don't walk around crying. I spent my childhood learning not to cry. I've adjusted to situations because I don't want to get killed."

Rapping as 50 Cent seemed a safer way than dealing to help provide for himself and son Marquis, born in 1997. Around that time Run-DMC's Jam Master Jay (mysteriously shot dead in 2003) spotted his talent, and the

Trackmasters produced his first LP, *Power Of The Dollar*, on Columbia. But, scared no "buzz" was building on his one shot at ghetto escape, he released the almost literally suicidal single 'How To Rob', threatening violence to a string of rappers, hoping for notoriety. In May 2000, massive retaliation came when he was shot by an unknown gunman – once in the cheek, once in the hand, and seven times in the legs. In the hospital, he was dropped by his fearful label, and his album was shelved.

For the next two years, with a like-minded posse, G Unit, he clawed his way back up from the underground, sneering at mainstream rap's separation from the streets, and rashly starting a new feud, with Ja Rule. Irv Gotti, head of Ja's label Murder Inc. – under FBI investigation for links to drug crime – was associated in 50's mind and lyrics with his shooting. The subsequent second-party punching of Ja and stabbing of 50 seemed traceable to the conflict, too. This was the bloody background that Eminem bought into when he announced on New York radio he was a 50 Cent fan, then swiftly signed him to a $1 million deal on Shady/Aftermath. There, he would be produced by Eminem and Dre.

It was Eminem's manager, Paul Rosenberg, Shady's self-styled "business side", who pushed for the move. "I was blown away by [50's potential]," he told *Hip-Hop Connection*. "I realised what a huge thing it could become. I kept trying to push Eminem to focus on 50 Cent but he was recording his record at the time and didn't have any time to listen to it. Then when he was done with it and got into it, it was later in the game and there was already a bidding war going on. That probably cost us a few dollars. But in hindsight, it didn't matter."

As Eminem's first major protégé, 50 was guaranteed attention. But the overdose of ghetto reality in his life made him almost too good to be true for Interscope's marketers. His album *Get Rich Or Die Tryin'*, released in February 2003, was shamelessly sold with a cover showing his topless, tattooed, breathtakingly sculpted body, with a chest looking tough enough to bounce bullets off. Booklet photos posed him in starkly lit, empty inner city streets, somewhere between a fashion shoot and a crime scene, with a baseball bat draped over his shoulders. Crisp dollar bills were shoved down his pants by a hand carefully turned to show its bullet wounds, while wide-eyed, set-lipped challenge burned from his face.

To white eyes he gave off the frisson of Mike Tyson in his animalistic prime. The concentration on his physical condition and presence typed him as a brutal black man, even as he was objectified and sexualised as much as any female R&B star, or hip-hop video honey. In the inner city, though, his history and image sent a different message. On a British TV documentary, black and white youths from areas like 50's own said his being shot made them admire him more. He knew what they were going through; his raps were real.

For Eminem, his story's new cast-member sent equally ambiguous signals. The demographic trade-off was similar but more risky than it had been with Dre. Next to 50 and his scars, Eminem could again seem like the skinny white dilettante he had once been scorned as. On the other hand, the more pictures of him that appeared with 50, Dre, and D12, the more black he might appear by association. No one white has yet been signed by Shady Records.

The final awkward twist was that, as Eminem started to offer black acts the patronage Dre had once bestowed on him, the brief historical inversion that had made Dre and Timbaland (with his find Bubba Sparxxx) black Colonel Parkers with pet white Elvises could seem reversed. If Eminem's unique popularity made him not just an honourable white novelty in hip-hop, but its king and king-maker, resentment was bound to follow; within the year, it would.

Creatively and commercially, though, *Get Rich Or Die Tryin'* was a triumph. 'Wanksta', on the massively successful *8 Mile* soundtrack, was a carefully placed preview of 50's qualities, as he wittily dismissed fake gangstas with his trademark taunting drawl. The album that followed was a full-scale attempt by Eminem and Dre to replicate their own successes with a fresh face. They contributed to almost all its tracks. The guinea pig-like nature of 50's position was playfully admitted in the video to his first enormous hit, 'In Da Club', a return to top visual form for Eminem, in which he and Dre were mad Frankensteins, assembling the monstrous 50. On 'Patiently Waiting', one of two Em guest-raps, he extended the idea: *"Take some Big and some 'Pac and you mix them up in a pot . . . and what the fuck do you got?/ You got the realest and illest killas, tied up in a knot."*

Dre's back-room role was strangely under-sold. *Get Rich . . .* was released on his Aftermath imprint as well as Shady, and he produced four tracks (including singles 'In Da Club' and 'If I Can't'). With his trusted LA keyboardist Mike Elizondo heavily involved, he used stabbing organs and strings to give 50 knockout pop punch. But Eminem was close behind, having his hand in almost everything Dre didn't. A mixture of the glum and the epic, his developing string and synth-heavy style was darker and narrower than Dre's, as if his early hopelessness had stayed in him.

Get Rich Or Die Tryin' was an instant phenomenon, selling nine million in a year, beating *The Eminem Show*'s early sales. On Eminem's July UK tour, it was 50's support slot that attracted fevered press attention, not rap's former demon king. Eminem seemed in danger of being outshone by his sky-rocketing, more obviously "authentic" protégé, even as it was the white star's imprimatur that made this hardcore street material approachable for such unprecedented masses. It was an awkward ambiguity addressed on *Get Rich*'s 'Patiently Waiting', where 50 loyally toasted Em as *"my favourite white boy . . . I owe ya for this one"*, before bemoaning *"this white man's world"*. Eminem meanwhile tried to maintain his dangerous aura even alongside his bullet-riddled charge, by making his second outrageous verbal visit to the destroyed World Trade Center: *"You put your life in this, nothing like surviving a shot/ You know about death threats, 'cos I get a lot/ Shady Records was 80 seconds away from the Towers/ them cowards fucked with the wrong building, they meant to hit ours."*

50, for one, had no doubt his boss was still relevant. "Em himself is nowhere near done," he told *Bang*. "There was a point where he was really unexcited by hip-hop, he thought there was nothing going on. Em uses so much of himself that we know who Hailie is, we know who Kim is, we know his relationship with his mom. He's using his life and as a person he's gonna grow, he's gonna feel new experiences, and you never lose something to rap about when you use yourself in your music."

The charge that Interscope and Eminem were exploiting 50's really violent ghetto life was also rebuffed. 50's next release, *Beg For Mercy* by his crew G Unit, was not on Shady but his own new G Unit Records, exactly replicating Eminem's founding of Shady with D12's album, after being on Dre's Aftermath. It looked more like a chain of saved lives than one rapper's enslavement by another. As 50 pointedly told *Vibe*, "I own G Unit Records. I own G Unit Clothing. These are my deals that I made happen with the people *I* put in place. Every situation I've been through has enhanced my character, and when I get past it all, I'll become what God wants me to be."

Beg For Mercy gave no clue as to whether the intelligent, learning man who spoke those words would soon appear on record. It mostly coarsened the Bad Black stereotype of his solo CD, as if all 50 had to offer was his "authentic" past, with monotonously martial music and thoughtless themes of rough sex and violence. But its sales the week of its November release – 377,000 in the US alone – proved that Eminem's name, re-inforced by 50's, now guaranteed rap gold. Though on 50's label, and mostly the work of his Long Island producer Sha Money XL, the cover still credited "PRODUCTION BY EMINEM AND DR. DRE" (Em's crucial contribution? "Additional Production" on two tracks). 50 was spreading the Shady empire, the production line of which now rumbled night and day.

Luis Resto, now Eminem's right-hand man at Detroit's 54 Studios alongside guitarist-mixer Steve King, revealed their work rate, as the three men assembled music for new albums by Eminem, D12 and Obie Trice: "When Eminem's in Detroit, we work together every day. A lot of times we're writing for all three projects. You go in and you're jamming, doing music, and it gets spread here and there. Some stuff goes to Eminem, some to Obie and some to other artists. We sit down and write and we parcel it out. Marshall takes home CDs and he listens to them, some things intrigue him, some things not so much – you keep backlogging the ideas, and see what comes of it."

Detroit's Obie Trice barely bothered to hide his resentment at Shady's over-stretching. "The reason why it took so long to get my album done," he offered, "is because Eminem was into a lot of shit. We didn't get a chance to really get into the studio like we wanted to. He dropped D12's album, he dropped *The Eminem Show*, then he went off into the movie thing. So *8 Mile* came about, the *8 Mile* soundtrack came about, all the time he's busy doing this, busy doing that. I can't get into the studio with him, I can't get into the studio. Then around the *8 Mile* movie, 50 Cent was getting signed, he was coming to the table with an album damn near done. Then boom we dropped 50 Cent first. He had the momentum, this what you want to hear? He had the momentum, he had the buzz, he had all that shit from New York, he's been shot nine times, yes, yes, you get what I'm saying? So, Obie Trice, now I'm here, that's the thing. Why it took so long? We don't want to know about that . . ."

Obie Trice's début, *Cheers*, was Eminem's most sustained work since *8 Mile*. He had a producing hand in almost every track, rapping on four. Obie, 23, with an adored five-year-old daughter, Kobie, made good company for doting dads 50 and Em. But he was a different proposition from 50, a natural joker and dirty ladies' man. He raised a glass of Hennessy Cognac on *Cheers*' cover, happy to party and, at an Eminem-like 5′ 8″, wasn't eager to fight. Raised on Rakim, he was a similarly clear, confident rapper, with a sensitive side. Though the album's big hit was the comic 'Got Some Teeth' (with a hilarious video of Obie explaining disastrous, drunken one-night stands to Eminem's TV interviewer, despite his minimum standards in a woman: *"hopefully, she got some teef . . ."*), its best track was 'Don't Come Down'. A shamed lament at his drug-dealing youth, when his mother disowned him, it countered Eminem's mother-cursing career. Its dramatic orchestral soul sound, sped-up, sampled Seventies female vocals and Steve King's shamelessly stretched guitar solo was Em's most imaginative production on the record, too: a rap power ballad. It was a style he would return to.

His guest-raps, meanwhile, though hardly full-blast, had intriguing touches. 'Lady' was a lighter variant on 'Superman', warning would-be lovers that if they did snare him, his insane jealousy would leave them the trapped ones, branded and shackled to the bed. 'We All Die One Day' imagined him as the al Qaeda shoe-bomber, while 'Outro' favourably compared him to his President: *"I don't send my soldiers to war if I ain't in the middle of the shit with them."*

Obie's own essential good humour, though, was too often smothered in trite sexist and violent bragging. And Eminem's production was not skilful or varied enough yet (over-fond as it was of repeating sounds, beats and even tunes from earlier successes) to save his second protégé from sounding half-baked, a potentially useful Joker in the Shady pack who had been misplayed. When I saw Obie's UK début at the intimate London venue the Scala, it was enjoyable enough – at least until a shambolic sexy dancing competition between girls in the crowd for a Shady jacket, fun only for the harmlessly hot-blooded rapper. As he nervously clutched at his Detroit baseball cap, and the crowd went wild only at Eminem's name, he hardly seemed ready for the big leagues, and Shady did not seem the new star-stuffed Motown. *Cheers*' million US sales did, though, confirm Eminem's Midas touch.

His most creatively successful 2003 release, however, was for the sound-track to the documentary *Tupac: Resurrection*, where he would produce the first musical meeting of rap's rival martyrs, Biggie and Tupac. The scale of the honour was humbling to Eminem. To reporters, he recalled feeling as if he and the childhood-damaged Tupac were growing up together, and his unreal daze as he watched 'Pac's death on Gilbert's Lodge's TV. His 'Runnin' (Dying To Live)' built on the lesson of *Cheers*' 'Don't Come Down', again sampling and treating a soulful Seventies record. This time, it was Texan blues-rocker Edgar Winter's forgotten, bleak cry – *"Why am I dyin' to live, if I'm just living to die?"* Speeded to a girlish pitch, over surging strings, rolling brass, splashes of Luis Resto's piano, clattering break-beats and excerpts of crackly interviews and defiant raps from Tupac and Biggie, and police radio news of Tupac's death, Winter's soaring vocal was powerfully redemptive, a resurrection prayer from the pit of his own despair. Winter himself wondered how Eminem had ever heard it, the old-school mark of sampling respect. In its complex arrangement and primal pop force, it showed significant progress, at last, in his producing. Eminem's own guest-rap on Tupac's 'One Day At A Time' meanwhile suggested they were both immortal originals. The presence of Eminem and 50 on *Resurrection*'s two other unreleased tracks though prompted a more uneasy thought: that, thanks to sharing Tupac's corporate home, Interscope, Eminem was expanding his empire to annex rap's most potent myth.

The only ripple in Eminem's calm private life now was revealed in another recording. On *Cheers'* 'Lady' he gallantly told a lover: *"I'm a bachelor, bitch, and I ain't in no fast hurry to run out and find another Mrs. Mathers, because technically, me and Kim ain't back fully, but we still make booty calls occasionally, but be damned if I end up back in a pattern where we end up back in that tavern . . ."*

As his grandmother had already told the *New York Post*, in October 2002, Kim had returned to live in Eminem's mansion. "They're back together and I think Marshall is very happy about it," Betty Kresin said. "He loves Kim and Hailie, and Kim is the mother of his child. He is a terrific father, and very family-oriented. I'm not surprised he wants that stability. I want him to enjoy his life. Everybody deserves a piece of the pie."

His attempts at relationships during their separation had always seemed sad and half-hearted. He had a brief fling with Brittany Murphy on the set of *8 Mile*, where he once again ruined his misogynist rep. "He was one of the first people I've met that made me feel comfortable with being every aspect of myself that I would want to possibly be," Murphy gushed when it was over. "But he came, and went." Mariah Carey, meanwhile, revealed that they had dated in only the most desultory way, never making love. "Maybe he thinks because nothing happened he'd look bad," she puzzled, after he dissed her on 'Superman', and it was rumoured he would release old, erotic phone-messages from her. "I don't know what the hell he's doing. Doesn't it seem a little bit girly? Like we're in a catfight."

Compared to these brushes with showbiz romance, Kim, who still knew him as Marshall, would always win. The defensiveness in 'Lady', trying to guard against the *"pattern"* of conflict whenever he inched open his heart to her, was understandable. One of the stolen, unfinished raps on the *Straight From The Lab* EP, 'I Love You More', switched tone between tenderness and violent rage, suggesting their relationship's old bruising nature remained: *"Do you hate me? Good, because you're so fucking beautiful when you're angry."* They often seemed more like the squabbling, inseparable siblings they were first raised as than lovers.

Kim giving birth to another man's child five months before their reunion was announced must have wounded Eminem, of course. But in the early months of 2003, it seemed the dream ending he had imagined for his life as a teenager would come true: his adolescent sweetheart by his side for good, and now with a darling daughter, too. Whatever his protestations, they appeared as a couple around Detroit as he attended gigs and industry conferences, Kim as always staying silent in public, but unmistakably his.

Then in September 2003, after a year of this latest truce, Kim left again. It was claimed she was furious that Eminem had put Hailie's life in danger, by putting her on a track on an underground mix tape which continued 50's, and therefore his, feud with Ja Rule (with its alleged influence on 50's stabbing). The latest trouble had begun when, on 'Warrior's Song (Loose Change)', Ja crowed: *"Eminem, you claim your mother is a crackhead and Kim is a known whore/ So what's Hailie gonna be when she grows up?"* Eminem's retaliation, 'Hailie's Revenge', brought his 7-year-old into the battle. *"Come here, baby,"* he said. *"Bring Daddy his Oscar." "OK." "We're going to shove it up Ja Rule's ass." "Daddy,"* Hailie cooed, *"is Ja Rule taller than me?" "No, honey. You guys are the* same size.*"* Hilarious as it was, it showed Eminem once again exploiting those around him for raps without thought of the consequences. But parallel events suggested Hailie's mother had problems of her own.

On June 10, 2003, at 2.30 am, Kim's white Cadillac was seen by police driving erratically near 12 Mile Road. When she was stopped, two bags of cocaine were found in her car, and one on her person. Police checks also found her driving licence had been revoked in 2000, and she had previously been arrested for coke possession in July 2001, being released as there was doubt that it was hers. Then, on September 29, police were called to a party at Warren's Candlewood Suites hotel, after complaints of loud music and yelling. Kim allegedly told them the room was in her name, and that her guests had taken marijuana and Es.

Charged separately with possessing a controlled substance and maintaining a drug house, she faced serious jail-time, as her ex-husband had three years before. On November 7, she compounded her problems, vanishing from sight when due in court, provoking two arrest warrants. "Her family and her children are praying for her," her attorney told the press. "We are really concerned." On November 13, Eminem was temporarily granted full custody of Hailie.

On November 19, Kim reappeared, posting $53,000 bail. She was made subject to electronic tagging, and drug and drink tests and counselling. On December 19, plea-bargaining saw her admit drugs possession and her driving violations, while other charges were dismissed. She was sentenced to two years probation and regular drug tests, much as Eminem had been. She was warned another slip would mean prison. But unlike her ex-, she could not help herself. On February 6, 2004, she was jailed after failing a urine test, and admitting cocaine use to her probation officer. "She obviously has a drug problem and on her own it wasn't being addressed," assistant prosecutor Dan Gillian said. A year of penal drama, including, Eminem alleged, Kim hacking off her tag to go on the run like a true outlaw, or addict, tentatively ended with her October release.

America's severe drug laws, separating a mother from her child when she had harmed no one, may have seemed more immoral than Kim's actions. But her inability to respond to relative leniency by cleaning up even for a short while suggested either genuine addiction, or a fatal feeling of drift, a lack of the will which had let Eminem straighten out. It was a devastating end to their latest reunion. But by now, it was clear only death would separate them for good.

Mother Debbie, by contrast, seemed almost invisible to Eminem now. There was talk of her appearing in an *Osbournes*-style reality show, after her son refused point-blank. She then made the news on January 22, 2004, when 16-year-old James Knott pointed a silver pistol at her at an 8 Mile gas station, dragging her out of her car by her hair and stealing the vehicle, before his swift arrest. "I tried to contact Marshall," she sniffed, "but he apparently must not be in town." He no longer cared.

Whatever he thought of Kim's incarceration, meanwhile, one court ruling at least raised a smile. On October 18, the terroriser of his childhood, De Angelo Bailey, had his suit for defamation in 'Guilty Conscience' finally dismissed. To rub it in, Judge Deborah Sevitto appended her decision with a 10-verse rap, refuting *"stories no one would take as fact/ they're an exaggeration of a childish act"*. "I don't know how the Court of Appeal would look at something like this," said Bailey's stunned attorney.

But a more serious threat was coming to Eminem's placid world, a time-bomb from long ago that would blast the discomfort some still felt at this white boy rapping right to the surface. On November 18, Ray "Benzino" Scott and David Mays, co-founders of *The Source*, held a press conference to unveil exclusively an unreleased Eminem track, 'Foolish Pride'. It included these words:

> *"I'll get straight to the point/ Black girls are bitches . . . All the girls I like to bone have big butts/ No they don't 'cause I don't like that nigger shit/ I'm just here to make a bigger hit."*

There was much more on the same lines, along with a final verse vaguely lamenting that *"when black and white take different sides/ Unity never happens and we will subside"*. This "why can't we just get along" homily was neutralised by rumours of a still more offensive rap, with Eminem calling black people *"moon crickets"*, *"spear chuckers"* and *"porch monkeys"*.

Eminem released a statement to minimise the damage that day: "Ray Benzino, David Mays and *The Source* have had a vendetta against me, Shady Records and our artists for a long time. The tape they played today was something I made out of anger, stupidity and frustration when I was a teenager. I'd just broken up with my girlfriend, who was African-American, and I reacted like the angry, stupid kid I was. I hope people will take it for the foolishness that it was, not for what somebody is trying to make it into today."

A further apology soon followed, stating, "The song in no way represents who I was then or who I am today. In becoming an adult I've seen what hip-hop and rap music can do to touch millions of people. The music can be truly powerful, and it has helped improve race relations in a very real way. I want to use this negative attack on me as a positive opportunity to show that. So while I think common sense tells you not to judge a man by what he may have said when he was a boy, I will say it straight up: I am sorry I said those things when I was 16. And I don't want to let anybody turn this into an opportunity to promote their own bullshit agenda."

The talk of "agendas" was understood by everybody in hip-hop. Benzino, a veteran if unsuccessful rapper himself, had sided with Ja Rule in his feud with 50 and Em, attacking the latter in 'Pull Your Skirt Up', a nakedly race-barbed taunt that could have come from *8 Mile*'s climax, or the real black hostility Eminem had suffered early on. *"2003 Vanilla Ice"*, Benzino had called him – *"Five shades darker you'd be Canibus/ and no one would care about your complicated rhyme style/ . . . what you know about pimpin' on the block till you freeze?"* Amidst a barrage of responses to the *"83-year-old fake Pacino"* on 'I Don't Wanna', Eminem goaded: *"I would never have said shit if you had kept your mouth shut, bitch. Now what?"* Now he knew.

But the tape could not be dismissed so easily. It was like a recording of every half-admitted suspicion any black person had ever had of this freakish white boy appearing in their midst, gaining their confidence, then stealing one of the last things America let them call their own – hip-hop. Elvis had been the last white person *"to do Black Music so selfishly, and use it to get myself wealthy"*, as Eminem had reminded everyone on 'Without Me', with a wink. On 'Foolish Pride', the wink was gone. The rumour that Elvis was a racist had lasted half a century, and was now taken as fact by most young black Americans, without a shred of evidence. Now, here was a tape of his descendant, caught at last cackling behind their backs, when he thought they couldn't hear. "What else could be Eminem's Achilles' heel ?" the rapper himself said, understanding it all.

A vox pop for a special issue of *The Source* which cover-mounted CD excerpts of the tape in January found no major rap figure ready to condemn Eminem, except the morally bankrupt ex-con Suge Knight. But the lingering doubt the affair could leave was clear. "He's definitely equivalent to Elvis Presley in a sense that Elvis only thought that black people were good enough to be his servants," said Freddie Foxxx. "His goal is to do better than the people he stole from. What else do you expect from a white man? I'm sure he said the N-word a whole lot of times." Skillz: "If you say the word 'nigger' out of anger and frustration and call a black girl a bitch, I'm pretty sure you'll do it again." Petey Pablo: "I don't think you can really apologise for that, because you call me a nigger, then to me, that's always on your mind and that's what you think about us. That's the way you look at me." As *The Source* told its readers: "Remember this is a White rapper with the ability to influence millions who is saying these things to other White people behind closed doors." Like they all are, it went without saying.

In interviews and press conferences, Benzino floated arguments and theories that were riddled with holes, wondering why, for instance, the storm around Eminem was so much less than for black icons like Mike Tyson, Kobe Bryant, Michael Jackson and O.J. Simpson (charged, respectively, with rape, rape, child molestation and murdering his wife, not the rapper's crime of saying an awful word). But the wider sense of white conspiracy Benzino conjured around Eminem was not without substance. He compared it to the bleaching of the Middle Eastern Jesus into a white man: "Some people want to culturally keep their image up, and hip-hop has such a strong influence on these [white] people's kids that they probably first hated Eminem, but now they love him, just so that image can stay intact . . . that no matter what we do, they can always do it better than us."

Benzino and veteran black Detroit rapper and one-time Eminem friend Champtown went further, alleging a gradual "whitening" of the corporate staff at Shady by Paul Rosenberg. Adding to discomfort at Interscope's Shady-led dominance of rap in 2003, that empire could then be seen as truly colonial. So many scores were being settled by the magazine's sources, it was hard to give this credence. But the greater charge stuck. In corporate boardrooms and children's bedrooms, Eminem and Elvis would always be more welcome than Ice Cube and Little Richard. The King would always be white.

That was not Eminem's fault, though, and the idea that someone should be cursed forever for a stray, private outburst in adolescence, when set against his clear love for black American culture and deep friendships with black Americans since, was thought policing at its most extreme, as if the tape was an original sin that could never be wiped clean. As Eminem said on a retaliatory mix-tape: *"Oh sorry, yo, so so sorry, whoa/ But that was a long time ago/ When I was a Joe Schmo/ Rapping in Joe Blow's basement/ I apologised for it before, so/ Either accept it or you don't/ And let's move on/ If I ain't shown you that I've grown/ You can get the bone/ . . . Word on my daughter, I told ya/ That I love this culture/ Don't let 'em insult ya/ I'ma tell you once more again/ This is the environment I was brought up in."*

It was as dignified a response as his original apology, suggesting a man too comfortable in himself today to be over-worried by the attack. When *The Source*'s special issue hit the stands in January, its headline – "EMINEM: CLEANING OUT WHITE AMERICA'S CLOSET – THE HIP-HOP COMMUNITY RESPONDS TO MARSHALL'S

MADNESS" – and a feature comparing him to Nixon because "both were undone by recordings that were never intended to be heard" were too overblown to convince. The links between Eminem and corporate and racist ills in hip-hop which the magazine tried to force home were just too tenuous, making them seem a smokescreen for Benzino's vendetta. The blatant double-standard in vilifying him for once saying "black bitch", when misogynist language belittling black and white women (as well as the now malleable word "nigga") was so thoughtlessly rife in rap, was also inadequately addressed.

Interscope, no doubt fearing how bad the exposé might be, put Eminem on the cover of rival hip-hop magazine *XXL* with an interview anyway (headline: "EMINEM: IS THE BEST RAPPER ALIVE A RACIST?"). For the affair to really be the Watergate *The Source* so desperately wanted, though, the tape would have to have been the smirking, secret thoughts of Eminem now, not the ramblings of the spotty, unformed Marshall Mathers. The date of the recording therefore became a key issue, with *The Source* producing evidence from the MCA corporation that the tape in its possession had not entered production until 1993, when Marshall was 21 – the age of adult responsibility. Eminem, never at his most reliable when it came to his age and past, maintained it was from 1988, when he was 16. It hardly mattered in the end.

The most fascinating aspect of the affair, perhaps, was the investigation the magazine conducted, almost incidentally, into previously buried aspects of Marshall's life in those long gone days. It dragged us back to his Ground Zero, once more. And it found a forgotten story.

It showed us Marshall at 16, the year after he met his black future partner Proof, and the year he was booed off by black audiences at Detroit's Rhythm Kitchen. But this Marshall had white rapping partners, too. This Marshall lived in Warren's white suburb, the side of his life he had always blurred. There, from 1988 to 1993, he was a member of Bassmint Productions, with another MC, Chaos Kid, and two producing brothers, DJ Buttafingaz and Manix. Photos of them in 1991 showed four goofy, badly dressed white kids, clowning for the camera. The scrawny, satirically intense Chaos Kid looked like the contender. Marshall, with his finger up his nose, had not yet met Shady.

"*8 Mile* was not a documentary of his life," the adult Chaos Kid told *The Source*. "Hollywood would have liked to portray him as a white kid in the ghetto – the *only* white kid, struggling to come up, with no other white people around him when he first started recording. But we were all white. Eminem didn't even start working with black producers until '95."

A picture of Chaos Kid shows him looking at the camera with hungry, nervous eyes, writing on pages filled with words. Not an MC now, back then he too must have had Marshall's dreams. "For a while, I did influence him," he remembered. "But I was about Public Enemy and he was Naughty By Nature."

Bassmint Productions performed locally and recorded hundreds of freestyles in, naturally, a basement. "It belonged to the only dude in the neighbourhood who had a turntable and a fucking microphone," Eminem remembered to *XXL*. "We would skip school, go to his house, make tapes, do songs. The whole recording process then was to sit down and make goofy-ass songs. None of this was wrote – it was all fuckin' freestyle. We made a million fuckin' songs." As to racism, Chaos Kid remembered opting out of a spoof "Racist Rap Hour". "I know it's kind of hard for a black person to understand why white people that are in rap music would do this, but it was a joke. It was never meant to be released to the public."

In a letter to *The Source* after the publication of the piece, which he felt misrepresented him and had been written with "ulterior motives", Chaos Kid further clarified that those tapes were "suckering rhymes", meant to be as "goofy/stupid/ignorant/wack as possible. Marshall never used derogatory remarks about African-Americans in conversation – in fact, we both had real songs denouncing racism. Marshall Mathers is not a racist. Although the songs were in bad taste, they were not intended to be taken seriously or even heard."

Others were not so conciliatory – like Champtown, who claimed Bassmint "were rolling with [my] Straight Jacket Records from '91 to '95. Eminem was stiff with it at first. I definitely was responsible for his humour. I gave him the confidence to be funny. I used to be a jokerman back in the days. When I see Eminem, that was a part of me." From most of these people Marshall once knew, there was the same tone of hurt confusion. Head, Eminem's DJ for years, whose productions were retooled by Dre on *The Slim Shady LP*, and was then cast aside, was simply bitter. It seemed likely *The Source*'s tape originated with him. Manix had meanwhile angrily played Champtown the *"moon crickets"* recording, and the two men had hundreds more tapes stashed, their intentions for them unclear. Others cursed Eminem for not signing them, for hurting Detroit, not helping it; for leaving them behind.

They were like vengeful ghosts from Eminem's past clawing at his feet, as a closet he'd thought locked suddenly yawned wide. But it was too late for them. Marshall had been the one with the strength to succeed. And as Eminem, his responsibilities were not to the past. At the 54 Sound Studio, still in the heart of his old home, he was making a new album. The future was waiting.

15

MOSH

Eminem fully re-entered the fray in 2004, momentum building month by month. First, he fulfilled his responsibilities to D12, whose second album *D12 World* was released on April 27. His more mainstream fans still reluctantly tolerated the group as their star's indulgence. But the perception that D12 were just his lucky lackeys was addressed head-on with the album's first single, 'My Band', a daring dramatisation of everyone's worst suspicions of the group's true relationship behind backstage doors.

The amusing video showed Eminem being pampered, pawed by groupies, massaged (naked, he let it be known, if you froze the frame and looked really closely) and stealing the spotlight on stage, while the others gripe helplessly behind his back, in their cramped dressing room. *"I think everybody's all jealous and shit, because I'm the lead singer of the band,"* Em egotistically confides. *"This rock star shit – it's the life for me, and all the other guys, they just despise me."* When the others try to summon the nerve to confront their meal-ticket about their shoddy treatment, a very white, bratty Eminem asking, *"You got something to SAY?"* from stage-left shuts them up. Real simmering slights are also confronted, from D12's steep drop in popularity when, as usually happens, they tour without their star attraction (*"they say the lead singer's rock, and the group is not"*), to interviewers' disinterest in anything except Em (*"fuck Marshall, ask us the questions!"*). 'My Band' ends with lardy scatological supremo Bizarre revealing he's the real talent and going solo (actually, an appetising prospect).

The enduring contradictions of D12's existence were brought out more seriously in interviews. "We get asked about Eminem a lot," Kon Artis complained to *Hip-Hop Connection* with unfaked hurt. "I understand that. I mean, we're on his label after all, but sometimes they ask 10 questions and nine are about Eminem. I'm like, 'So why are you even interviewing me then?'"

The answer was obvious, if unflattering. D12 were like a girlfriend only Eminem knew why he loved, but who others had to tolerate to get to him. Kuniva had no illusions about the relationship's imbalance. But he also knew it was co-dependent, in a way outsiders missed. "There's a million things Em could be doing besides doin' an album with D12," he admitted to *Rolling Stone*. "But we're the only real friends he has. We grew up together, lived together, flipped burgers together. There's a bond between us that nobody can break. And there's a whole thing with him feelin' like he owes it to us. He knows without D12 there wouldn't be a Slim Shady."

The depth of that adolescent loyalty was revealed when, for the first time, Bizarre recalled Eminem's desperate efforts to fulfil the group's blood oath that whoever made it out "alive" would return for the rest. In his first weeks in LA after being signed in 1998, as Dre was magicking his life of poverty away, and the pressure to repay the Doctor with great work had begun, Eminem was begging his saviour to sign D12. "Marshall was tryin' to force us on Dre," Bizarre said. " 'This is my boys! D12!' And Dre said, 'Wait a minute – it's about you!' Dre told him, 'Build your house before you have your friends walk in it.' "

"They're my foundation," Eminem said simply. "If I lose my foundation, then what do I have? Just to be myself on a big-ass mountain, a little lonely rich bastard? Not only are these guys my friends, I don't trust nobody new that I meet. At all."

His bond with Dre was equally fierce. "Dre saved my life, literally *saved my life*, just by giving me a chance," he told *Vanity Fair*. "To me he's 'boss man'; if he needs something done, whatever I am doing is dropped – my loyalty always goes that way with him." The men who had stuck with him when he seemed doomed, and the man who scooped him from the abyss – all were loved not like colleagues, but family. Like Hailie and his half-brother Nathan (as well as his 8-year-old niece via Kim, Alaina, also living with him now), they were part of the ad hoc emotional core he had built to replace his parents, and help withstand his fame's crushing pressure. The unchecked, innocent force of Eminem's loyalty to this tight inner circle, inside which he could be himself, dwarfed vagaries of career and critics' opinions. Betrayed in his own mind almost since the womb, viewed by every new acquaintance through a star-struck prism, he'd stop a bullet for any of them, because they kept him alive. In the face of this, whether Kon Artis was good enough to share the mic with him was a pathetic consideration.

To anyone buying *D12 World*, though, it was deeply pertinent. Eminem was of course well aware of the disparity between his standing and his friends', and went deeper than 'My Band' to deal with it. First, he used himself as a commercial lure. Second single 'How Come' was again dominated by him, as he lamented a Detroit friendship that hadn't survived his fame. Proof took a verse. But it was an Eminem single in all but name.

'How Come' helped float *D12 World* in its star's slipstream. But further listening showed Eminem stepping back, as if he now wanted D12 to sink or swim on their own. Only the irresistible pop rush of 'Get My Gun', with its Sixties cop theme brassy bounce and Slim at his snarling best, was worth his fans' money. And though he produced nearly half the tracks, he absented himself altogether elsewhere. Only Bizarre's reliably disgraceful outbursts, raping grannies over the sink and raising crackhead pimp kids, papered over the longueurs. Rapid sales of 3 million, though, made D12 more than a charity case. As they conclude on 'Keep Talkin'': *"We ain't stoppin'. We ain't got to prove shit to y'all."*

Eminem's first new solo output in two years, 'Just Lose It', released November 8 with an album, *Encore*, scheduled for the next week, then suggested its maker was past "proving shit" too. So similar to his previous poppy first singles from albums that it excerpted 'Lose Yourself' and 'Without Me', even Eminem sounded bored as he asked once more: *"Guess who's back? Back again?"* With an LP title implying a brief coda to his initial extraordinary trilogy, the omens stank.

When *XXL* queried his choice of single, a man who had by now sold 50 million albums, and was by far Interscope's most valuable asset, showed an unwillingness to flex his power bordering on cowardice. "Well, you know, we had discussions about that – me and Dre," he hedged. "And it's not just me running that food chain. It's not just me calling the shots. I'm not necessarily my own boss, so to speak. Between me, the label and Dre, it's got to be a mutual decision. Do we come out with [a serious single] right out the jump, come out so serious and dark to where people don't even know the album's out because it ain't getting played on the radio?" As if, even in the ultra-conservative world of US airplay, the new Eminem single could ever be excluded. The gratitude that lingered to those that had signed and so saved him in 1998 mingled with the engrained cautiousness of a man who had once been unable to support his family (he still talked in 2004 about Hailie's college fund, though by now he could found her a college). He remained a frustrating mix of fervent radical and meek company man.

'Just Lose It''s video also recalled the playful style of 'Without Me', as Eminem employed MTV-notorious heiress Paris Hilton to slap him, and impersonated fallen Eighties stars Pee-Wee Herman, MC Hammer and Michael Jackson. *"What else could I possibly do to make noise?"* he wondered aloud, *"I've done touched on everything except little boys."* Accompanying images of Eminem dressed as Jackson with his nose falling off, hair aflame (Jackson's fate on a Pepsi commercial), and bouncing on a bed with kids naturally left the ex-King of Pop, mired in accusations of molesting children at his Neverland ranch, apoplectic. He dubbed the video "demeaning and insensitive". Fellow ageing Detroit legend Stevie Wonder, who had supported Eminem in earlier controversies, went further, all but calling him racist: "I was disappointed that he would let himself go to such a level. He has succeeded on the backs of people predominantly in that lower pay bracket, people of colour. So for him to come out like that is bull."

The tape of Eminem rapping *"nigger"* was almost audible beneath Wonder's words, which implied everything black was off-limits to the satire of a white man still under suspicion. Eminem contented himself with disposing of Jackson's complaints. "I thought it was blown way out of proportion," he told MTV. "Michael Jackson sitting on the edge of a bed with little boys jumping on it – that ain't nothing he didn't tell us."

A second track out just prior to *Encore* taunted a far more powerful enemy. 'Mosh', released as a video over the internet seven days before the US election on November 2, was the culmination of *The Eminem Show*'s anti-Bush vitriol, the most daring political statement by a major pop star in years, and proof Eminem's power as a lightning rod for his country's stormy subconscious still sparked.

The 2004 election was the most bitterly divisive since Nixon steam-rollered the idealistic liberal George McGovern in 1972, when Vietnam still staggered on, anti-war protests outside conventions were violently squashed, and Watergate waited in the wings. The Iraq war and Bush's Nixon-like venality had similarly schismed America. And so, although the Democrats' John Kerry was a weak candidate, the chance to unseat Bush partially unfroze the post-9/11 paralysis of the nation's allegedly radical rock stars. Bruce Springsteen, R.E.M., Neil Young, Creedence Clearwater Revival's John Fogerty, the Dixie Chicks, and token young person

Bright Eyes combined in the Vote for Change tour, timed to sweep through swing states as the campaign climaxed. The intentions were laudable, but the constituency of these mostly ageing, "classic" rock stars was narrow. And R.E.M.'s recorded reaction to the times, *Around The Sun*, like Springsteen's *The Rising*, saw them windily hem and haw, too mildly agonised to alter minds. The dormant tradition of protest songs – as anti-war protests once more swept the world – was revived in powerful, personal work from indie underground figures like Bright Eyes and Willy Mason. And previously apolitical old punks Green Day hit number one globally just after the election with *American Idiot*, a concept album about alienated adolescents in Bush's America. Generally, though, at this vital moment, rock arthritically fumbled its chance to make a stand, and a small difference.

By contrast, Eminem just plugged into his rage and let rip. 'Mosh' moved to a martial beat, galley-slave chants and lightning-lashed, rain-whipped ambience. It sounded implacable and apocalyptic. Its lyrics' *"final hour"* could equally refer to the election countdown, or the "end days" Christians Bush and Eminem would both recognise. As in 'White America', it re-imagined the frustrated burger-flippers of 'The Real Slim Shady' finding a purpose beyond spitting in food, becoming a revolutionary army led by Eminem's *"spark"* to the gates of the White House. There he wondered if the storm breaking over their heads was God's curse that their country had voted Bush inside, before delivering this seditious address: *"Maybe we can reach al Qaeda with my speech/ Let the President answer our high anarchy/ Strap him with an AK-47/ Let him fight his own war/ Let him impress Daddy that way . . . no more blood for oil."*

'Mosh' raised the stakes as high as a pop song could reach, Eminem taking a generation's leadership upon himself and promising *"I won't steer you wrong"*, even as he asked them to give him *"hope"* and *"strength"* as they marched shoulder to shoulder. This was no 'We Shall Overcome' passive protest, instead describing insurrectionary *"mosh pits outside the Oval Office"*. *"Stomp, push, shove, mush, fuck Bush, until they bring our troops home, COME ON,"* Eminem exhorted, his unfaked fury on the final words hitting harder than polemic. His patriotic love for his country, its citizens and the free speech it guaranteed – tested by him for so long – struggled directly with the McCarthyite poisons the War on Terror had let loose, a battle he saw ending in his own assassination: *"No more psychological warfare to trick us into thinking we ain't loyal/ . . . Look into his eyes it's all lies the Stars and Stripes have been swiped / washed out and wiped and replaced with his own face / Mosh now or die / If I get sniped tonight, you'll know why.*"

'Mosh' 's video made its intentions still more explicit. At first distributed from the Guerrilla News Network website, and made by the avowedly left-wing Ian Inaba, Eminem's collaboration with such brazen radicals took him far outside normal corporate channels. Only his fellow working-class Michiganite Michael Moore stood so far to the left, while in America's media mainstream. The animated video showed Eminem angrily reading a board pinned with clippings reporting Bush's declaration of war and tax cuts for the rich, then pulling on a black hoodie and taking to the street. In other corners of America, a black man was harassed by cops, a young soldier was reassigned to Iraq, and a single mother was evicted from her home. All yanked black hoodies over their heads and joined a mass march on the White House, a new army of the night. The video ended with them crashing through police lines, and voting.

"We all honestly believe it could have a significant impact [on the election]," one of its makers, Steve Ogden, told *NME*. Co-artist Kevin Elam added: "I think this video has very little to do with pushing *Encore*. My belief is that Mr. Mathers is rightfully bringing an anthem to the fight against the corrupt system and secretive Bush administration."

"Most of it is in the song, and I would prefer to leave it at that," Eminem told *Vanity Fair*. "But my personal opinion – and I'm just one person who happens to speak to a lot of people – is that we live in the best country there is, and this guy is fucking it up. There's people over there in Iraq dying and we can't get a straight answer why. My personal take is that when 9/11 happened, you had bin Laden. It was an attack on America from one guy, and all of a sudden we're going after someone we haven't heard about in fucking 10, 12 years. It's like two people are standing here and one punches you in the face and you don't do anything back to him – you punch the other guy in the face."

"We got young people over there dyin', kids in their teens, early twenties who should have futures ahead of them. And for what?" he asked *Rolling Stone*. "I'm not 100 million per cent on Kerry. I don't agree with everything he says, but I hope he's true to his word about his plan to pull the troops out. I hope we can get Bush out of there, and I hope 'Mosh' wasn't too little, too late. That it can sway some of the voters or open people's minds and eyes up to see this dude. I don't wanna see my little brother get drafted. Every motherfuckin' vote counts."

Of course, when the votes were counted, Bush did win, with a substantial majority. Even if Eminem had fully followed through on his radicalism, and made 'Mosh' *Encore*'s first single, the result would not have changed. He had anyway participated heavily in Detroit voter registration drives earlier in the year, so could hold his head up. But the final failure of nerve in the release of 'Mosh' still haunted him, when he spoke to MTV.

"I feel like the election was a big let-down," he said. "We did our best to get 'Mosh' out as soon as we could. But do I wish it could have come out two weeks earlier? Yes." That showed hardened resolve, after this damning admission to *XXL*: "We were trying to get 'Just Lose It' out there. We didn't want to get 'Mosh' out there and be too political. Eminem's never been too political." No one believed that now.

The 'Mosh' story was not quite over. The song finished with a dedication to *"the future of our next generation"*, and children's voices giggling, *"Can you hear us?"* The majority of young voters had sided against Bush, and a re-shot ending to the 'Mosh' video spoke to them. Instead of voting, Eminem's hooded army now marched into the Supreme Court, with placards protesting everything from the war to First Amendment infringements. Vice-President Dick Cheney appeared to suffer one of his regular heart attacks, while Donald Rumsfeld impotently grimaced, and John Kerry cried tears of joy. "Voting was only part of the video's message," director Ian Inaba explained. "It was a larger call to arms for a generation alienated by a system that only sees young people as consumers, criminals or cannon fodder. In this alternate ending, we remind those who were inspired by the first version to not give up the fight. In our corporate-controlled duopoly, you have to take other measures to have your voice heard."

'Mosh' had seen its writer glowingly compared by the *Asian Times*' terrorism expert to those on May '68's Paris barricades, and was declared "the most important piece of mainstream dissent since the '60s" by *New York* magazine. Though compromised in its release and maybe ineffectual, it still gave Eminem, so recently a feared folk devil, fresh respect.

Encore itself arrived on November 12, three days earlier than planned, to counter the usual internet leaks. Eminem's nemesis on his fifth album had seemed likely to be the maturity which had pacified his private life. *Encore* defeated expectations by both embracing that maturity, and being his most adolescently outrageous, gut-bustingly funny effort since *The Slim Shady LP*.

'Mosh' was part of an opening salvo addressing entries in his diary since last we met: the racist lyrics, his beef with *The Source*, and Kim's coke busts. As he rapped in reference to *The Eminem Show*'s supposed finale, *"the curtain just don't close for me"*. But for this latest Act, he shocked with a new kind of daring: admitting that he had grown up, and no longer lived by rap's adolescent rules. Having offended liberals and censors with six years of homophobia, misogyny and murder, he went out on the only limb left, rap's own macho code, and leapt off.

'Like Toy Soldiers' began the heresy. Sampling forgotten Eighties star Martika's 'Toy Soldiers', a number one hit about teen heroin addiction, in a chorus which speeded her into helium self-harmony, the song exhaustively detailed the tangled beefs between 50, Ja Rule, Eminem and *The Source*. Drained by the futile exchanges, fearful of a Tupac-style fatality, Eminem then unilaterally disarmed: *"Don't get it twisted / It's not a plea that I'm coppin' / I'm just willing to be the bigger man . . . 'cause frankly I'm sick of talkin' / I'm not gonna let someone else's coffin rest on my conscience."* Suddenly, Eminem was a high-minded parent, not a kid in the play-ground. Instead of rucking, he was walking away. For a form partly based on the swapped street-insults of "the dozens", this was new terrain. Eminem now reserved battle-raps for the President.

Next up for reassessment was his attitude to women. Where before positive thoughts had been tucked away in odd phrases or turns of tone, *Encore*'s three Kim songs for the first time presented a rounded picture. 'Puke' saw him react to the turmoil her jail-time had put their family through, projectile-vomiting at the thought of her. But it was very far from the murderous vileness of 'Kim', admitting a residue of love: *"If you only knew, how much I hated you / For every motherfucking thing you've ever put us through / Then I wouldn't be standing here, crying over you."* He concluded softly: *"But what else can I do? / I haven't got a clue / Now I guess I'll just move on / I have no choice but to."* Even as the vomit flew, he sounded baffled by their romantic ruin.

'Mockingbird' and 'Crazy In Love' then opened fresh emotional vistas. In the former, as the tune of the nursery rhyme 'Daddy's Gonna Buy You A Mockingbird' was picked out by Luis Resto's piano, he tried to explain to his children why Kim had gone away. Flexing his functional singing voice, he reminisced about her good points as a mum back when they were struggling together – pretending some of her presents for Hailie were from him when he couldn't afford any, and sitting crying when the $1,000 she'd scrimped for Hailie's college fund was stolen. He had never rapped so affectionately about a woman before, not even on the callow *Infinite*. Seemingly responding to Hailie's hurt eyes with each word, he evenly apportioned blame for their divorce: *"Papa was a rolling stone and Mama developed a habit / And it all happened too fast for either one of us to grab it."* Surely thinking of his own dad's disappearance, he promised secure love for his daughter and niece: *"Daddy's still here / I like the sound of that, yeah / It's got a ring to it, don't it / Ssshhh, mama's only gone for a moment . . ."*

It was partial atonement for Dad's serial psychotic dissing of Mum as recently as 'Puke', a realisation at last that it did no good to their daughter. The apparent sentimentality of 'Mockingbird' might itself induce puking in some. But, for anyone who had followed Eminem's rage-contorted route to it, its soft emotional exposure brought a tear.

'Crazy In Love' then flipped to love's X-rated extremes, the sex and violence that kept Em and Kim coming back for more. The best example yet of his penchant for screamingly speeded soft rock samples, Heart's Wilson sisters joined this disco-soul paean to rough love. Its prototype was 'Love You More', the bootlegged *Straight From The Lab* track (now out officially on *Encore*'s Collector's Edition). Written before coke and contempt split the couple again, that had been a murmured confessional, the only mature evidence of how he felt when inside their affair. It wasn't for the faint-hearted, but then neither were they. *"I punch you in the mouth,"* he fondly reminisced, *"fist-fights, we tear this mother out . . ."* Their love and hate were wild bonds expressed equally in fighting and fucking. The Kinks' Ray Davies, oddly, was among the few other pop writers to risk exposing this uncomfortable underside to passion (in later songs like 'Animal'). Eminem, perhaps emboldened by the half-buried experiment of 'Love You More', now returned to the theme.

'Crazy In Love' was lightly fictionalised. "The song is technically about finding my dream girl that I could have this kind of relationship with but probably will never find," he told *Vanity Fair*. "But I will say that me and Kim have been to that place before." Eminem's sexual and emotional ideal *"let me beat the shit out of you before you beat the shit out of me"*, a wild child (described as 24) tough enough to take him on, but also the yawning void in his ad hoc family: *"the wife who never divorced me"*. Though the violence seemed nearer the truth than 'Kim''s hysterical throat-slitting, and could be construed as disturbing, the fierce feeling behind it also burst to the surface. *"You are the word that I'm looking for when I'm trying to describe how I feel inside,"* he declared of this dream Kim *"as crazy as I am"*. If you could accept soulmates who beat each other black and blue, this troubling, reckless song unpeeled that sexual psyche. This was Slim's bruised muse.

Back in the real world, he listed his parental rules to *Rolling Stone*, including these: "Never lay a hand on them. Let them know it's not right for a man to ever lay his hands on a female. Despite what people may think of me and what I say in my songs – you know, me and Kim have had our moments – I'm tryin' to teach them and make them learn from my mistakes."

As to the trauma of Kim's trials on their family, he told *Vanity Fair* it had been the "toughest year" of his life. "But with her bein' on the run from the cops," he added to *Rolling Stone*, "I really had no choice but to step up to the plate." Explaining Kim's absence to Hailie and Alaina had been "one of the hardest things I ever had to go through." And as he started to talk about why he had gathered Alaina and Nate into his family, he let slip why he was so desperate to shield them from pain. "My little brother was taken away by the state when he was eight, nine," he explained, shining a little more light into their life with Debbie. "I tried to apply for full custody when I was twenty [three years before the state intervened], but I didn't have the means. They had come and got him out of school. He didn't know what the fuck was goin' on. The same thing that had happened in my life was happening in his. And then Kim's niece was born. Watched her bounce around from house to house – just watchin' the cycle of dsyfunction, it was like, 'Man, if I get in position, I'm gonna stop all this shit.'" His pride in what he'd achieved peeped through for a moment. "And I got in position and did."

And what of Kim, he was asked in October. Were they together now? "No, not necessarily," he answered *Vanity Fair*. "But because we share parenthood we have this mutual respect for each other [for Hailie's sake]." Their relationship was "neutral at best", he told *Rolling Stone*; romance seemed "pretty much out the window". But in *Vanity Fair*, he still couldn't move beyond her. "There's things I went through with Kim that I could never experience or go through again," he admitted. "From back in the early days, Kim had been there, fought with me, in fights, fought *dudes*, in fights. I'm kind of stuck between this place. I don't think I could ever fall in love with her again. Or anyone, for that matter."

Fellow celebrities he'd dated had been "crazier than I am". "Insecurity" stopped him believing anyone else loved him, not his fame. Memories and fantasies – the stuff of *Encore*'s love songs – were all he could trust.

The album's overall tone, though, was far less dark. Instead, for eight straight tracks, it welcomed back snickering Slim Shady, all but retired on the jail-haunted *The Eminem Show*. The standard was consistently high, sides conclusively split, even after six years' familiarity with his schtick. He deliberately slurred and slid on seemingly freestyled words, mockingly questioning his talent then proving it, like a tightrope walker bouncing on one toe. Even if 2004 had been his "toughest" year, on a deeper level the stability of his mature existence seemed to have released something in him, allowing his talent free play. Michael Moore might applaud 'Mosh', but *Encore*'s guiding spirit elsewhere seemed to be Barney the *Simpsons* barfly (imitated several times), or *Beavis And Butthead Do America*.

Most of these Slim songs were the result of a late recording burst in Florida with Dre (who, surprisingly, had a bigger hand in *Encore* than any previous album). 'Rain Man' defined the record's mix of growth and schoolyard regression, as Eminem tied himself into parodical politically correct knots over the appropriate attitude to gayness, with equal reference to *The Bible* and lesbian porn: *"Who's to say what's fair to say, and what's not to say – let's ask Dr. Dre !"* Em ploughed on to describe a macho gridiron player reaching between a fellow footballer's legs for the ball and *"accidentally"* falling dick-first into his ass. *"Is that gay?"* he earnestly wondered. *"I just need to clear things up. Till then, I'll just walk around with a manly strut . . ."*

This followed on from his "confession" to fucking Dre on *The Eminem Show*, and his *"beer goggles"* play for the long-suffering Doc in the video for 'Just Lose It' (with its repeated muddling of *"boys"* and *"girls"* to dance with). In a virulently homophobic genre (where his pal 50 could still casually say in 2004, "I ain't into faggots. I don't like gay people around me"), the man who once rapped *"hate fags? Yes"* now seemed extremely comfortable with his sexuality.

Such shifting attitudes were the best defence of the truly free speech he insisted on, but which had made him so many enemies. The 32-year-old Eminem had seen more of the world and its values than Detroit's ghetto, and had pushed past his old prejudices. Increasingly, and in a simpler way than when he had shoved misogynist fury into the open where it had to be dealt with, he was a force for good. If you let someone pour their uncensored soul out long enough, perhaps this was the result.

Encore ended with the sound of Eminem gunning down the audience to this latest "show", before turning the pistol on himself. The CD showed the rapper with a gun in his mouth, and a suicide note. Taken with his promise in the concluding, title track that *"I don't ever wanna leave this game without at least saying goodbye"*, and his disgusted laying down of his mic at the end of 'Like Toy Soldiers'' video, some eagerly speculated that *Encore* truly was his final bow.

That time might come soon. But not yet. "I kind of want to finish my music thing first," he told *Rolling Stone* in a telling phrase, when asked about his movie career (the latest rumours of which involved him playing a Marshall-like bullied stripling who becomes a supervillain, in an adaptation of Mark Millar's comic *Wanted*). After the strain of his *8 Mile/Eminem Show* multitasking, he continued, "I felt like I was really neglecting life at home. I want to remain in control of things, where I can stay in the city and go home at night to my kids."

Encore ensured his day-job was still secure. It sold 700,000 in the US in its first weekend, his appeal entirely undiminished. December then gave a clue to his post-rapping future, with the release of *Loyal To The Game*. The ninth posthumous album by his old hero Tupac, it was the first record entirely produced by Eminem.

Liner notes by Tupac's fiercely loyal mother Afeni Shakur revealed Eminem's eagerness to contribute. "[Many] vow that they are 'here for me' and 'here for Tupac' or for whatever I may need," she wrote. "Yet in the same conversation they ask if I have $150,000 to send their way, or if there is an unreleased Tupac verse for the single on their next album." In contrast came "the gift of generosity given to me by a young man who not only asked for nothing in return for his services, but refused to accept anything I offered . . . I must personally thank Marshall Mathers."

A far more ambitious undertaking for Eminem than *Tupac: Resurrection*, the contrast between *Encore* and Tupac's old raps was striking. Tupac was left mired in the romanticised criminality and macho feuds which had contributed to his early death. Eminem, given time to grow up, had left such stifling self-destruction behind. As he freely admitted when duetting with his dead hero on 'Soldier Like Me': *"I don't walk around like no G, 'cause that ain't me."*

Whether he would make his mark as a producer wasn't really answered on *Loyal To The Game*. Leaning on Luis Resto's understated keyboards, his work was simply atmospheric, without the imaginative leaps of true studio auteurs like the Neptunes or Kanye West. He was at his best when sampling unlikely white musicians, like old pals Elton John (supplying a duet the sexually insecure 'Pac might have baulked at), and Dido, seemingly only affecting when kidnapped by the man whose 'Stan' made her. These tracks added to Eminem's story too, recalling almost forgotten cast members, distant relatives in his growing "family".

The insecure, angry boy raised by his real mother, Debbie, seemed almost gone now. He had been replaced by Mr. Mathers, the responsible adult his kids' friends saw at school field trips or reading to the class, a man who had come through his life's maelstrom cleansed. And yet, in the studio, Slim Shady still breathed.

"There's that fine line of walking where I have fans that I don't want to let down," he pondered to *Vanity Fair*. "I don't ever want to become soft. I don't want to compromise my music for my life at home. It's almost like I do live a double life. When I get behind those gates and I go home, I'm Dad."

Slim's final end might come when that double life tore. How would he choose, he was asked, between a happy family and fame's needs?

"If there ever comes a day where I would have to pick one or the other," he said at once, "I already know what it would be. I would walk away from all of this if I had to."

16

THE KILLING

April 11, 2006, 8 Mile after dark. Proof had been out prowling and partying all night. He had been the same since he was a teenager, never wanting to let go of the wild times until the last bar closed. That Monday night had begun at the Coliseum strip club with his friends, Mudd, Horny Mack and Chop. "We at the titty bar chillin'," Mudd said later. "Got the booth, drank a little, hollered at the DJ." They moved on to a second strip bar, Club Rolex, four men in their early thirties exuberantly getting off on the heat of naked women and hip-hop.

Finally, they walked into that last bar, the CCC Club (also known as the Triple C to locals). The doors closed behind them. At 4.30 am, Proof was laid out on the club's floor, three bullets in him, the life gone from his eyes.

The Triple C was a typical place for a Detroit night to end up, one way or the other. It was a squat red building with a steel door and no windows, on a desolate stretch of road; a tomb-like holding tank for those in no hurry to go home, where the risk of sudden violence is part of the bill for seeing what the next hour brings. "There was a barber shop next door, and a 7-Eleven type place. A pawnbrokers across the road. Very little else for miles," the *Independent*'s Guy Adams tells me of visiting the place in 2009 after it had been shut down. "It didn't look like a fashionable joint. It looked like a retail unit that had been converted into a sort of bar, with blacked-out windows and a few pool tables. It's on a reasonably busy road in a very deprived area. If you wanted to go for a drink, you'd be very short on options. So the dregs end up there." Mudd admitted as much to *XXL*. "It was kind of a shady spot. Cats always had they pistols . . . because Detroit's a gangsta-ass city, and there's a lot of cats that want to play gangsta here. Certain cats get down, and the East Side has the reputation for being the grimier side of town."

The first police version of how Eminem's best friend Proof, given name Deshaun Holton, was shot dead there aged 32, reeks of bloody pointlessness. Proof had been playing pool with a Desert Storm veteran, Keith Bender, Jr., 35. When a dispute between them became violent, Bender's cousin, Triple C bouncer Mario Etheridge, 28, fired warning shots into the ceiling. According to witnesses quoted in the Detroit press, Proof then pistol-whipped Bender and shot him in the head. As Proof stood over his victim, threatening to shoot again, Etheridge shot Proof three times: twice in his chest, and once in his head. April 14's *New York Times* reported a Detroit police statement that Proof had fired first, and Etheridge's lawyer, Randall Upshaw, telling WXYZ-TV: "The understanding of every witness we've spoken to is that Proof pulled out a weapon. Proof shot Keith in the face, and Keith was unarmed." On the morning, April 19, that Proof was buried, Bender also died of his injuries. On April 27, the police announced neither Proof nor Etheridge had entered the club armed. On September 20, Etheridge was convicted only of carrying a concealed weapon and discharging it, the bouncer having acted "in lawful defence of another" in killing Proof. During the trial, four witnesses claimed Proof had fought a man at the club before Bender.

Less damning memories of Proof's part in the shoot-out at the Triple C eventually emerged from the friends who had walked in there with him; three men at the tail-end of the sort of hedonistic trawl through Detroit's shady clubland that was an almost nightly ritual for Proof. "Wild Woody's on Wednesday, Tuesday was Northern Lights, Mondays we would hang at a titty bar called Jon-Jon's, Saturday was the State Theater," Mudd recalled fondly. "If I wanted to see him or find him, I would know where to go." Devoted family man and promoter of Detroit hip-hop as he was, rich man as he must have been after D12's great success, he still lived hungrily in his city's heart.

Anthony Bozza, a journalist uniquely trusted among Eminem's inner circle, quoted H. Mack, himself shot through the hand by a stray bullet, in a report on the shootings for the *Observer*. "The fight wasn't just the two of them [Proof and Bender], everyone in the club was involved. Guns started goin' off. P. hit the guy, and then his cousin Etheridge fired shots into the ceiling . . . Yeah, they were fighting over some bullshit but [I do not believe] P. would ever, ever shoot someone over the bullshit. It was all just fucked up."

Mudd, real name Reginald Moorer, had been a friend of Proof since school days, and a member of his early Detroit rap crew 5 ELA. He dismissed Mack's version of events: "I heard at the time Horny Mack's story changed so many different times." And in a long, emotional interview with *XXL*, Mudd remembered Proof's last minutes in intimate detail.

Everyone but Mudd was searched as they entered the club. "I had my pistol on me, of course. We had some drinks, everybody buzzed up." In the early hours of Tuesday, the place was quiet. Frustrated by the lack of girls, Mudd left Proof and the man he'd later know as Keith Bender playing pool, and stepped outside. Meeting two girls from previous strip-club stop the Rolex, Mudd drifted back inside, where Proof joined him in boisterous flirting. Distracted by his own girl, Mudd didn't notice the argument between Proof and Bender start. As their heated voices grew louder, he heard Bender shout: "I don't care who the fuck you are." The pair were separated, Mudd telling Bender: "Calm down. It ain't that serious." As Proof placated the club's owner, and peace seemed restored, Bender sucker-punched Proof in the face. The crowd scattered to let them fight. The bouncer Mario Etheridge fired shots in the air. Mudd reached for his gun, but Proof tackled him onto the pool table, demanding the pistol then grabbing it. Walking back deliberately to where he and Bender had fought, Proof fired his pistol into the ceiling. Bender lunged at him to renew their struggle. Shots were fired, and both men fell. Smoke hung over the scene as if it was a Wild West gunfight. Blood pooled under the bodies. "There was this look in Proof's eyes. He wasn't there any more."

Mudd went outside with H. Mack and Chop. He couldn't dial 911. He couldn't remember where his car keys were. He couldn't find his car. Mudd picked his pistol up where his dead friend had dropped it. Then he went home.

Many police witnesses disagree with Mudd's memories. He even heard H. Mack had told the story of Proof the cold executioner. The truthfulness in Mudd's account comes in the blank spots of inattentiveness, the sudden jumps in action he was too slow to stop; the slurred skips in time and explosions of drunken danger which are hazards of establishments such as the Triple C at the wrong end of the night. Everyone is drunk, and anything can happen. The whole truth is hard to reach.

"It wasn't anything out of the ordinary for Proof to get drunk and fight," Mudd told *XXL*. "He had that personality, the Derrty Harry [Proof's other D12 alias], scrap-happy type." Eminem later confirmed his friend's "dual personality" in his autobiography, *The Way I Am*. "He wasn't one to back down. If you pushed the wrong button, something could go off in him." Whatever really happened that morning – and in Mudd's account there is a messy internal logic to everyone's actions that a skilled novelist would envy – Proof marched towards his fate.

There was one further detail in the narrative Mudd told to *XXL*. Each protagonist had met as schoolboys at Osborn High, whose wall Proof had been sitting on when 15-year-old Marshall Mathers walked up, and they both rhymed "first place" with "birthday". It was a chance meeting as significant to Eminem as Lennon and McCartney colliding at that Liverpool church fête in 1957. It was in Osborn's cafeteria that Proof made Eminem battle-rap, and began his hip-hop education. He became his mentor and, Eminem bluntly admitted in *The Way I Am*, the white boy's "ghetto pass". That pass led Eminem to a gated community outside Detroit's city borders. It wasn't in Proof to leave. "I found out that Proof and Keith Bender were at Osborn together," said Mudd. "Everybody in the place knows each other from somewhere . . . It almost seemed like this was some high-school grudge shit, as petty as it is." Proof died aged 32 in a fight left over from the school yard during a game of pool. Another member of D12, Bugz, had been killed in a row over water pistols. The waste waiting in Detroit for its sons was a crying, relentless shame.

"I can't even bring myself back to the place I was when I heard what happened to Proof," Eminem wrote in *The Way I Am*. "I have never felt so much pain in my life . . . It was the worst day of my life. I just remember thinking, NOT PROOF, NOT PROOF, NOT PROOF. Proof was kind of my rock . . . His death brought me to my knees . . . This is the biggest tragedy I can imagine, aside from something happening to one of my kids."

Eminem drove to the hospital to see his friend's body at 7 am on the day of his death. Two days later, Swift called Mudd from the studio where he and Eminem were holed up, phoning lawyers and acquaintances, desperate to know how Proof had died. About 100 friends gathered at one of Detroit's surviving rap meccas, St. Andrews Hall, as news of the death spread. On April 18, his body lay in a 24-carat gold casket in the city's Fellowship Chapel, as mourners filed past for 12 hours. On the morning of April 19, 2,000 filled the church, and many others packed its car park to listen to the two-hour service on loudspeakers. Dre, 50 Cent and D12's remnants were among those in the pews. Anthony Bozza observed Eminem all in black, moving slowly, "hunched over . . . crying with

[Proof's family], hugging them, and rocking back and forth." Before a horse-drawn carriage took Proof on the long ride to Woodlawn Cemetery, and before the Good Life Lounge held one last raucous hip-hop party in his honour, tributes were paid.

Obie Trice, who Proof had also mentored, changing Obie's name from Obie 1 back to his real one as he was about to rap at The Hip-Hop Shop, pleaded with tears in his eyes. "We been comin' up in this struggle and we killin' each other. Yeah, I know you 'hood, you gangsta. We all from the 'hood. Detroit is the 'hood. We all killin' each other, dawg, and it's about nothin'." Bozza reported Eminem admitting his absolute debt. "Without Proof, there would be a Marshall Mathers, but there would not be an Eminem, there would not be a D12 and there would not be a Slim Shady."

Everyone commented on Proof's boundless generosity, to individuals and to Detroit hip-hop, for which he was the catalyst, and Eminem the explosion. Public tributes to Keith Bender, Jr., who died the morning Proof was buried, were harder to find. By everyone's account he didn't pull a gun, and was just as dead.

Proof's most concrete memorial stood well away from his association with Eminem, or his aid to others. His solo album, *Searching For Jerry Garcia*, had been released on August 9, 2005. He avoided the Shady and Aftermath empires, which would almost have assured him a hit, putting the album out on his Iron Man imprint. The release date was the tenth anniversary of Garcia's death. Always the hip older brother to Eminem, whose taste in rock stopped at blowsy power ballads, Proof admired the Grateful Dead's late leader as a "genius . . . who went against the grain". He was also a Miles Davis fan, who Mudd remembered had till recently been into "pills and weed-smoking . . . deep into metaphysics. Anything that he was doing, he was fully aware of the concepts . . . very intelligent . . . very spiritual." Proof was, by this description, a thug pothead, a black Detroit hippie bohemian.

Searching For Jerry Garcia portrayed him riven by contradictions and, like Eminem, painfully abandoned by his father. It began with Proof in his dressing room at the Detroit Hip-Hop Recognition Award feeling a worthless failure, and ended with a suicide note. In between pimp and gangsta stories, Proof's rough lisping voice and bittersweet soul samples listed the sins of a broken man, regretting hot temper and neglected daughter. There were declarations of toughness with fists or pistols, along-side premonitions of death. But then it's almost impossible not to find premonitions of death in hip-hop albums. Proof didn't prophesy or seek his doom.

On his album's last track, however, he did leave one major, metaphysical hip-hop song. 'Kurt Kobain' showed this was the man who had once schooled Eminem, and still texted him advice and lyrical ammunition till his death. It was styled as a suicide note. Gospel-soul organ snaked through the music, and in the lyrics Proof flinched at his own touch, breathing in again, feeling too much. He was out on the existential edge, as he gave parting advice to those close to him. This Proof would rather be "real" than alive. His voice only found a sickly enthusiasm as he ordered Eminem not to cry on his grave. He asked his friend not to let riches change them, but felt it already had. 'Kurt Kobain' kept true to its namesake, and ended with a gunshot. In its dying seconds, the organ became the wheezing sound of a life-support machine or spectral waiting room, as if the song had slipped to the other side. "Love . . . killed me," Proof exhaled. The real man his friends had loved was full of vigorous life. But in his final piece of art, he considered his failings and his end. It was a last will and testament to hip-hop's possibilities and the cause of personal authenticity. That cause sent him through the doors of the Triple C. It made the song a parting gift.

The problems that would cripple Eminem's life for the next three years had begun when Proof was still alive. They would make the most famous rapper in history vanish and become a creature of rumour: hip-hop's Howard Hughes.

The first warning sign flashed on August 17, 2005. Eminem had just finished a 23-date US tour in Detroit. But he would not be leaving home for the Anger Management 3 tour's European leg, which was due to climax on September 17 with a prestigious gig for 80,000 fans at Ireland's Slaine Castle. "Eminem is currently being treated for exhaustion, complicated by other medical issues," Interscope announced.

Two days later, truer news seeped out. Eminem was "in the hospital [in Brighton, Michigan] under doctors' care" for addiction to sleeping pills. He would spend six weeks in rehab, officially attempting to kick the sedative Ambien. But it would transpire he had other problems. The rehab failed. "I wasn't ready to go," he would reflect to the *Guardian* later. "So when I came out I relapsed right away, within a week." That July, he had denied Proof's comment to a Detroit newspaper that he would retire after the Slaine Castle gig. But such thoughts were swirling round his mind. "I was sitting in rehab reflecting for the first time in a while," he told the *Guardian*. "I felt like I needed to pull back from the spotlight, because it was getting out of control."

The December 5 release of a greatest hits collection put a full stop to his major label story to date. Its title, *Curtain Call: The Hits*, completed the conceit of *The Eminem Show* and *Encore*. All he could do now was leave the theatre. Hearing his biggest singles in one place made Eminem the subject of nostalgia for the first time, mixed with amazement at the scope and sustained potency of his six years' work. The youthful cheek of the unprecedented Slim Shady's introduction on 'My Name Is'; the comic unifying of a generation of burger-flippers in 'The Real Slim Shady'; the slashing barbs at the Columbine killings and class as 'The Way I Am' rounded on his tormentors; the motivational anthem 'Lose Yourself'; his prayerful responsibility for hip-hop's fans in 'Sing For The Moment' and its practitioners in 'Like Toy Soldiers'; and richly emotional conversations with his own family in 'Cleanin' Out My Closet' and 'Mockingbird': this was chart pop at its most resourcefully ambitious, by a pop star reckoning with every problem and pleasure that was put in his way. On top of these, 'Stan' sounded like a miracle. How on earth had such a perfectly twisted piece of fiction ever been a hit? Who else could have written it, or made us listen?

Not Eminem in 2005, or ever again, you were tempted to think, listening to the new tracks scattered through *Curtain Call*. 'Fack' was sex-crazed doggerel inspired by a *South Park* episode: Slim Shady regressing to his sick childhood. 'Shake That' was a dumb party tune about sex. The scattershot humour of *Encore* songs such as 'Ass Like That' plunged lower in throwaway efforts which seemed designed to piss on the legacy surrounding them. This was the first clear sign that whatever was wrong with Eminem was infecting his music.

Curtain Call's last new track, 'When I'm Gone', redeemed the record. It was Eminem's final single of 2005, and in most countries would not be followed up for four years. In the mode of 'Mockingbird', it was heavy on syrupy strings from Luis Resto's keyboards, and addressed Hailie with near-mawkish sentiment. But the anger that made it bite came from Hailie, here confronting her dad in a series of dreams that he crashes through like a hall of mirrors. He was here and Mom would be back, he had sung at the conclusion of 'Mockingbird'. Now he was the one abandoning Hailie to write another song and start another tour, even physically attacking the mother who looked so much like her. Real events blurred, as they do in bad dreams, and Eminem found himself taking the stage in Sweden while Hailie wailed for help with Kim back home, perhaps after her suicide attempt in 2000. But then, there was Hailie accusing him from the crowd, and the stage curtains folded around him, trapping him in the dark. His daughter's words came in Shady's angry growl, and confronted him with current sins: a man whose debased authenticity now amounted to guiltily gulping pills, just as he'd rapped about.

The song became a death-dream, sharing the wish for posthumous comfort to loved ones of Proof's 'Kurt Kobain'. But the only corpse left behind in 'When I'm Gone' is that of Slim Shady, who has a bullet put in him. "Slim Shady eventually became a metaphor for the trappings of fame for me," his creator explained in *The Way I Am*. "I was basically saying, I don't want this life any more . . . he'd become so famous he had damn near destroyed my family."

The video for 'When I'm Gone' showed where the song began, and where Eminem wanted it to end. It starts in a shadowy AA-style meeting. "Hi, my name is Marshall Mathers," the newest recruit says, replacing the jittery fun of "My name is . . . Slim Shady" with sober confession. When the song's nightmares are reversed and erased – the plane which would have flown him to Sweden turning to ash without him on it – Eminem finds himself miraculously back with Hailie and Kim (played by actresses, as always). They embrace under the blue skies of a home he'll never leave. "I don't ever want to become soft. I don't want to compromise my music for my life at home," he had told *Vanity Fair* only a year before. But he had already known then that if he could have only one, the music would stop.

'When I'm Gone' entered the Top 10 on either side of the Atlantic, while *Curtain Call* topped Christmas charts and sold 2.5 million in the US. That was the only predictable thing to hang onto as Eminem entered a period of buffeting change. His new video was, it turned out, more than wishful thinking. His relationship with Kim, "neutral at best" and the subject of 'Puke' at worst, when she became a coke-snorting fugitive from justice in 2004, had evolved again: she was now his fiancée for the second time. The first most people had seen of her in years was on the cover of *Hello!* magazine on February 1, 2006, which announced: "A New-Look Eminem Remarries His Childhood Sweetheart". As in previous photos, she seemed to dwarf her lover, in a tuxedo for the occasion as he squinted at the camera.

The invitations were touchingly hopeful: "This day I will marry my best friend, the one I laugh with, live for, love. Kimberley Anne Mathers and Marshall Bruce Mathers III. On January 14 at 5 pm they hope you will join them as they exchange vows and the celebration of their new life together." They repeated the vows from their first marriage at Michigan's Meadow Brook Hall mansion, walking down the aisle as Luis Resto tinkled 'Mockingbird' on the piano. Proof, Eminem's best man, was at his side. Hailie (then 10), Alaina (12), and the newest adopted member of what sometimes seemed to be the groom's family of saved refugees, Whitney, Kim's three-year-old by another man, formed the bridal party. Debbie Mathers-Briggs, reportedly very ill now, was not invited. He "should get a prenup this time", grandmother Betty Kresin advised, un-impressed. They did, the week before. It was still a romantic, sweet-natured day. On April 5, 82 days later, Eminem filed for divorce.

"We decided [to get married] on January 14," Kim soon explained to *People* magazine. "Marshall wanted to do it because it was our fifteenth year together from our original day we started going out. And even on that day I said, 'Let's just go through the ceremony and not sign the marriage license.' Because I was just afraid of what would happen if we had to go through a divorce, our kids. And then 41 days later, February 25, Marshall left."

The day after papers were filed, Kim was explicit about the reasons when she rang a Detroit radio show. "He's having problems with, you know, his problem that he had," she said, referring to his pill addiction. "Right after he came home from his rehab we started having a few prob-lems, and I thought it was going to be in our best interest to delay the wedding. But he really pushed it and I really thought it was going to be something that worked this time. I don't really necessarily want to get divorced. I was hoping he was going to come home and say, 'I got us a counsellor, let's go.' But you know, it didn't work out that way. I got an attorney at the door instead."

Eminem put his side across in a statement that afternoon. "The details surrounding my marriage and subsequent filing for divorce are private, and I had hoped to keep them that way for the sake of my family. However, a few of Kim's statements . . . this morning need to be addressed. First, her allegations regarding my status post-rehab are both untrue and unfortu-nate. Second, she was aware that I was filing for divorce. We both tried to give our marriage another chance, and quickly realised that a wedding doesn't fix the underlying problems."

That spat aside, Kim needn't have worried about the split, which was conducted in the mood of 'Mockingbird', not 'Puke'. On December 19, divorce was amicably finalised between a couple who "conducted themselves with dignity and respect", presiding judge Antonio P. Viviano observed (years before, he had spared Eminem jail for pistol-whipping John Guerra). Custody of the children would be shared. Kim and Eminem remained entwined.

But by now Eminem's world was narrowing and darkening almost daily. Only six days after he filed for divorce Proof was shot dead. As Eminem went into shock, he wondered if he had left his best friend at risk in some karmic balance. He had cast his friend in the character of the rapper's posse-member who is shot dead for his boss's beef in the video for 'Like Toy Soldiers'. There, Proof's body jerked and flapped on the operating table, smeared with blood that also covered the shirt and hands of Eminem, who clutched his wide-eyed head in horror, too late.

"It was a year before I could really do anything normally again," he wrote in *The Way I Am*. Sometimes, he stayed in bed. Sometimes, he couldn't walk, paralysed by grief. Brain "scattered", "I wasn't making sense when I spoke, so everyone was trying to keep me off TV and away from the press." Slim Shady was dead, Eminem was shutting down, and Marshall Mathers was falling apart.

The death of Proof, on top of his divorce, accelerated a deeper, more secret malaise. A cancelled tour and a quick rehab spell for sleeping pills didn't sound serious. But between *The Eminem Show* and *Encore*, recreational gulping of the sedatives Ambien, Vicodin and Valium became an addiction. The latter album would become an unlistenable repository of bad memories for him. "I remember going to LA recording [*Encore*] with Dre and being in the studio high, taking too many pills, getting in this slap-happy mood and making songs like 'Big Weenie' and 'Rain Man' and 'Ass Like That'," he told *Vibe* in 2010, when the truth was out. "Dre would just laugh. He didn't understand what was going on. Nobody understood what was going on with me or why I was acting so fucking goofy."

Proof's death "gave me a real legitimate excuse, in my own head at least, to take more drugs," he told the *Guardian*. "I didn't care if my drug problem got worse at that point so I took more pills. And the more I said fuck it and took more pills, the higher my tolerance got." He was taking "10 to 20 Vicodin" a day and countless Ambien and Valium, just to sleep, he told *Spin*. Proof's death had also made him fearful. "He started to worry that he might be next," an associate told the *Independent*. "It also made him realise his responsibilities. He didn't need any more money, and he hated being away from his daughter, so he decided that he wouldn't leave her alone to go touring any more."

But this wasn't the happy, family-friendly ending of 'When I'm Gone'. It seemed more like an excuse to lock the world out, and entomb himself. He divided his time between his two gated houses on Detroit's wooded outskirts – a six-bedroom, nine-and-a-half-bathroom behemoth with swimming pools and helipad in Rochester Hills, and a smaller, more discrete mansion in Clinton Township. When I wandered Detroit in 2002, Eminem was still a regular weekend visitor to his old haunts. When Guy Adams went on his trail for the *Independent* in February 2009, he seemed more like a ghost. "No one had seen him at all," he says. "Everyone knew someone who'd seen him – 'a friend of a friend saw him three weeks ago in a bar . . .'"

Every rapper in Detroit knew Eminem was still working. "He's never stopped recording. Ever," Terry Simaan, owner of local hip-hop label Oh Trey 9 told Adams. "I hear they've got over 300 songs in the can." No one Adams spoke to even considered their local hero had lost it. "Everyone kept the faith. They all think he's a genius."

Perhaps only Eminem knew that the pills had given him crippling writer's block. "I never stopped working, but I had a problem I was hiding," he told the *Guardian*. "A combination of writer's block and being lazy . . . I couldn't write a line to save my life." The man whose dense, cryptic notebooks were part of his myth now freestyled in the studio, rather than focus on words. The mush of barely there, mumbled lyrics which made *Encore*'s comic songs sound so daring in isolation now seemed the product of a dissolving, stoned mind. "I had this slurry tone," he told *Spin* of the failed recordings he made next. "It sounded like I was talking-rapping. I'd become so fucking lazy. Songs where I would talk about eating so much and getting fat and saying, 'Fuck it, I don't care.'" The rumours of 300 recordings were true. Only one would be salvaged. The writer's block lasted four years, and Eminem never stopped recording hazy, despairing shit.

Songs on his 2009 album *Relapse* retrospectively sketched the sloth and furtiveness of a functioning addict. He spent the morning slumped nude on his sofa in '3 a.m.', idly musing if it was too early for naked breasts on

TV. 'Déjà Vu' plotted his addiction's course, as rap's most gifted and wealthy man decides to get wasted until the kids walk in from school, and stashes pills in his porn video boxes, so his beloved, worried children won't find them. He feels alone and shivers as his home's gates close behind him, but doesn't really struggle. "My Dad's gone crazy," this song's Hailie clearly thinks, no longer joking.

As the pills muffled his mood, Eminem would creep down to his basement and eat "nachos and popcorn, just sitting around getting fat," he told *Spin*. "I just gave up." In his basement cinema, he watched the *Rocky* films, *Boogie Nights* and *Shooter* 150 times each, clinging to the comforting familiarity like a child to nursery tales. He may also have seen himself in Rocky Balboa's humbling and gutsy resurrection in each film, so like the story spun around his own character in *8 Mile*; he may have felt closer to the seedy decline of *Boogie Nights'* ageing porn star Dirk Diggler. The *Rocky*-style willpower that pounds through 'Lose Yourself' had left him.

Watching the rap world go by in the summer of 2006, he became consumed with jealousy at the latest hot talents, Lil Wayne and Kanye West. He thought of firing off a battle-rap, showing the upstarts who was still boss. But he knew he was no longer good enough. The man who once happily called out Clinton and Bush would be crucified.

He did put out one album on December 5 that year. *Eminem Presents The Re-Up* was part of his vague plan to withdraw from front-line rapping and fame, to focus on producing and promoting his Shady Records protégés. The Shady Midas touch was fading now, but Obie Trice (himself shot while driving in Detroit on New Year's Eve 2005, though he quickly recovered), 50 Cent and D12 gamely helped Eminem prop up Stat Quo and new signings Bobby Creekwater and Cashis. It was a lively old-school mix-tape, nothing more. Eminem's own contributions, though, were strong and revealing. 'Public Enemy #1' was a promising scenario of Eminem as a target for FBI assassination, recording furiously before the bullets hit. On 'We're Back', he felt slighted he wasn't ranked as a "hip-hop legend, which amazes me." Best of all, the stark 'No Apologies' admitted he was "wounded", but furiously restated his need to rap in a flurry of aggressive rhymes, "to salvage me inside". This music wasn't "for you, it's for me". The most surprising evidence of abiding talent was Eminem's illustrations of the rappers on the sleeve. The life-long fan of Marvel Comics who'd become his own super-villain, Slim Shady, drew a decent line.

Nothing followed from this flicker of life. As 2006 became 2007, Eminem completed half-a-dozen secret trips to Dr. Dre's studios. He arrived with no real songs and left the same way. He felt he was wasting the time of the producer who had helped save his life almost a decade before. He went to a few Narcotics Anonymous and AA meetings in Detroit, but was stared at like "Bugs Bunny" when he walked in, he told *Spin*.

In December 2007, he finally hit rock bottom, 10 years after the events of the song of the same name when, penniless and despairing of amounting to anything as a rapper, he had overdosed on Tylenol 3 pills. Trying out some new blue pills he'd been handed this time, he overdosed on methadone. The last thing he remembered was saying goodnight to his children. He was found collapsed in his bathroom. He woke up in the ambulance. "They say that if I got to the hospital two hours later then I would be gone," he later told *Vibe*. The thought terrified him. He was photographed in a wheelchair at the hospital. It was announced he had pneumonia. His jarring visit to rock bottom in 1997 had kickstarted his greatness. Now, he stirred again.

17

INFINITE

Eminem's brush with death barely dented his addiction at first. His methadone overdose had been equivalent to "shooting up four bags of heroin," doctors warned him as they detoxified his body. "My kidneys, my organs, everything was shutting down," he later told *60 Minutes*. He hadn't even known, or cared, what the blue capsules he had gobbled were. "I was just taking anything that anyone was giving me," he confessed. Sweet-talking hangers-on were always ready to help, many working from plush surgeries. "Where you're famous, doctors will kiss your ass because they love the celebrity," he told *Vibe*. "'Oh, I can call Eminem and get him on the phone right now. Oh, hi, Marshall, how are you doing? Do you need that [prescription]?' . . . You tell them what you need. You don't need to go in and see them. They will just write you a [prescription] because they want that connection with you." On 'Déjà Vu', he wondered what Elvis would do in his place. In his echoing mansions, watching TV and eating junk food, doped by sycophant physicians and discovered almost dead in his bathroom, he was learning every day.

The methadone had hardly been flushed from his system when, in January 2008, he relapsed. The *National Enquirer* spotted him puffily out of shape in a car park. They sneered at his "droopy man-breasts" and ran photos under the headline: "EMINEM STARTING TO LOOK LIKE AN M&M". He had been gone so long that sightings of him had slipped from paparazzi snaps for the pop pages to true Howard Hughes terrain: wheelchair-bound with "pneumonia" one month, worryingly fat the next. Few bothered to join the dots to this showbiz ghost's rehab stay of two years before.

Privately, though, the overdose had shaken him. Early in 2008, he admitted his addiction, and began to truly fight it. He checked himself back into hospital, and began the classic addict's 12-step programme with a sponsor, and a rehab counsellor he still sees once a week. His earlier rehab had been disrupted by star-struck fellow addicts asking for autographs, and pocketing his notebooks, pens and hats. This time, a man with a better understanding of what Elvis, or Eminem, might do was his saviour. "Elton John calls me once a week," he told *Spin*. "He used to tell me stuff like, 'You're going to start seeing certain things you've been overlooking.' And it came true. I'd walk around like, 'Damn, that tree looks crazy, look at all those leaves!' Things I didn't notice when I was fucked up." On April 20, 2008, he stopped taking pills.

Like a montage from the *Rocky* films he'd also been addicted to, he burned off his flab with legendary Detroit boxing trainer Emanuel Steward. "Eminem's a workout maven, and one of those healthy mind, healthy body people," a Steward associate told the *Independent*. As the opiate cloud that had oppressed his mind lifted, he tentatively started to write. "I had been writing songs without beats," he told the *Guardian*. "I was making beats in my head and writing lyrics down just like I used to . . . I had a couple of songs and a few loose verses. In hindsight I was doing mind exercises, getting myself back in shape." He elaborated on the process to the *New York Times*. "I'd stack a bunch of words and just go down the line and try to fill in the blanks and make sense of them. For three or your years I [hadn't been able] to." He had read a dictionary as a boy, in his hunger for words. Now he was a student again. As if he had been in a coma or suffered a mild stroke, he had to relearn his rapper's language.

In June, he nervously rang Dr. Dre. "I wasn't sure if I was ready," he remembered to Anthony Bozza in the *Guardian*. "But I called him anyway and was like, 'Yo, homie, I think I'm starting to come out of this writer's block.' He was like, 'All right. That's what I like to hear.' "

Eminem was fearful before his latest trip to Dre's studio in Orlando, Florida, desperate not to let his mentor down again. In two weeks, they blazed through 11 songs. Dre kept things simple, handing Eminem beats to choose from and write words to. He'd record them till his voice was hoarse. Then as he recovered, he'd start writing again. "When we were done I felt like I did when we made the first two records," he recalled to the *Guardian* in wonder. "The word 'relapse' kept playing over and over in my head." He worried the mood would peter out back in Detroit. "But we came back and it never stopped . . . it was a whole shit-storm . . . these thoughts that I could not control." He snapped awake in the middle of the night, thinking of lines he had to write down. To the *New York Times*, he talked of "the lid" blowing off his creativity: "In seven months I accomplished more than I could in three or four years doing drugs." Again like Elvis in his last years, he had got used to lazily recording aimless sessions in his home studio. Now he bought a new facility in Ferndale, Detroit, Effigy (leaving loyal musicians from the albums made at Studio 54, including Luis Resto, behind). It was stocked with his favourite old arcade games, a soda fountain, a barbecue and a giant mixing desk bought from Dre. At least for the half-hour drive from his house to the studio, he would have to face the world to make music. On October 15, 2008, during a late-night interview on Shade 45, a satellite radio station he part-owns, he announced he was working on a new record: *Relapse*. The comeback had begun.

His first substantial work in three years, *The Way I Am*, was published the next week. Touted as an autobiography and certainly going deeper than his first book, 2000's annotated lyrics collection *Angry Blonde*, it remained more like the "scrapbook for my fans" Eminem had originally intended. A man who had only read two picture-free books, a dictionary and LL Cool J's autobiography, preferring to absorb language from rap records and the vividly colourful fictions of Marvel comics, was never going to use the medium to say anything definitive about himself. This wasn't Bob Dylan's *Chronicles*, revelling or even interested in the literary form. Instead it offered crumpled mementoes such as a hand-written flyer for the teenage Marshall's fledgling business painting jeans and jackets in hip-hop styles ("Call M + M" . . .), and photos of him as a young unknown stoked to have opened for the Wu-Tang Clan in Staten Island, and performing, his eyes wild with unvarnished passion. Forty-five pages of his fabled lyric sheets were the centrepiece. Fragments of future great songs could be spotted amidst a sometimes staggering density of phrases and stanzas, ink colours and even handwriting changing on a single page of hotel stationery as he stocked lyrical ammunition, in the days when his mind and pen never stopped. Younger rappers poured ideas into mobile phones and BlackBerries, and in his depression Eminem had tried to copy Jay-Z's technique of storing lines in his head then freestyling in the studio. But in this way at least, the true Eminem was an old-fashioned writer, thoughts shooting from his mind onto worked-over, scribbled pages. "I've got some letters from some crazy people, and it looks like this," Anderson Cooper said, when Eminem showed him some sheets during a *60 Minutes*

TV interview two years later. "Either all in capitals or scrawled on pages." Eminem chose not to rise to the bait from this interrogator from the mainstream world, mildly offering: "Yeah, well. That's probably because I'm crazy." Told the rapper saved all his rhyme books, Cooper suggested they might one day go in an Eminem museum. "Maybe," the rapper said, interested. He took his achievements seriously now, and spoke of them as art. "I always was good at English," the high school dropout let his posh interviewer know.

"The guy has been out of the mix and not interacting with a lot of people, let alone a writer," Sacha Jenkins, Eminem's ghost-writer, told the *New York Times* of interviewing him for the book. "But this was an opportunity for him to get a lot of stuff off his chest, especially in the wake of the death of his best friend." Eminem addressed Proof's loss head-on in the introduction. It was a steady beat beneath what followed, stories inevitably circling back to some crucial kindness or intervention. He vividly recalled Proof fist-fighting him till his knuckles were bloody, knocking him down but never keeping him there, outside the house Debbie had moved him to in Detroit's East Side ghetto. Proof was training him to fight back, and survive. When Marshall was living with Kim at her mother's in an attic too cramped to even stand, and becoming "hermit-ish" as he obsessively recorded demos – exactly as he had just been behaving for three years as an adult superstar in a gated mansion – it was Proof who dragged him out to The Hip-Hop Shop, and his future.

"Guns and violence have been around me my whole life – in my family life, in my social life, everywhere," he also revealed in *The Way I Am*. He had often spoken of his Uncle Ronnie's shotgun suicide in 1992, but now gave new details of the moment he heard: "I just threw the phone down and dropped to my knees." And then there was another uncle, Todd Nelson, who "allegedly ended up murdering a dude in a supermarket parking lot", and on release from jail in 2004, "blew his brains out on my birthday". These violent deaths had already taken "chunks out of my life", Eminem said, before Proof's. Physical abuse was a constant presence around his family. "It's no surprise I became who I am. Someone I don't really want to be."

There was almost no mention of the drug abuse that had defined his recent life, which stayed limited in the public mind to his seemingly successful 2005 rehab spell. The book was, he told the *New York Times*, "more about Eminem and less about Marshall". Paul Rosenberg told the paper: "This is the end of the first chapter of his career. Em's looking forward now." But his new album *Relapse* would similarly content itself almost entirely with surface feelings. "This is not really an emotionally driven album," he told the *Guardian* truthfully. His rehabilitation was still too fragile to dig deeper.

He talked further on the theories behind *Relapse* to the *Guardian*. "I was hearing all these things about what if Em comes back and the different ways he needs to reinvent himself as a completely different person. Dre was just like, 'Man, people just want to see you, they just want to hear you get the fuck out there again' . . . I don't feel like I need to reinvent myself. I feel like I just need to go back to doing what made me me in the first place." Dre explained his thinking to the *New York Times*. "I talked to my son about it, and he was like: 'The kids want to hear him act the fool. We want to hear him be crazy, we want to hear him be Slim Shady and nothing else.' "

In February 2009, 'Crack A Bottle', the first official release from *Relapse*, broke the US record for most downloads in a first week with 418,000, making it his first home number one since 'Lose Yourself'. Leaked in rough form the previous October, it was a swaggering reunion with Dre and 50 Cent. More crucially it resurrected Slim Shady. Shot dead by his creator on his last record, he twitched back to life with the inevitability of Frankenstein's monster. Eminem announced his return like a boxing MC, while the music recalled a three-ring circus.

A series of videos were released through April, stoking anticipation for *Relapse*'s release on May 15. '3 a.m.' began with Eminem waking in a forest, looking at his slashed hands, and gradually recalling the rehab centre where he had slaughtered a nurse and everyone he could find with a butcher's knife, trailing bloody footprints and finger-smears behind him. Eyeballs staring as he sank into a bath of blood in a serial killer's dank gothic basement somewhat like Stan's lair, he finally looked around him and screamed as he realised what he'd done. Eminem could still act. But the video was far less disturbing than the one he'd made for 'Just Don't Give A Fuck' as an unknown in 1998.

The video that defined *Relapse*, though, was for 'We Made You'. A virtual remake of 'Without Me', a comeback single after far less time away, Eminem rattled through a new repertoire of comic guises: a topless lumberjack ready to pleasure a negligee-wearing Sarah Palin; waiting in *Psycho*'s shower for Jessica Alba; Eminem fan Dustin Hoffman's *Rain Man* character to Dre's Tom Cruise; on the deck of *Star Trek*'s *Enterprise* and a morphing Transformer. Finally he rushed back to rehab, lusting for Amy Winehouse. His eyes, so blackly shark-like sometimes, looked empty at the end. 'We Made You' got Eminem on TV. But its superficial riffs on his old themes ran through *Relapse*.

When fans finally played the first new Eminem album in five years, they found the skits at least were as sharp as ever. Accompanying interviews had at last acknowledged the depths of his addiction. Now, Dominic West, the British star of the great crime series *The Wire*, was on hand as "Dr. West" to prepare the rapper for the outside world. His advice on the 12-step programme ("Steps? There are a lot of them aren't there? Christ, I don't even know them all . . .") and how to respond in the company of drinkers ("Take a drink – take the edge off!"), till his voice monstrously warps and he hurls pills at Eminem, who wakes shaking from his nightmare, was a wonderful sketch. Aghast manager Paul Rosenberg and tough label boss Steve Berman ("Lemme guess – another album about poor me, I'm so famous it has ruined my rich little life – am I onto something here?") rejoined the company. Like *Relapse*'s cover image of Eminem's face composed from thousands of coloured pills, they showed how lightly he meant to treat his years of torment. "The overall theme of the record is to have a centre," he explained to the *Guardian*. "[*Encore*] feels a little too self-loathing to me . . . like I'm pissing and moaning about whatever . . . I beat up the subject of what was me."

He looked forward to being hated again on 'Medicine Ball'. It was impossible to feel so strongly about songs such as 'My Mom', a bored addendum to 'Cleanin' Out My Closet'. Its claims that Mathers-Briggs had crushed drugs into his meals as a kid to keep him docile, making him repeat her cycle of addiction 30 years later, was something he broadly believed. But when the next song, 'Insane', sailed into far fantasies of his mom-sanctioned childhood rape by a step-father, who could care?

'Bagpipes From Baghdad' was a sheer comedown from 'Mosh''s political engagement, allying Arabic music to another dig at old flame Mariah Carey. The rape and murder of fellow rehab habitués Lindsay Lohan and Britney Spears, and of stray pick-ups on rainy nights, were part of a serial killer theme on 'Same Song & Dance', 'Stay Wide Awake' and '3 a.m.', among others. "I did find myself watching a lot of documentaries on serial killers," he told the *Guardian*'s Anthony Bozza. "I always had a thing for them . . . going back through my DVD collection and watching movies about killers sparked something in me." They helped bring Slim back. "I did everything I could to lapse into the old me. When you relapse, you go into your old ways harder than before."

This Slim, though, carried no threat. The women he abused and hunted and corpses he piled high had no weight. *Relapse* was scrubbed moronically clean of content. Eminem's truest comment on the album came in the *New York Times*. "At the end of the day, it's just words. That's all it is to me." And it was here that *Relapse* conversely touched dazzling greatness. Only a year before, Eminem's command of language had been struck dumb. Now he rapped with born-again zeal, throwing his crutches away to sing and dance. The even swing and clean sound of Dre's beats provided regular structure into which he poured exercises in rapping dexterity. Stanzas, phrases and words were stretched, squeezed, broken and stitched with Sinatraesque relish. What he said mattered less than ever before. How he said it showed him rapping himself back to life.

There were two exceptions. 'Déjà Vu' was an intimate narrative of his drug decline. 'Beautiful' was a desperate plea during it. The first verse and a half were written sitting on the end of a hospital bed in rehab. He finished it when he relapsed once he got home. That accounts for the naked depression it described, of a man writing only to stop his mind floating away, but who feared his rapping was finished. His only consolation: he'd be hard to follow. This snapshot of Eminem in the pit found him paranoid in rooms which chilled as he entered them, where crawling yes-men howled at his jokes. His penchant for power ballads did see a sample of Queen and Paul Rodgers' 'Reaching Out' add warmth. The video changed the subject to Detroit, as he wandered through the rotted suburban streets of his past, and accusingly watched Depression-style poverty in America's former powerhouse. Somehow, a song written in a lost place became inspiring. "It reminds me of what that space is like and what never to go back to," he told the *Guardian*.

Relapse was a US number one of course. Eminem's promotional blitz included an interview on TV's *Jimmy Kimmel Live!*, where he looked lean but wired with nerves. The show's audience of 200 laid-off Michigan car industry union members was then flown back home to Detroit for his 30-minute set at the MotorCity Casino Hotel. He played with his homophobic image at the MTV Movie Awards, when Sacha Baron Cohen, in character as Austrian fashion designer Bruno, planted his near-naked ass in the rapper's mortified face, a stunt which made global headlines. He even added to his record's cartoon style by co-starring in a Marvel comic, *Punisher/Eminem: Kill You*. But *Relapse*'s reviews were poor. *Vibe* noticed its mastery of the hip-hop form while calling it "patchy". Rock magazines mostly agreed with the *Village Voice*: "a dank echo chamber wherein he continues his 'shock tactics' in pointless isolation." US sales stalled below two million. Its predecessor *Encore* sold five million, and 11 million worldwide (where the album before that, *The Eminem Show*, managed 19 million). *Relapse* simply wasn't enough. Eminem's initial plan to cull Relapse 2 from its prolific sessions wasn't the answer (a compromise Christmas release, *Relapse: Refill*, added seven songs).

Eminem instead proved his renewed energy with a second comeback. On June 18, 2010, he released a brand-new album, *Recovery*. In every interview, he disowned *Relapse*. "I've grown up so much just in the last couple of years since I've been sober," he told *Vibe*. "*Relapse* didn't reflect that or where I really am mentally." To *Spin*, he said: "It was a regression, me rhyming to shock people again. 'How much fucked-up shit can I say?' . . . after a while, people get used to it, and the joke is dead." He put the change most succinctly into a *Recovery* song, 'Talkin' 2 Myself', where he bravely admitted he no longer ruled. He described his mental shift to *60 Minutes*. "I had to go back and listen to some of my older music, and try to figure out why those songs off *Relapse* weren't making me feel like those used to . . . [and] just put the emotion back in." *Relapse*'s relieved gush of words was refined. "I started choosing words carefully," he said to *Spin*, "as far as striking an emotional chord."

The skits were gone. They had helped make his first five major-label albums seem one long story. *Recovery* scrubbed that past, and started again. The comforting presence of Dre was also abandoned (bar one track, 'So Bad'). Instead, Eminem sought fresh sounds from various producers, most prominently Just Blaze and DJ Khalil. The even sheen Dre had given *Relapse* was replaced by music closer to Eminem's own tastes: the fuzzed guitars, choirs and sometimes cloying emotion of full-blown soft rock. Aqueous keyboards and Steve McEwan's high vocal on 'Space Bound' made it Pink Floydian Eminem; the guitars on 'Talkin' 2 Myself' could have been The Police. 'Going Through Changes' sampled Black Sabbath's 'Changes', and irresistibly recalled Ozzy Osbourne's sappy duet version with daughter Kelly. The *NME*, attuned to what was hip in a rock world, rooted for Eminem in his mother's '70s album collection, cautioned against " 'crossover' songs that just come across as naff as a Care Bear teddy clutching a stuffed heart". This was doubtless a factor in *Recovery*'s commercial success. But this music also helped turn the key to relentlessly heightened feelings in Eminem, as his rapping regained its rasping threat, even as he shamelessly crooned choruses. A year before, he had rapped with numb euphoria at being able to do so at all. Now the anaesthetic had worn off, the therapy of sponsors and friends had dug deep, and Eminem was quivering with pain, rage and wounded pride.

The new image on the album cover and videos showed a mature Eminem, hair and clothes dark, face gauntly sharp from a year's worth of workouts: a sleek 37-year-old professional. The opening track 'Cold Wind Blows' set the mood. He danced like a cartoon character when his feet were scorched by lightning bolts, and God promised hell if he continued his evil rapping. He begged himself to calm down, futilely. If he still tried too hard with the shock tactics, this was in the context of tough, committed wordplay.

Shady and the jokes stayed leashed, as the theme continued of a rapper reclaiming his kingdom. 'Talkin' 2 Myself' bravely admitted "you're no longer the man", while the sound of his own fans' laughter at his decline spurred him on. 'No Love' then paired him with Lil Wayne. As he confessed in 'Talkin' 2 Myself', he had been consumed with jealousy at the younger man's success during his addiction, but had known an attack then would have been the pathetic gesture of a flabby has-been. The man acknowledged as the period's top rapper had already paired with Eminem and the other contenders, Kanye West and Drake, on the latter's 2009 single 'Forever'. Now, Eminem let Lil Wayne take 'No Love''s first half. He was at his best, his cool, cracked drawl outlining a punished, unregretted life. Eminem's rejoinder burned with resurrected intent. His first words were: "I'm alive again". Building metaphors for his own brilliance, his rapping picked up pace like a man running on the spot till his feet blurred. Then he cockily slowed for more feeble MCs to catch up, before lines spat with such intense speed it felt like he had launched into space. Egged on by Wayne, he more than matched him, and his own fabled 2001 guest spot with Jay-Z on 'Renegade', when he had bested the then king. "I had to resort to other things to make me feel [like] that," he told Jonathan Ross on his TV show. "Now, rap's getting me high."

'Not Afraid', the first single and a US number one, also had a renewed sense of mission, and the pride of a Detroit underdog. The video showed him standing on a roof as if contemplating suicide, and walking straight through zooming traffic, a common metaphor for a panic attack. But then he punched through the back wall of a hall of mirrors, and became a superman, flying onto that roof. Eminem added a speech straight from his counselling sessions to the video's start. Observing he had to "get to that place, to get to this one", he concluded: "Just follow me. I'll get you there." The positivity was echoed in this *Recovery* sleeve note: "THIS ALBUM IS DEDICATED 2 ANYONE WHO'S IN A DARK PLACE TRYIN' 2 GET OUT. KEEP YOUR HEAD UP . . . IT DOES GET BETTER!" It was a far cry from 'Kim', but close to his heartfelt sentiment in *The Way I Am*: "I want to bring people together. I feel that can be my biggest contribution to hip-hop. [Slim'd] be like, 'What the fuck? You got soft,'" he admitted to *Spin*. "[But], if I can make songs to inspire people and try and help them, fuck, why not?"

Recovery's sentimentality was shameless. But it combined with Eminem's harder-edged sense of himself as a rapper, as on the song which started the album's climactic emotional payload, 'Almost Famous'. This rehearsed the story of Eminem's rise, putting himself back in the desperate mood of his Hip Hop Shop battles when everything was at stake. Irony missing from *8 Mile* and 'Lose Yourself' saw singer Liz Rodriguez play fame's siren voice, cackling, "Be careful what you wish for . . ." This was the mature perspective of a man who had found fame to be the glass-walled cage he was pictured in on a Detroit street in *Recovery*'s booklet. 'Almost Famous' still remembered, and missed, the raw excitement of getting there.

Recovery's second single, 'Love The Way You Lie', was another US number one. It returned to the theme of a mutually violent, passionate relationship, as explored on *Encore*'s 'Crazy In Love'. It gained a frisson from guest star Rihanna, recently in the news for being battered by her then-boyfriend Chris Brown, prettily singing she loved the pain. Her status as the year's top R&B star equally helped the song's crossover success, perhaps in spite of its theme.

Relapse's most surprising disappointment had been its avoidance of Proof's death. "I tried to write a song for you but nothing was good enough," Eminem admitted in its sleeve notes. "It took me so long to get out of that place where I couldn't even speak about it without crying," he confessed to *Vibe*. *Recovery* put this right. 'Going Through Changes' followed his depression right onto the operating table after his overdose, where Hailie's voice reaches him and pulls him back from death. 'You're Never Over' imagined Proof as the guardian angel who made him think of his daughter in time. This song was a cry of love from Eminem, feeling old, alone and "insane" without his friend, but determined to "rise from these ashes" in his honour. He didn't rap its choruses, but sang with naked feeling, as if with grieving friends at Proof's wake. As fuzzed guitars and synths pounded the song home, a hard heart might think, not for the first time on *Recovery*, of some old Eighties Foreigner ballad. But the bombast was built around the most exposed vocals of Eminem's life.

Recovery was a startling success. It was a sustained transatlantic number one, selling 714,000 in its first week in the US. By October 2010, global sales already touched five million. Gavin Martin in the *Mirror* summed up the critical temperature: "*Relapse* offered gory imagery aplenty, but *Recovery* packs real emotional weight . . . he would be the first to admit that his *Recovery* is by no means complete. But at least it often connects with the rude health that helped make him great in the first place."

Eminem no longer really toured, preferring to put his family first. "It's hard on the body," he observed to the *New York Times*. "It used to be a big trigger for me with drinking and drugging." He was content with four high-profile US gigs with Jay-Z, starting at Detroit's Comerica Park on September 2. A three-night trip to Europe was caught by the *NME* when he headlined Scotland's T in the Park festival. They saw him "bound" on stage, "his rapping tongue . . . sharp – every syllable arrowing through the chilly Scottish sky," as T's biggest crowd in years moshed before him.

D12 shuffled on with him for a while. But the Shady empire they had been foot-soldiers for, once meant to rival Motown, had fallen in his absence. D12's four other survivors had been equally distraught from Proof's death. Their follow-up to 2004's *D12 World* also had to wait in Shady parent Interscope's corporate line for Eminem to surface. Kuniva spoke to the *Detroit Free Press* on their future in 2008. "I've read the blogs where people are so fucking cruel: 'Why do they call it the Dozen when two members are dead?'" Bizarre put out three solo albums independently, telling *XXL*, "I'm trying to get away from the whole Eminem thing." He added to *Complex* of their erstwhile star's D12 involvement now: "He's at the point in his career where he needs us to stand on our own, and he'll come for the finishing touches . . . We can't be on my man's left nut sack."

Cashis's Eminem-produced *The County Hound EP* sold only 6,700 copies its first week; his *The Art of Dying* LP was shelved. Obie Trice quit

Shady in 2008, tired of waiting on a label finally dependent on one distracted man. His last album for them, *Second Round's On Me*, showed an X-ray of the bullet still lodged in his head, where stray lead sloshed and froze when he moved. He mixed armed defiance to his enemies with soulful, socially informed regret. 'Obie Story' described a clever little boy with a loving mother, damned to drug-dealing and violence by the gunshots which echoed down his street and America's slave legacy of black people not "born equal". Eminem's production was careful, Obie's rapping strong. This fine bulletin from a hurt man refusing to leave Detroit's streets showed what Shady Records could have been.

The folk devil who had capered through the UK in 2001 had also disappeared. Eminem was a beloved old entertainer now. One reaction to *Recovery*'s success was simply that people were pleased to have him back. "For right-wing Americans, his name is still enough to conjure up this visceral fear of everything he stands for," the *Independent*'s LA correspondent, Guy Adams, considers. "They still believe the old George Bush line that he's more dangerous than polio. He's very well respected and widely liked, but he's not modish. He's not a real celebrity at the moment in the sense that Kanye West is. He was in the major newspapers every single day for five or six years, and now he's not. I think if he stuck a baseball cap on, he could quite happily walk down Rodeo Drive in Hollywood and not be recognised by paparazzi. He doesn't exist in that world."

Eminem finished the decade as its biggest-selling artist, *Billboard* declared. But the man who, at his peak in 2002, had seemed ready to take on the mantle of a great American like Allen Ginsberg, writing about and wrestling with his country when he wrote about himself, had been reduced by American fame. He no longer raged at presidents, or even seemed interested in how the racial schisms he once picked at had been bridged by Obama. He no longer felt able to see America at all. "I stay at home a lot because I can't go anywhere without a huge entourage," he believed in *The Way I Am*. "Sometimes I'll go out just to prove I can do it. I'll leave my neighbourhood and go to where a lot of people are . . ." Sometimes, he cruised back to the streets where he once lived in Detroit, a ghost now, unable to walk freely there ever again. "I'll go back and remember . . . how life was back then," he explained to *Spin*. "How much of a struggle it was. As time goes by, you might get content and forget things." He tried to explain these roots to his daughters too. "Why *should* we live like that?" they sniffed, even Hailie too young to remember when he couldn't buy her clothes. They were a millionaire's children, living behind his mansion's gates. His old compadre Royce Da 5–9 didn't see much difference. "He's always been a homebody," he told *Vibe*.

Eminem at 38, isolated by fame, mourning his best friend and, he told *Vibe*, often laying awake since his overdose fearing his own death, could seem a tragic figure. But he and his teenage sweetheart Kim shared their children seamlessly, and loved each other ("We're a good team now," he wrote in *The Way I Am*), and he was the world's most successful rapper. *Recovery* showed this American life could still be mined for music. His competitive urge to stay on top had become its own, self-generating subject. "Realistically, if I don't rap, what the fuck am I going to do?" he asked *Vibe*, knowing the answer. "It's too late to just be unfamous at this point." All Marshall Mathers' dreams had come true. He was learning to live with them.

ACKNOWLEDGEMENTS

The Origins Of The Urban Crisis: Race And Inequality In Postwar Detroit by Thomas J. Sugrue (Princeton, 1996) was particularly helpful on the history of Detroit; *Have Gun Will Travel* by Ronin Ro (Quartet, 1998), *A Change Is Gonna Come* by Craig Werner (Payback, 2000) and *Westsiders* by William Shaw (Bloomsbury, 2000) were all useful in thinking about hip-hop and Eminem.

Thanks also to Anthony LeQuerica for Detroit hospitality, and Sebastian Krop for Detroit driving, both beyond the call of duty.

And to Sarah Jezzard and Andrea Nettleton, for making my life better.

DISCOGRAPHY

ALBUMS

Infinite (Web Entertainment, 1996)
The Slim Shady LP (Aftermath/Interscope, 1999)
The Marshall Mathers LP (Aftermath/Interscope, 2000)
The Eminem Show (Aftermath/Shady/Interscope, 2002)
Encore (Aftermath/Shady/Interscope, 2004)
Encore Collector's Edition – includes extra tracks 'We As Americans', 'Love You
    More' and 'Ricky Ticky Toc' (Aftermath/Shady/Interscope, 2004)
Curtain Call: The Hits (Aftermath/Shady/Interscope, 2005)
Relapse (Aftermath/Shady/Interscope, 2009)
Relapse: Deluxe Edition – includes extra tracks 'My Darling' and 'Careful What
    You Wish For' (Aftermath/Shady/Interscope, 2009)
Relapse: Refill – includes extra tracks 'Forever', 'Hell Breaks Loose', 'Buffalo
    Bill', 'Elevator', 'Taking My Ball', 'Music Box', 'Drop The Bomb On Em'
    (Aftermath/Shady/Interscope, 2009)
Recovery (Aftermath/Shady/Interscope, 2010)

With D12:
Devil's Night (Shady/Interscope, 2001)
D12 World (Shady/Interscope, 2004)

With various artists:
8 Mile (Shady/Interscope, 2002)
Eminem Presents: The Re-Up (Shady/Interscope, 2006)

SINGLES/EPS

As Soul Intent:
'Fucking Backstabber'/'Biterphobia' (Mashin' Duck, cassette only, 1996)
As Bad Meets Evil (with Royce Da 5–9)
'Nuttin' To Do'/'Scary Movies' (Beyond Real, 1998)

As Eminem:
The Slim Shady EP (Web Entertainment, 1998)
'Just Don't Give A Fuck'/ 'Brain Damage' (Aftermath/Interscope, 1998)
'My Name Is' (Aftermath/Interscope, 1999)
'Any Man' (Rawkus, 1999)

'Guilty Conscience' (Aftermath/Interscope, 1999)
'The Real Slim Shady' (Aftermath/Interscope, 2000)
'The Way I Am'/'Bad Influence' (Aftermath/Interscope, 2000)
'Stan' (Aftermath/Interscope, 2000)
'Without Me' (Aftermath/Shady/Interscope, 2002)
'Cleanin' Out My Closet' (Aftermath/Shady/Interscope, 2002)
'Lose Yourself' (Shady/Interscope, 2002)
'Sing For The Moment' (Aftermath/Shady/Interscope, 2003)
'Business' (Aftermath/Shady/Interscope, 2003)
'Just Lose It' (Aftermath/Shady/Interscope, 2004)
'Like Toy Soldiers' (Aftermath/Shady/Interscope, 2005)
'When I'm Gone' (Aftermath/Shady/Interscope, 2005)
'Crack A Bottle' (Aftermath/Shady/Interscope, 2009)
'We Made You' (Aftermath/Shady/Interscope, 2009)
'3 a.m.' (Aftermath/Shady/Interscope, 2009)
'Beautiful' (Aftermath/Shady/Interscope, 2009)
'Not Afraid' (Aftermath/Shady/Interscope, 2010)
'Love The Way You Lie' (Aftermath/Shady/Interscope, 2010)
'No Love' (Aftermath/Shady/Interscope, 2010)

With D12:
'Shit On You' (Shady/Interscope, 2001)
'Purple Pills' (Shady/Interscope, 2001)
'Fight Music' (Shady/Interscope, 2001)
'My Band' (Shady/Interscope, 2004)
'How Come' (Shady/Interscope, 2004)

GUEST APPEARANCES

'5 Star Generals' single – Shabaam Sahdeeq (Rawkus, 1998)
'Green And Gold' on *Green And Gold* EP –-The Anonymous (Goodvibe, 1998)
'Trife Thieves' on *Attack Of The Weirdos* EP – Bizarre (Federation, 1998)
'We Shine' on *Episode 1* EP – Da Ruckus (Federation, 1998)
'Fuck Off' on *Devil Without A Cause* LP – Kid Rock (Atlantic, 1998)
'ThreeSixtyFive' single – OldWorlDisorder (Beyond Real, 1998)
'The Anthem' single – Sway & Tech (Interscope, 1999)
'Hustlers And Hardcore' on *Behind The Doors Of The 13th Floor* LP – Domingo (Roadrunner, 1999)
'Get You Mad' on *This Or That* LP – Sway & Tech (Interscope, 1999)
'Busa Rhyme' on *Da Real World* LP – Missy 'Misdemeanor' Elliott (EastWest, 1999)
'The Last Hit' on *Home Field Advantage* LP – The High & Mighty (Rawkus, 1999)

'Watch Dees' on *Heavy Beats Vol. One* EP – DJ Spinna (Rawkus, 1999)

'Macosa' single – The Outsidaz (Ruffnation, 1999)

'Forgot About Dre' (also single) and 'What's The Difference' on *2001* LP – Dr. Dre (Aftermath, 1999)

'If I Get Locked Up Tonight' – Funkmaster Flex & Big Kap, with Dr. Dre (Def Jam, 1999)

'Dead Wrong' (also single) on *Born Again* LP – Notorious B.I.G. (Bad Boy, 1999)

'Rush Ya Clique' on *Night Life* EP – Outsidaz (Ruff Life, 2000)

'Get Back' on *The Piece Maker* LP – Tony Touch (Tommy Boy, 2000)

'Stir Crazy' on *Tell 'Em Why You Madd* LP – Madd Rapper (Columbia, 2000)

'The One' – Royce Da 5–9 (Game, 2000)

'Don't Approach Me' on *Restless* LP – Xzibit (Loud, 2000)

'Renagade' (sic) on *The Blueprint* LP – Jay-Z (Roc-A-Fella, 2001)

'My Name' (also single) on *Man Vs. Machine* LP – Xzibit (Loud, 2002)

'Rap Superstar' on *Skull & Bones* LP – Cypress Hill (Columbia, 2002)

'Patiently Waiting' and 'Don't Push Me' on *Get Rich Or Die Tryin'* LP – 50 Cent (Shady/Aftermath/Interscope, 2003)

'Lady', 'We All Die One Day', 'Hands On You' and 'Outro' on *Cheers* LP – Obie Trice (Shady/Interscope, 2003)

'One Day At A Time' on *Tupac: Resurrection* LP – Tupac (Amaru/Interscope, 2003)

'911' on *Koastra Nostra* LP – Boo-Ya T.R.I.B.E. (The Oglio Entertainment Company, 2003)

'Welcome to D-Block' on *Kiss Of Death* LP – Jadakiss (Interscope/Ruff Ryders, 2004)

'Warrior Part 2' on *The Hunger For More* LP – Lloyd Banks (G-Unit/Interscope, 2004)

'Soldier Like Me' and 'Black Cotton' on *Loyal To The Game* LP – 2Pac (Amaru/Interscope, 2004)

'We Ain't' on *The Documentary* LP – The Game (Aftermath/G-Unit/Interscope, 2005)

'Lean Back (Remix)' on *All Or Nothing* LP – Fat Joe (Atlantic, 2005)

'Hip Hop' on *Hannicap Circus* LP – Bizarre (Sanctuary/SonyBMG, 2005)

'Drama Setter' on *Thoughts Of A Predicate Felon* LP – Tony Yayo (G-Unit/Interscope, 2005)

'Pimplikeness' (with D12) on *Searching For Jerry Garcia* LP – Proof (Iron Fist, 2005)

'Gatman And Robbin' on *The Massacre* LP – 50 Cent (Shady/Aftermath/Interscope, 2005)

'Off To Tijuana' on *Bulletproof* LP – Hush (Geffen, 2005)

'It Has Been Said' on *Duets: The Final Chapter* LP – The Notorious B.I.G. (Bad Boy, 2005)

'Welcome 2 Detroit' (also single) and 'No More To Say' on *The People vs.* LP – Trick-Trick (Motown, 2005)

'There They Go' on *Second Round's On Me* LP – Obie Trice (Shady/Interscope, 2006)

'Smack That' (also single) on *Konvicted* LP – Akon (Konvict/Up Front/SRC/Universal Motown, 2006)

'Pistol Poppin'' on *The County Hound EP* – Cashis (Shady/Interscope, 2007)

'Touchdown' on *T.I. vs. T.I.P.* LP – T.I. (Grand Hustle/Atlantic, 2007)

'Peep Show' on *Curtis* LP – 50 Cent (Shady/Aftermath/Interscope, 2007)

'Who Want It' on *The Villain* LP – Trick-Trick (Time Entertainment/Koch, 2008)

'Chemical Warfare' on *Chemical Warfare* LP – The Alchemist (ALC/E1, 2009)

'Psycho' on *Before I Self-Destruct* LP – 50 Cent (Shady/Aftermath/Interscope, 2009)

'Drop The World' on *Rebirth* LP – Lil Wayne (Universal Motown/Cash Money, 2010)

'Airplanes, Part II' on *B.o.B. Presents: The Adventures of Bobby Ray* LP – B.o.B. (Grand Hustle/Atlantic, 2010)

'Love The Way You Lie, Part II' on *Loud* LP – Rihanna (Def Jam, 2010)

'Celebrity' and 'Where I'm At' on *The Hunger For More 2* LP – Lloyd Banks (G-Unit/EMI, 2010)

'Roman's Revenge' on *Pink Friday* LP – Nicki Minaj (Young Money/Cash Money/Universal Motown, 2010)

'Living Proof' – Royce Da 5–9 (2010)

'All She Wrote' on *No Mercy* LP – T.I. (Grand Hustle/Atlantic, 2010)

NOTABLE COMPILATION APPEARANCES

'Any Man' on *Rawkus Presents Soundbombing 2* (Rawkus, 1999)

'Bad Guys Always Die' with Dr. Dre, on *Wild Wild West* soundtrack (Interscope, 1999)

'Murder (Remix)' on *Next Friday* soundtrack (Priority, 1999)

'Off The Wall' featuring D12, on *The Nutty Professor 2* soundtrack (Universal/Def Jam, 2000)

'Forever' (also single, with Drake, Kanye West, Lil Wayne) on *Music Inspired by More Than A Game* soundtrack (Zone 4/Interscope, 2009)

VIDEOS

Up In Smoke – tour documentary (Universal, 2000)

Eminem – video compilation, 'Just Don't Give A Fuck' to 'Stan' (Universal, 2001)

The Slim Shady Show – cartoon (Universal, 2001)

All Access Europe – tour documentary (Universal, 2002)
Eminem Presents: The Anger Management Tour – tour documentary (Interscope, 2005)
Live From New York City 2005 – tour documentary (Eagle Rock, 2007)

FILMS

The Wash (dir. DJ Pooh, 2001)
8 Mile (dir. Curtis Hanson, 2002)

TV

Entourage, Series 7 finale – as himself (2010)